UK AIRFIELDS PAST AND PRESENT

A DIRECTORY OF AIRFIELDS FROM 1908 TO 2018

GRANT PEERLESS

FONTHILL

Fonthill Media Language Policy

Fonthill Media publishes in the international English language market. One language edition is published worldwide. As there are minor differences in spelling and presentation, especially with regard to American English and British English, a policy is necessary to define which form of English to use. The Fonthill Policy is to use the form of English native to the author. Grant Peerless was born and educated in the United Kingdom; therefore, British English has been adopted in this publication.

Fonthill Media Limited
Fonthill Media LLC
www.fonthillmedia.com
office@fonthillmedia.com

First published in the United Kingdom and the United States of America 2020

British Library Cataloguing in Publication Data:
A catalogue record for this book is available from the British Library

ISBN 978-1-78155-792-1

Typeset in Sabon 10pt on 13pt
Printed and bound in England

Foreword

As with all books about airfields, the big dilemma is deciding which to include and which to leave out. This is not usually a problem with military airfields as most of them have a significant history, but civil airfields are a different case. Many pre-Second World War aerodromes often hosted just a few flying circus or joy-riding type events and were closed for the rest of the time. In the post-war period, many RAF airfields were used for civil flying, sometimes just for crop-spraying and gliding. Farm strips and microlight sites can be here today and gone tomorrow or often move their location by a few fields. I have not included seaplane, airship, or balloon bases except were they had an associated landing ground.

My criteria for including current civil airfields in this directory is that generally they must have at least a 500-m runway, five or more resident aircraft (ten in the case of predominantly microlight sites), and appear on Ordnance Survey maps or support scheduled services. There are always exceptions to the rule: Deanland's runway is only 457-m long, but it is home to around forty aircraft whereas Marshland has an international civil aviation organisation (EGSI) designator and an 800-m runway, but probably only one resident aircraft.

I have referred to 'aerodromes' prior to the Second World War and 'airfields' after the war. Opening dates are when the first aircraft arrived, not necessarily when the site was officially opened. Airfields referred to as 'private' are those not included in the various flight guides. Counties are generally those formed following local government reorganisation in 1974 (London from 1965) as it is not practicable to include the many unitary authorities now in place. I have not provided counties for Irish airfields, merely referring to them as NI (Northern Ireland).

Aircraft types and units stated as being based at airfields are not necessarily every type ever in residence but a representative selection. In the case of Fleet Air Arm airfields, many types were based at the respective airfields for short periods only while on 'shore leave' from aircraft carriers. The numbers of aircraft probably based at airfields are only approximate as they frequently move to other locations.

There are bound to be errors in an undertaking of this magnitude, for which I apologise.

Grant Peerless
St Albans
October 2019

Acknowledgements

This book is dedicated to my good friend and well-known aviation journalist and photographer Richard Riding, who sadly passed away in January 2019. Richard was co-author on two of my previous books on Elstree and Leavesden Aerodromes and was a great help with this publication. He supplied many of the photographs from his extensive collection as well as being a mine of information.

Many other people helped with compiling this book, but I would particularly like to thank Peter Howarth of the Airfield Research Group, who provided useful details of First World War aerodromes, and Tony Yarnold, who flew me in his Grumman American AA-5 G-PURR and AG-5 D-ENTO to over 120 of the airfields contained in this book. These two aeroplanes feature in many of the photographs in this book.

Contents

Abbreviations

A&AEE	aircraft and armament experimental establishment
AAC	army air corps
AACU	anti-aircraft cooperation unit
AALG	automobile association landing ground
AAP	aircraft acceptance park
ACGS	air cadet gliding school
AEF	air experience flight
AFEE	airborne forces experimental establishment
AFS	advanced flying school
AFU	advanced flying unit
ALG	advanced landing ground
ANS	air navigation school
AOP	air observation post
ARD	aircraft repair depot
ASR	air-sea rescue
ATA	air transport auxiliary
BAe	British Aerospace
BAT	blind (later beam) approach training
BEA	British European Airways
BOAC	British Overseas Airways Corporation
C&M	care and maintenance
CAACU	civilian anti-aircraft cooperation unit
CAG	civil air guard
CFE	central fighter establishment
CFS	central flying school
CRO	civilian repair organisation
ELG	emergency landing ground
FAA	Fleet Air Arm
FLG	forced landing ground
FRU	fleet requirements unit
FTS	flying training school
GA	general aviation
GC	gliding club
GTS	glider training school
HCU	heavy conversion unit
HGCU	heavy glider conversion unit
LG	landing ground
MAP	Ministry of Aircraft Production
MCA	Maritime and Coastguard Agency
MOS	Ministry of Supply
MTCA	Ministry of Transport and Civil Aviation
MU	maintenance unit
OCU	operational conversion unit
OTU	operational training unit
PRU	photographic reconnaissance unit
RAE	Royal Aircraft Establishment
RAF	Royal Air Force
RAuxAF	Royal Auxiliary Air Force
RFC	Royal Flying Corps
RFS	reserve flying school
RLG	relief landing ground
RNAS	Royal Naval Air Service
SAR	search and rescue
SBAC	Society of British Aircraft Constructors
SLG	satellite landing ground
SOE	special operations executive
STOL	short take-off and landing
TDS	training depot station
TWU	tactical weapons unit
UAS	university air squadron
USAAF	United States Army Air Force
USAAS	United States Army Air Service
USAF	United States Air Force
VGS	volunteer gliding squadron

Abbots Bromley, Staffs

This RAF station opened as a RLG for Burnaston in June 1940 and was used by an elementary flying school operating Tiger Moths and Magisters. Flying ceased in July 1945, and the airfield closed in February 1948. Just to the south-west is an unlicensed grass strip at Yeatsall Farm, which opened before 1992; it is home to over twenty private aircraft.

Aberdeen (Dyce), Grampian

Construction work commenced in October 1933 and the aerodrome was opened officially in July 1934. Various airlines operated scheduled services until civil flying ceased in September 1939. Before this, in June 1937, an AACU was formed, which operated Tutors, Hectors, and later Ansons and Whitleys until April 1941. A coastal patrol flight was set up in December 1939 with Tiger Moths and Hornet Moths, but it was disbanded in May 1940. In January 1940, Spitfires were the first of many based fighter units, followed by Hurricanes, Blenheims, and Beaufighters, which stayed until November 1944. An OTU arrived in February 1943 equipped with Spitfires, Mosquitoes, Masters, and Oxfords; it was resident until January 1945. A BAT flight of Oxfords was based there from July 1941 to August 1944, and some civilian scheduled services were operated from February 1942 to May 1944. Fighters were based again in April 1945 when Spitfires, Mustangs, and Vampires were used until March 1957. It returned to civil use at the end of 1945 as Aberdeen airport, but the RAF still had a presence with a VGS and a UAS as late as 1981.

Aberdeen (Kintore), Grampian

This civil aerodrome opened in May 1935 and was used by a few scheduled services until the late 1930s. It was used as a RLG for Dyce during the Second World War and finally closed around 1949.

Aberdeen (Seaton), Grampian

This short-lived civil aerodrome opened in May 1934 for scheduled services, but operations moved to Kintore a year later.

Abergavenny (The Byre), Gwent

This unlicensed grass airfield opened before 2003, which is home to around ten light aircraft.

Aberporth, Pembrokeshire

This aerodrome opened in September 1940 with an AACU, which operated Queen Bees, Henleys, Tiger Moths, Battles, Hurricanes, Martinets, Lysanders, Blenheims, and Dominies. The Army stayed until April 1946 when the station was placed on C&M. Post-war, it became a RAE establishment and received regular visits from Ansons, Devons and Pembrokes on communication duties. A VGS was based from 1996 to 2001 when it passed into civil use as West Wales Airport. It has one licensed hard runway and an unlicensed grass strip.

Abingdon, Oxon

This RAF bomber station opened in September 1932 and was home initially to Gordons, Harts, and Hinds, which were followed by Battles, Whitleys, Ansons, and finally Wellingtons. The last bomber departed in September 1946. A BAT flight operated from January 1941 to April 1943 with Oxfords and Whitleys. In October 1945, Transport Command took over and operated Dakotas, Yorks, Hastings, Valettas, Beverleys, and Andovers until September 1970. An overseas ferry unit was based from March 1951 to April 1953, which used a wide variety of types. A MU arrived in June 1976 and dealt mainly with Jaguars, Hunters, and Hawks. Several UASs were resident over the years starting with Tiger Moths in April 1941 and finishing with Bulldogs, which departed in July 1992. It then closed to flying, but a VGS operated from the airfield with Vigilants until 2016 and an air and country show takes place every May.

Abbotsinch

See Glasgow.

Aboyne, Grampian

This unlicensed airfield with two hard runways opened in 1965 and operated mainly as a gliding site by the Deeside GC. Around thirty gliders are based. It is also open to visiting light aircraft.

Abridge (Loughton Air Park), Essex

This civil aerodrome opened in November 1932 but proposed scheduled services did not materialise, although a couple of flying clubs took up residence. When Stapleford Tawney aerodrome, 3 miles away, opened in 1934, use of Abridge slowly declined and it finally closed in August 1937, although some limited flying may have taken place after this.

Acaster Malbis, Yorks

This RAF station opened in January 1942 as a satellite for Church Fenton and was home initially to Airacobras. These only stayed for three months and were replaced by Oxfords, which remained until January 1943. It was then developed into a bomber base and reopened in 1944 but did not host any operational units. It was only used for circuit training by Halifaxes of nearby HCUs but flying ceased in late 1944, and it closed in February 1946. It reopened for civil flying around 1974 due to its proximity to York racecourse and some flying still takes place.

Acklam, Yorks

This civil airfield at Sandy Flatts Farm was opened around 1947 and used by Acklam Aviation until they moved to West Hartlepool in 1949. It closed in 1952.

Acklington, Northumberland

This RFC second-class night LG, known as Southfields, was in use for home defence with Be2s and Fe2s from early 1917 to June 1919. Following expansion, it reopened as a RAF airfield in December 1937 and was initially home to an armament training school equipped with Seals, Henleys, and Whitleys. These departed in September 1939, and the station then became the north-east's main fighter base, a role it was to keep until September 1960, apart from a spell of inactivity from 1951 to 1956. Fighters operated over the years included Gladiators, Hurricanes, Spitfires, Defiants, Beaufighters, Typhoons, Mosquitoes, Mustangs, Meteors, Vampires, and Hunters. A FTS arrived in July 1961 with Provosts and Jet Provosts and stayed until June 1968. A SAR flight was stationed from October 1957 to October 1975 equipped with Sycamores, Whirlwinds, and Wessexes; when they left, flying ceased.

Acton, Gt. London

This civil aerodrome opened in 1910 and was known as the London Aviation Ground. A factory on the site built a few DH9s in 1919 and afterwards a couple of experimental long-distance aeroplanes. The Ruffy-Baumann Flying School was resident in 1917–18, but the aerodrome closed in early 1920. The former factory was taken over by the MAP in September 1940, and de Havilland produced components for the Mosquito and Anson until June 1945.

Addington, Gt. London

This civil aerodrome opened in 1930, but it was little used and closed in 1933, the resident aircraft moving to Gatwick.

Aintree, Merseyside

The racecourse was first used as an aerodrome in 1909 and was used sporadically until the outbreak of the First World War. The RFC arrived in 1916 and in 1917 National Aircraft Factory No. 3 was established, building F2bs until late 1918. A storage and salvage unit was also set up, which was in use until December 1919. It reopened for civilian scheduled services in 1924, but it was soon found that it was too small for heavily loaded aircraft to operate from; it finally closed around 1939.

Akeman Street, Oxon

This RAF station opened in June 1940 and was used mainly as a RLG for Brize Norton and Little Rissington until closure in April 1946. Types using the grass airfield included Tiger Moths, Harvards, Oxfords, and Albermarles.

Alconbury, Cambs

This RAF station opened as a satellite to Upwood in May 1938, Battles being the first residents; they were followed in 1940 by Blenheims, Wellingtons, and later Stirlings. The USAAF started to arrive in August 1942 with B-24s followed by B-17s in January 1943 and stayed until June 1945. The base was returned to the RAF in November 1945 but remained inactive until June 1953 when the Americans returned. They operated C-47s, B-45s, B-66s, WB-50s, F-100s, and later RF-4Cs, F-5Es, TR-1s, A-10s, U-2s, and C-130s. The USAF remained until the airfield closed to flying in April 1995.

Aldeburgh (Hazelwood), Suffolk

This RNAS night LG opened in August 1915 as a sub-station for Great Yarmouth and used initially for home defence. From August 1918 it was used by a marine observers school operating Be2s, DH6s, DH9s, Snipes and Kangaroos until flying ceased in September 1919.

Aldergrove

See Belfast.

Aldermaston, Berks

This was planned as a RAF bomber OTU when it opened in July 1942, but it was home instead to the USAAF. They operated mainly transport types and gliders including C-47s, C-53s, CG-4s, and Horsas until February 1945. Between July 1943 and April 1945, Vickers assembled and test-flew Spitfires from the site. In May 1946, it became BOAC's training headquarters and they used Dakotas, Oxfords, Yorks, Haltons, and Vikings until the company departed in November 1948. Some transport flights continued until April 1950 when the airfield closed and was taken over by the Atomic Weapons Research Establishment.

Alderney, CI

This civil aerodrome opened in June 1935 as a request stop on Jersey Airways' services. Regular scheduled services commenced in April 1936 and continued until the German forces invaded in June 1940. It returned to civil use in 1947, a hard runway being provided in 1968. Scheduled services still operate, and the airport is open to visiting aircraft.

All Hallows (Sheerness), Kent

This RFC third-class night LG was used for home defence from October 1916 until flying ceased in July 1919. Types operated included Be2s, Be12s, and FK8s. It was used for civil flying during 1935, but there is no record of its use after this.

Alloa (Forthbank) Central Region

The British Caudron Company was established here in 1914 and built G3s, Be2s, Avro 504s, and Camels up to the end of the First World War. It was used during the 1920s by light aircraft.

Alrewas, Staffs

This unlicensed airfield at Sittles Farm opened in 1993 for the Sittles Flying Club. It has two grass runways and around twenty residents.

Alton Barnes, Wilts

This RAF station opened in 1935 as a RLG for Upavon and was used by Avro 504s and Tutors. These were followed by an elementary flying school, which operated Tiger Moths, Magisters, Masters, and Oxfords until flying ceased in July 1945. The airfield closed in 1947.

Andover (Weyhill), Hants

This RFC TDS opened in August 1917 and was home to various units operating Fe2s, DH4s, DH9s, RE8s, F2bs, O/400s, Snipes, and Avro 504s until April 1920. RAF Bomber Command arrived in September 1923 and used Fawns, Foxes, Sidestrands, Harts, Virginias, Atlases, Hinds, and Battles until May 1939. It then transferred to Fighter Command, which operated Hectors, Blenheims, Ansons, Whitleys, Mustangs, and Oxfords during the Second World War. It was used briefly by USAAF P-38s between February and July 1944. Various other units used the airfield during and after the War including a communications flight (until January 1960), an AOP flight equipped with Austers, and a helicopter squadron. A communications flight returned in April 1964 and operated Ansons, Pembrokes, Bassetts, and Devons until the RAF departed in March 1976. Some flying by fixed and rotary winged aircraft continued until flying ceased around 1984.

Andreas, IoM

This RAF station opened in October 1941 and was home initially to various squadrons of Spitfires until September 1942. A gunnery school arrived in May 1943 equipped with Wellingtons, Martinets, and Ansons, which stayed until September 1946 when the airfield closed. Flying still takes place from two of the wartime hard runways, both unlicensed, and some twenty aircraft are based there, along with the Andreas GC.

Andrewsfield (Great Saling), Essex

The USAAF station opened in April 1943 with B-17s, but these were later replaced by B-26s. RAF Mustangs then arrived, followed for a short time in March 1945 by the first Meteor jet fighters. The Mustangs stayed until the airfield closed in November 1945. It reopened in 1972 for private flying from a single licensed grass runway and is today a thriving GA airfield with over sixty residents.

Angle, Pembrokeshire

This RAF station opened in June 1941 as a satellite for Brawdy and was home to various units operating Hurricanes, Spitfires, Whirlwinds, Swordfishes, Defiants, Masters, Wellingtons, and Proctors. Flying ceased in January 1945 and the airfield closed soon after.

Anglesey (Llangefni), Gwynedd

Predominantly an airship station, it opened in September 1915 and closed in 1919 but was also used as a LG. A coastal patrol flight operating DH6s was based here from June to August 1918. Mona airfield is just to the east.

Annan, Dumfries and Galloway

This RAF station opened in April 1942 and was home for most of its short life to an OTU, later a TEU, which operated Masters, Hurricanes, Martinets, Lysanders, Typhoons, and Oxfords until flying ceased in May 1944. It was then used by a MU for storage until the end of the war.

Ansty, Warks

This RAF station opened in June 1936 and was used by a succession of training units until March 1953. Types operated included Harts, Hinds, Demons, Audaxes, Magisters, Tiger Moths, Ansons, and Chipmunks. An adjacent shadow factory produced 1,000 Mosquitoes and 750 Oxfords during the Second World War. It was used post-war by Armstrong Siddeley for engine testing.

Anthorn, Cumbria

RFC day LG known as Solway House was in use during the First World War. Following expansion, it reopened in September 1944 for the FAA as HMS *Nuthatch* and was used for the receipt and dispatch of aircraft. Over 5,000 aircraft of twenty-five different types passed through the unit, including Martinets, Avengers, Mosquitoes, Seafires, Sea Hornets, Firebrands, Sea Furies, Fireflies, and Sea Balliols until flying ceased in February 1958.

Anwick (Ruskington Fen/Sleaford), Lincs

This RFC second-class night LG was used for home defence from September 1916 to June 1919. Types operated included Be2s, Fe2s, F2bs, and Avro 504s. It reopened in September 1939 as a decoy for RAF Digby but closed in August 1942. A private airstrip at Old Manor Farm opened before 1982 on part of the old airfield and is home to several light aircraft.

Various light aircraft including Grumman American AA-5 in front of the control tower at the former USAAF bomber base of Great Saling, now known as Andrewsfield on 16 October 2008. (*Grant Peerless*)

Appleton Wiske, Yorks
This RFC second-class day and night LG was used for home defence from January 1917 to August 1919.

Apuldram, Sussex
This ALG opened in June 1943 and was used initially by RAF Typhoons but for only a month. Spitfires arrived in April 1944 and stayed until August 1944 when the temporary airfield closed.

Arbroath, Tayside
This FAA station opened in July 1940 as HMS *Condor* and was used initially by a deck landing school and for observer training. It went on to become home to numerous units operating a variety of types until fixed-wing flying ceased in June 1954, although a station flight continued until July 1968. Types based included Swordfish, Albacores, Walruses, Sharks, Ansons, Fireflies, Barracudas, Sea Otters, Sea Hornets, and Sea Furies. It was used instead of Dundee for scheduled services for a brief period in the early 1960s. Helicopters, mainly Wessexes and Sea Kings began using the airfield in July 1966 and continued until October 1992. An ACGS was formed in May 1958 and transferred to a VGS whose Vikings were based until 2016. The airfield is to remain open indefinitely.

Arlington (Hailsham), Sussex
This RFC first-class day and night LG was used for home defence from December 1916 to 1919.

Arran (Shiskine), Strathclyde
This civil aerodrome was used by scheduled services from July 1935 until December 1938. Private light aircraft were also based here.

Ascot, Berks
A stores and repair depot was set up on the racecourse in 1916 with an associated LG, which stayed until 1929. It was used by USAAF L-4s during the Second World War.

Ashbourne, Derbys
This RAF training station opened in July 1942 and was equipped with Wellingtons, Whitleys, Blenheims, Albermarles, Ansons, Martinets, and Oxfords. Flying ceased in March 1945 and the airfield was used by a MU until it closed in 1954. Flying resumed from part of the airfield in the late 1960s until about 1975 including use by a sky-diving club. It is still used occasionally by light aircraft, and a few microlights are based on an area known as Bradley Moor.

Ashcroft (Winsford), Cheshire
This unlicensed airfield opened in 1991 as Bryan's Landings with four grass runways and home to around twenty aircraft. It is now known as Ashcroft Farm. Just to the east is another grass strip at Ash House Farm at which a few aircraft are based.

Ashford (Great Chart), Kent
This ALG opened in June 1943 and was home to RAF Hurricanes, Mustangs, Spitfires, and latterly Meteors until the temporary airfield closed in October 1944. USAAF P-47s were based briefly between April and July 1944.

Ashingdon (Canute Air Park), Essex
This civil aerodrome opened in 1931 and was used by a couple of flying clubs and other light aircraft. Phoenix Aircraft Construction Company was also resident here. Use of the aerodrome declined as the more suitable airport at nearby Southend came into use and Ashingdon closed in 1936.

Ashington, Northumberland
This RFC home defence flight station opened in October 1916 and was used by Be2s, Be12s, Pups, Scouts, and F2bs until June 1919. A coastal patrol flight equipped with DH6s arrived in June 1918 and stayed until flying ceased in June 1919.

Ashwell, Herts
This civil aerodrome on the site of a former speedway track was used by light aircraft from about 1932 until the outbreak of the Second World War.

Askern, Yorks
This RAF station was in use between February 1944 and May 1946 by an ACGS.

Askernish
See South Uist.

Aston Down, Glos
This RFC training station known as Minchinhampton opened in late 1917 and closed in June 1919. Types operated included Avro 504s, SE5s, Camels, Snipes, and DH6s. Following expansion, it reopened as RAF Aston Down in October 1938 and became home to various units operating Spitfires, Hurricanes, Defiants, Harvards, Gladiators, Blenheims, Masters, Whitleys, and Battles. A MU was resident from February 1939 until September 1960, dealing with Albermarles, Spitfires, Typhoons, and

Lancasters. The CFS used the airfield as a RLG up to February 1976; part of it is now used by light aircraft as well as the Cotswold GC, which was formed in 1967. Over sixty gliders and light aircraft are based here.

Atcham, Salop

This opened as a RAF fighter station in September 1941; the first residents were Spitfires, which stayed until May 1942. The USAAF then took over with Spitfires, P-38s, and P-47s and these remained until February 1945. The airfield was then handed back to the RAF and flying ceased in April 1946.

Attlebridge, Norfolk

This RAF station opened as a satellite to Swanton Morley in June 1941 with Blenheims the first residents, followed by Bostons until September 1942. The USAAF then arrived with B-26s and, later, B-25s but stayed for only a year. After the laying of hard runways, USAAF B-24s arrived in March 1944 and stayed until April 1945 when all flying ceased, although the site did not close finally until 1959.

Atwick (Hornsea), Humberside

The RNAS set up a home defence flight on the racecourse in August 1915 equipped with TB8s. It was classified as a first-class night LG in April 1916, and the RFC continued to use it for home defence. It became home to a coastal patrol flight in May 1918, which operated DH6s until flying ceased in January 1919.

Aubourn, Lincs

This Microlight strip at Blackmoor Farm has around fifteen residents.

Audley End, Essex

This unlicensed airfield opened before 1974 with one grass runway. It is home to around thirty based aircraft and a restoration company.

Aylesbury (Haddenham/Thame), Bucks

Intended to be Aylesbury airport, it did not open officially until August 1939, but very little flying took place before it closed for the war. Before this, from July 1937, it saw use as a RAF RLG and the Hordern Richmond Company built a factory here in 1939 to produce propellers. The RAF arrived in September 1940 with an OTU operating Battles and Ansons and this was replaced by a GTS in the following December. This used Tiger Moths, Kites, Hotspurs, and Hectors until it departed in January 1943. Its place was taken by an ATA training and ferry pool, which operated Tiger Moths, Magisters, Arguses, Proctors, Dominies, and Ansons until April 1945. After the war, the site was taken over by Airtech, who carried out major maintenance on Halifaxes, Stirlings, Dakotas, Consuls, and Rapides. This company remained at the airfield until the 1990s. Gliding recommenced in 1963 when the Upward Bound Trust was set up and continued until the airfield closed in December 2018.

Ayr, Strathclyde

This RFC aerodrome opened on the Racecourse in September 1917 and was used by a school of aerial fighting and later as a flying instructors school. Types operated included Avro 504s, Camels, DH2s, F2bs, SE5s, DH9s, Dolphins, 0/400s, and RE8s until flying ceased in January 1919. About 1 mile to the north-east, a RAF fighter station known as Heathfield opened in April 1941 and was home to Spitfires, Defiants, Beaufighters, Hurricanes, Mosquitoes, and Typhoons until May 1944. It then transferred to the FAA as HMS *Wagtail* and was used mainly by aircraft on 'shore leave' until closure in April 1946. Many naval types used this facility including Corsairs, Hellcats, Fireflies, Wildcats, Avengers, and Seafires. From 1951 to 1957, the USAF used the site for storage. It was used by light aircraft in the 1960s and '70s and is now part of Prestwick airport.

Babdown Farm, Glos

This RAF station opened as a RLG for Hullavington in July 1940 and was used by training units operating Harts, Audaxes, Masters, Hurricanes, and Oxfords until June 1945 when it was placed on C&M. It was then taken over by a MU and closed in January 1948.

Bacton, Norfolk

This RNAS night LG opened in August 1915 and was used as a RLG for Great Yarmouth until March 1919. Various types were operated including Camels and DH9s.

Badminton, Avon

This unlicensed grass strip on the Badminton Estate was opened before 1982; it is available to visiting aircraft and a couple are based there.

Bagby (Thirsk), Yorks

This unlicensed airfield with a single grass runway was opened in the 1970s and is home to over fifty light aircraft.

The small grass airfield at Bagby on 20 September 1997 featuring a few light aircraft, including Cessna 150 G-BCKV by the control tower. (*Grant Peerless*)

Baginton

See Coventry.

Bainton, Cambs

This RFC night LG was used for home defence with Be2s and Be12s during 1916.

Balado Bridge, Tayside

This RAF station opened in March 1942 as a satellite for Grangemouth and was used mainly by an OTU, followed by a TEU until June 1944. Types operated included Spitfires, Hurricanes, Masters, and Battles. An air fighting unit equipped with Harvards was briefly resident from September to November 1944 after which military flying ceased. After the war, McDonnells broke up surplus naval aircraft on the site including Harvards, Fulmars, Fireflies, Martinets, Barracudas, and Expeditors; this continued until at least 1955. Light aircraft—including those of the Loch Leven Aero Club—and gliders used part of the airfield from 1946 to 1957 when it closed. Part of the northern wartime airfield has reopened and is used mainly by microlights but also gliders and occasional light aircraft. They operate from one hard and three grass runways, all unlicensed. Around ten aircraft and gliders are based here.

Balderton, Notts

This RAF bomber station opened in June 1941 as a satellite for Finningley with the first residents being Hampdens. These were replaced with Manchesters, Lancasters, and Halifaxes, which stayed until January 1944 when the USAAF arrived with C-47s and C-53s. They departed in the following April, when the Lancasters returned and stayed until April 1945. For a year from April 1943, Horsa gliders were stored, and between November 1943 and April 1944, Meteor jets were test-flown. A MU took up residence in June 1945 and the airfield closed in 1954.

Balhall (Balmain), Tayside

This RFC day LG was in use during the First World War. It was used as a RLG by training aircraft based at Montrose between 1940 and 1945, including Harts, Masters, Oxfords, Harvards, Ansons, and Tiger Moths.

Ballyhalbert, NI

This RAF fighter station opened in June 1941with Hurricanes, which were followed by Spitfires, Beaufighters and Mustangs. The FAA began to arrive in November 1943 and operated numerous types but predominantly Seafires; in July 1945, it became HMS *Corncrake*. Seafires, Corsairs, Hellcats, and Harvards were used until the Navy departed in November 1945. It was then transferred to Coastal Command and closed in 1946.

Ballykelly, NI

This RAF Coastal Command station opened in June 1941 and was home to Fortresses and later Liberators until June 1945. After a brief period on C&M, an anti-submarine school was set up in the following November, which operated Lancasters, Neptunes, and Shackletons until June 1970. Coastal Command returned in March 1952 and employed Shackletons until flying ceased in March 1971. The FAA were frequent visitors from December 1942 until 1971 and operated most types in naval service, latterly helicopters. The Army took over when the RAF departed and operated Gazelles and Lynxes from the airfield until March 2008.

Ballywalter (Millisle), NI
This aerodrome was used by the RAF as an ELG between 1918 and 1922. It became a SLG in June 1941 and stored mostly Wellingtons until closure in March 1945.

Balsdean, Sussex
This gliding site was operated by the Southdown GC from 1931 to 1933.

Banbury, Oxon
This civil aerodrome opened in 1931 and became an AALG in 1933 but only until 1934. Flying then continued on a limited basis until the outbreak of the Second World War.

Banff (Boyndie), Grampian
This RAF station opened in April 1943 and was used initially for training with Oxfords until August 1944. It then became a fighter base and was used by the famous 'Banff Strike Wing', which operated mainly Mosquitoes but also Beaufighters and Mustangs until August 1945. Flying then all but ceased, although a station flight continued until 1946. Part of the wartime airfield reopened for private flying by the Banff Flying Club in 1976 but closed in the early 1980s.

Bangor, Gwynedd
This LG was used by a RAF coastal patrol flight equipped with DH6s from July 1918 to January 1919.

Bangor, NI
This basic LG was used by US Navy aircraft during 1918.

Bardney, Lincs
This RAF bomber station opened in April 1943, the first and only residents being Lancasters, which stayed until April 1945. The airfield closed to flying at the end of 1945 but reopened as a Thor missile base in July 1959 until May 1963. The Lincoln Aero Club was resident from 1956 to 1958 and the Lincolnshire GC was based briefly during 1978.

Barford St John, Oxon
This RAF station opened in June 1941 as a RLG for Kidlington and was used by Oxfords until February 1942. Bomber Command then took over and the airfield became a satellite for Upper Heyford and used by Hampdens, Wellingtons, Ansons, and Masters. It was in use by the Gloster Aircraft Company from May 1943 for flight-testing their E28/39 prototype and also early marks of Meteor. The airfield closed in March 1946.

Barham, Kent
This unlicensed airfield at Clipgate Farm opened before 1992 with around a dozen resident aircraft that use a single grass runway.

Barking (Creekmouth), Gt. London
This civil aerodrome opened in 1909 and was used by Handley Page to build and test-fly a few experimental aeroplanes until they departed in 1912 to a new site at Cricklewood. It was taken over by the RNAS in June 1916 as a proposed airship factory, but it never materialised.

Barkston Heath, Lincs
This RAF station opened in September 1940 as a RLG for Cranwell and was used by Oxfords and Tutors until December 1942. It then became inactive until February 1944 when the USAAF arrived with C-46s, C-47s, and C-109s. They departed in April 1945 when it was returned to the RAF and closed in the following June. It reopened in its former role as a RLG in February 1949 until 1968 and again from 1989. Types operated included Meteors, Jet Provosts, Tucanos, Bulldogs, Dominies, Jetstreams, Fireflies, and Tutors. It was reactivated as a Bloodhound missile base between 1983 and 1991. It is still in use for training and is now home to Prefects.

Barmby Moor
See Pocklington.

Barnsley Park, Glos
This SLG opened in June 1941 and was used to store various aircraft including Hurricanes, Bostons, and Hudsons until September 1945.

Barra (Northbay), Hebrides

Some civil landing strips were situated on the beach and licensed in August 1936. It was used by scheduled services until the outbreak of the Second World War. After the war, scheduled services resumed and continue to the present day.

Barrow-in-Furness (Walney Island), Cumbria

During the First World War, an airship factory here was provided with a LG. A site three-quarters of a mile to the north was intended as the municipal airport for Barrow, but the Second World War intervened, and it opened instead as a RAF station in December 1941. The first residents were a gunnery school operating Lysanders, Blenheims, Defiants, Masters, and Ansons, which stayed until June 1946. In September 1945, an AACU was formed, which flew Vengeances, Spitfires, and Oxfords until February 1946. An ACGS was based between May 1947 and September 1955, and Starways opened a facility in 1950. The airfield is now operated by BAE Systems, and their executive aircraft are based here together with approximately twenty other types including gliders of the Lakes GC (which arrived in 1964). Two licensed hard runways are available.

Barry (Carnoustie), Tayside

This RNAS LG was in use from May 1915.

Barton, Gt. Manchester

This civil aerodrome for Manchester opened officially on 1 January 1930, although flying had commenced in 1928. Scheduled services commenced soon after opening and continued until they transferred to the new airport at Ringway in 1938. In 1936, Fairey Aviation assembled and test-flew Hendons and later Battles here before moving to Ringway in June 1937. An elementary flying school was set up in October 1937, which operated Tiger Moths and Ansons; however, this closed on the outbreak of the Second World War when the airfield was requisitioned by the MAP. This organisation was responsible for assembling over 700 Proctors and the repair of Hurricanes, Fulmars, and Corsairs. An RFS operated between October 1948 and March 1953 with Tiger Moths, Chipmunks, and Ansons. Civil flying resumed after the war and continues to the present day, with well over 100 light aircraft, which have the use of four licensed grass runways, being based here.

Barton Abbey (Lower Heyford), Oxon

This SLG opened in September 1941 and was used to store mostly Spitfires and Wellingtons until it closed in February 1945.

The iconic control tower at Barton, Manchester's first airport, on 27 May 2012. It opened in 1930 and is still in operation today. (*Grant Peerless*)

Barton Bendish, Norfolk

This short-lived RAF station opened in September 1939 and was home to Wellingtons, Tomahawks, and Lysanders until flying ceased in September 1941.

Barton-in-the-Clay, Beds

This civil aerodrome opened in November 1935 when Luton Aircraft Ltd set up a short-lived factory. Private flying took place until the outbreak of the Second World War, including some by the Bedford School of Flying. From July 1940, it was used as a RLG for Luton by Magisters, Harts, and Tiger Moths until flying ceased in early 1943.

Bassingbourn, Cambs

This RAF training station opened in March 1938 and was home to Blenheims, Wellingtons, Oxfords, and Ansons. Following the laying of hard runways, B-17s and B-24s of the USAAF arrived in October 1942 and stayed until May 1945. It was returned to RAF Transport Command in June 1945 when Liberators, Lancastrians, Yorks, and Dakotas were operated here. The USAF returned in August 1950 with B-29s followed by RB-50s, but their stay was short-lived as they departed in May 1951. The RAF then took over and operated Mosquitoes and Meteors in the training role. These were replaced with Canberras in 1952; they remained until the airfield closed to flying in May 1969.

Bath (Lansdown), Avon

This AALG opened in 1931 and continued in use until about 1984. It was popular on race days as it adjoined Bath Racecourse. The racecourse itself was used as a RLG for RAF Lulsgate Bottom, known as North Stoke between March 1943 and July 1945. Oxfords, Masters, and Harvards were the main users.

Battersea Park, Gt. London

This temporary ELG was in use by the RNAS from October 1914 to 1915.

Battlestead Hill, Staffs

This RLG for RAF Burnaston opened in May 1941 and closed in July 1945. It was used mainly by Tiger Moths and Magisters.

Bawtry, Yorks

This AALG was in use between 1933 and 1939.

Baxterley, Warks

This unlicensed airfield at Charity Farm opened before 1998 with a single grass runway and around eight based aircraft.

Beacon Hill (Morpeth), Northumberland

This RFC third-class night LG was used for home defence from October 1916 to July 1917.

Beaulieu, Hants

This civil aerodrome, known locally as East Boldre, opened in 1910 and was used for flying training until 1912 by the New Forest Flying School. It was taken over by the RFC in December 1915 and used mainly for training, becoming a TDS in July 1918. Most types of the period were operated here, including Avro 504s, Be2s, RE8s, JN4s, Camels, and Dolphins until flying ceased in March 1920. About 2 miles to the east, an AALG was in use from the 1920s until 1938. Just east of this, a RAF station opened in August 1942. The first residents were Liberators and Halifaxes followed by Typhoons that stayed until March 1944. These were replaced by P-47s and B-26s of the USAAF for a few months until August 1944. It was handed back to the RAF in September 1945 and then became the home of the AFEE. This unit operated Stirlings, Halifaxes, Lancasters, Yorks, Dakotas, Hadrians, Hotspurs, Hamilcars, Hoverflies, Valettas, and Hastings until September 1950 when flying ceased. It was assigned as a USAF standby base from January 1953 but not used and reverted to the RAF in October 1955, finally closing in November 1959.

Beaumont, Essex

This RFC night LG was used for home defence from April to August 1916.

Beccles (Ellough), Suffolk

This airfield was built for the USAAF in 1943 but was taken over instead by RAF Coastal Command in August 1944, which operated Mosquitoes, Warwicks, and Walruses. The FAA arrived in April 1945 with Barracudas but only stayed for a short while. The last based RAF aircraft were Warwicks, Sea Otters, and Mosquitoes, but all had departed by October and the airfield closed in December 1945. Part of the site reopened as Beccles Heliport in 1965, and fixed-wing flying returned in 1997 using part of a wartime runway, which is now licensed. Around twenty light aircraft are based.

Beddington
See Croydon.

Bedfield, Suffolk
This RFC second-class night LG was used for home defence from April 1916 to June 1919.

Bedford
See Thurleigh.

Bedford (Castle Mill), Beds
This civil airfield opened around 1953 with one grass runway and closed around 2005.

Bedford (Kempston), Beds
This AALG, also known as Marsh Leys, was in use from about February 1933 to September 1939.

Beechwood Park, Herts
This SLG opened in May 1942 and was used to store Blenheims, Spitfires, Hurricanes, Seamews, and Stirlings until closure in March 1946.

Bekesbourne (Canterbury), Kent
This RFC home defence flight station opened in April 1916 and was used by FK8s, Be12s, FB19s, SE5s, and Camels until closure in June 1919. It reopened as a civil aerodrome in 1920 for the Kent Flying Club and the CAG arrived in 1938. Flying ceased in September 1939, but the airfield was used in May and June 1940 by a few Lysanders.

Belchamp Water, Essex
This private grass strip at Waits Farm opened in 1966 and around six light aircraft are based here.

Belfast (Aldergrove), NI
This AAP opened in October 1918, dealing mainly with V/1500s until closure in December 1919. The RAF retained a presence with F2bs from October 1920 until February 1923. Bombers arrived in May 1925 in the shape of Vimys, Hyderabads, Virginias, Wallaces, Hinds, and Heyfords, which were present until January 1941. Scheduled services were operated from 1934 until they moved to Sydenham in 1938. In 1936, an armament training flight was set up, which became an air observers school and finally a bombing and gunnery school. It used Heyfords, Hinds, Wallaces, and Battles until disbandment in July 1940.

The main use of the base during the Second World War was coastal patrol and meteorological flights using Bulldogs, Gladiators, Hudsons, Ansons, Beaufighters, and latterly Liberators. The FAA put in a brief appearance in November 1939 with Rocs, Skuas, Swordfish, and Sharks until departing in July 1940. Another important occupant during the war was a MU that dealt with Wellingtons, Hampdens, Blenheims, Ansons, Corsairs, Oxfords, and Stirlings and carried on until finally leaving in April 1978. The meteorological flight resumed in September 1945 with Halifaxes and Hastings until July 1964 and a RAuxAF squadron arrived in July 1946 equipped with Mosquitoes, Spitfires, and Vampires until disbanding in March 1957. Coastal patrol duties recommenced in April 1952 with Shackletons and continued until April 1959.

A flight of ASR Sycamores was based there from May 1960 to August 1962. Aldergrove became Belfast Airport in September 1963, but a military presence remains to this day in the shape of the army, which arrived in September 1957 with Austers and went on to operate Siouxs, Beavers, and Lynxes. They currently operate mostly Islanders and Defenders. A UAS/AEF was set up in June 1943 with Tiger Moths, Bulldogs, and currently Tutors.

Belfast (Malone), NI
The first municipal airport in the UK was licensed in April 1924 and used for short-lived airmail services by Northern Airlines until about May 1925, when it closed. It may have been used for flying displays after this date.

Belfast (Nutts Corner), NI
This RAF Coastal Command station opened in June 1941 with Liberators, Hudsons, and Fortresses. An OTU equipped with Wellingtons arrived in March 1943 and stayed until the following January. It was transferred to Ferry Command in January 1943 and types handled included B-17s, B-24s, and C-47s. The FAA took over in July 1945 as HMS *Pintail* and operated Corsairs and Seafires until they departed in March 1946. It became Belfast Airport on 1 December 1946 and remained as such until September 1963 when it was replaced by Aldergrove.

Belfast (Sydenham), NI
An aerodrome on the edge of the harbour was licensed in September 1937 but not opened officially until 16 March 1938. Scheduled services were operated up to the outbreak of the Second World War. Shorts set up a factory in 1936, which initially produced Bombays and Herefords but went on to build over 2,000 Stirlings from 1940 and later Solents, Britannias, Canberras, Belfasts,

Skyvans, SD3-30/60s, and Tucanos. Shorts were taken over by Bombardier in 1989. An elementary flying school arrived in January 1939 and used Tiger Moths, Magisters, Harts, and Demons until the following September.

The RAF arrived in June 1940 and a variety of units were based here, operating Demons, Bostons, Blenheims, Lysanders, Ansons, and Masters. The RAF departed in December 1946 and scheduled services then recommenced. An ACGS continued flying until November 1952 and a UAS/AEF until January 1992, latterly with Bulldogs. The FAA arrived in June 1943 and commissioned the station as HMS *Gadwall,* but few aircraft were based there. It then became a repair yard and nearly 1,000 USAAF fighters were assembled and test-flown, mostly P-38s and P-47s until April 1944. Civil flying resumed after the war and regular scheduled services started again in 1983. Bombardier currently builds wings for the 'C' series airliner on the site. Today, the airport is known as George Best Belfast City Airport.

Belhaven Sands, Lothian

This LG on the beach was used by RAF Cuckoos from June to November 1918.

Bellarena, NI

This unlicensed aerodrome was opened in the early 1930s for the Ulster GC. It has two grass runways but gliding also takes place from the adjacent beach (Magilligan Strand) on Benone Strand and Downhill. The latter site was used by an ACGS from July 1947 to June 1949; around twenty residents, mostly gliders, operate from the main airfield.

Bellasize (Gilberdyke), Yorks

This RFC first-class night LG opened in April 1916 and was used for home defence by Be2s and Avro 504s until May 1919. It reopened as a RLG for Brough in November 1939 and was used for training with Blackburn B2s and Tiger Moths until July 1945 when flying ceased.

Bell Vue (Yarnscombe), Devon

This unlicensed airfield was opened before 1998 with one grass runway and is home to around ten light aircraft.

Belton

See Sandtoft.

Bembridge, IoW

This civil aerodrome was opened in the 1920s, becoming an AALG in 1933. Limited scheduled services called in until it closed for the duration of the Second World War. Britten-Norman set up a factory on the airfield in 1965, which produced Islanders and Trislanders, but has now departed. Today, it is home to around a dozen aircraft operating from an unlicensed hard runway (laid in 1979–80) and a grass strip. The Vectis GC is also based.

Benbecula (Balivanich), Hebrides

This civil aerodrome was opened in July 1936, supporting scheduled services until the outbreak of the Second World War. From August 1941, it was used by the RAF as an ELG, and in June 1942, Coastal Command arrived with Hudsons, later replaced by

Britten-Norman factory and control tower at Bembridge on 8 July 2005. One of their products, an Islander G-NESU, is parked on the grass together with a Rockwell R114 N395TC. The company moved to Lee-on-Solent in 2010. (*Grant Peerless*)

Fortresses and Wellingtons until June 1945. Scheduled services resumed in 1946 and continue to this day. Sea King helicopters of the Royal Navy were based between May 1975 and September 1988.

Benington, Herts

This private grass airfield at Whitehall Farm has been in use since the 1970s and is home to around six aircraft.

Benson, Oxon

This RAF station opened in April 1939 and was initially occupied by Battles, Ansons, and Wellingtons. Numerous units were based during the Second World War, many for only short periods, but the most famous was a PRU. This was formed in December 1940 and operated mainly Spitfires and Mosquitoes. These were followed after the war by Meteors and Canberras until the unit closed in March 1953. The King's Flight was based from September 1939 with a Hudson, a Flamingo, and a Q6; this later became the Queen's Flight, which operated Vikings, Devons, Herons, Andovers, 146s, and Wessexes. It relocated to Northolt in April 1995. Transport Command took over in March 1953 and employed Valettas, Hastings, Yorks, Twin Pioneers, Argosies, and Andovers until October 1993. The FAA put in an appearance in July 1953 and operated Attackers and Sea Hawks until March 1957. A UAS/AEF was formed in July 1992 with Bulldogs and is still flying today with Tutors. The station's role changed to rotary wing in October 1996 and Pumas and Chinooks are currently based there.

Benton, Tyne and Wear

This RFC second-class night LG was used for home defence from May 1917 to May 1919.

Bentra (Whitehead), NI

Also known as Larne, this was predominantly an airship station, but it had a LG attached, which was well used during 1917–18. No aircraft appear to have been based here.

Bentwaters, Suffolk

This RAF station opened in April 1944, the first residents from December of that year being Mustangs and Spitfires that stayed until September 1945. Meteors arrived the following October and stayed for just over a year when an OCU moved in with Meteors, Vampires, Tempests, Hornets, and Harvards until August 1949. The base was then inactive until transferred to the USAF in March 1951, who operated B-29s, F-86s, F-84s, F-101s, F-4Cs, F-5s, F-16s, and A-10s over the years until it closed in 1993. However, the runway is still occasionally used by light aircraft.

Control tower at RAF Bentwaters on 22 May 2011. The USAF vacated the base in 1993, but the Bentwaters Cold War Museum has a few static airframes on the site. (*Grant Peerless*)

Berneray, Hebrides

This ELG was used by the RAF from 1939 to 1945 and by air ambulance flights post-war until its closure in 1974.

Berrow (Pendock Moor), Worcs

This SLG was opened in April 1941 and closed in May 1945. It was also used by ATA Whitleys during 1942.

Berverley, Humberside

This RFC second-class night LG, which was situated on the racecourse, opened in March 1915 for use as a home defence flight station. It was used by various units operating Be2s, JN3s, Avro 504s, RE8s, Camels, and SE5s until flying ceased in June 1919.

Beverley (Linley Hill), Humberside

This unlicensed airfield with a single grass runway opened in 1991 for the Hull Aero Club and is home to around forty light aircraft including those of RM Aviation Microlight School.

Bewdley (Pound Green), Worcs

This unlicensed microlight site opened before 2006; it is currently home to around ten aircraft that use two grass strips.

Bexwell, Norfolk

This RFC ELG was used by home defence units from 1915.

Bibury, Glos

This RAF station opened in July 1940 as a RLG for South Cerney and was used by Oxfords, Harts, Harvards, and Ansons until November 1944. A few Hurricanes and Spitfires were based for a brief period between August and December 1940. Flying ceased in November 1944, and after some use by a MU, the airfield closed in 1945.

Bicester, Oxon

This RFC training station opened in 1917, equipped with Avro 504s, Pups, and F2bs until flying ceased in December 1919. Following expansion, it reopened as a RAF bomber base in January 1928; various types were operated from here, including Horseleys, Harts, Sidestrands, Overstrands, and Battles. During the Second World War, numerous units were based here, but the most ubiquitous type employed was the Blenheim, which was used in the training role until October 1944 when flying more or less ceased. An UAS operated Chipmunks between January 1959 and September 1975. The airfield closed as an active station in March 1976 but is now home to the Bicester Gliding Centre and Windrushers GC. Over 100 gliders and light aircraft are based here; they have the use of three unlicensed grass runways.

Bidford (Bickmarsh), Warks

This unlicensed airfield opened in 1964 with a single grass runway and is home to over fifty light aircraft and gliders. The Bidford Gliding and Flying Club is also based here.

Bidston, Merseyside

This civil aerodrome was used for a short time from 1920 by only small light aircraft.

Biggin Hill (Westerham), Gt. London

This RFC first-class night LG opened in April 1916 and was upgraded to a home defence flight station in December 1917. It was, however, used mainly for wireless and instrument testing with Be2s, FK8s, Pups, F2bs, Camels, and Snipes until July 1922. It then hosted a variety of units but predominantly AACU ones equipped with Snipes, Grebes, Vimys, Bisons, Virginias, Hyderabads, Horsleys, Wallaces, Bulldogs, Demons, Gauntlets, Henleys, Queen Bees, and Battles.

During the Second World War, it was a key Battle of Britain station, operating mostly Hurricanes and Spitfires, which stayed until June 1946. Transport Command arrived in March 1945 with Dakotas, but these departed in January 1946. A RAuxAF squadron took over in May 1946 and operated Spitfires followed by Meteors and Hunters until March 1957. An UAS/AEF was based from January 1957 to February 1959 with Tiger Moths, Harvards, Chipmunks, Prentices, and Provosts. The RAF ceased flying from Biggin in February 1959 when civil flying took over. The site is now Biggin Hill Airport with a single licensed hard runway and around 180 based aircraft. It is particularly popular with corporate jets.

Biggleswade, Beds

This RFC LG was in use between July and September 1917.

Billesley

See Kings Heath.

Billing, Northants

This civil aerodrome near the Aquadrome opened in around 1936 and was used for joy-riding in the late

The 1930s control tower, signal square, and 'C' type hangar at Bicester on 15 May 2018. (*Grant Peerless*)

Above: The grass airfield at Bidford (Bickmarsh) on 4 July 2008 featuring a few of the aircraft based there. (*Grant Peerless*)

Below: Cessna CitationJet D-CHAT in front of the control tower at London Biggin Hill Airport on 3 May 2011. (*Grant Peerless*)

1950s and early 1960s. It may have been used as a RLG from nearby Sywell after the Second World War. It closed in 1964.

Bilsborrow (St Michaels), Lancs

This unlicensed microlight site opened in 1983 with three grass strips and is home to around forty aircraft.

Binbrook, Lincs

This RAF bomber station opened in June 1940 with Battles and later Wellingtons, which were resident until September 1942 when it closed for hard runway construction. It reopened in May 1943 for Lancasters, which stayed until April 1946. These were replaced by Lincolns and, from November 1950, Canberras that stayed, on and off, until January 1972. The base was transferred to Fighter Command in April 1962 and supported squadrons of Javelins, Hunters, and Lightnings. The latter type remained until they were retired in April 1988 and the base then closed, although filming of Memphis Belle took place here during 1989.

Binsoe (West Tanfield), Yorks

This RFC third-class night LG was used for home defence from December 1916 to June 1919, mainly by Avro 504s.

Birch, Essex

This RAF station opened in April 1944 but was used only for a few days by USAAF A-20s. It was reactivated in March 1945 for RAF Dakotas and Horsas for a month or so, after which flying ceased, although an ACGS continued flying until early 1947.

Bircham Newton, Norfolk

This RFC training station was built in 1916–17, the first residents arriving in May 1918 in the form of DH5s, SE5s, Fe2s, Pups, Snipes, and later V/1500s. It closed in January 1920; following expansion, it reopened as a RAF heavy bomber base in 1923 operating Vimys, Aldershots, Fairey 3Fs, Virginias, DH9s, Sidestrands, Gordons, and finally Hinds until it transferred to Coastal Command in August 1936. Ansons were first to arrive, followed by Hudsons and later Blenheims, Wellingtons, and Warwicks. Numerous other units were based during and after the Second World War including AACU, meteorological and ASR Flights, FAA squadrons, aircrew holding units, and an air beam training flight, all using a wide variety of aircraft. Flying ceased in 1948, mainly due to the lack of hard runways and the station closed in December 1962.

Bircotes, Notts

This RAF training station opened in November 1941 and was used by Ansons, Hampdens, Lysanders, Martinets, Harvards, and Wellingtons. They departed by November 1944, but a communications flight remained until November 1945.

Birkenhead (Oxton), Merseyside

This civil aerodrome was used by the Birkenhead Flying Club during 1936 and 1937.

Birmingham (Adderley Park), W. Midlands

This airstrip was used by Wolseley Motors during the First World War to test-fly Be2s and SE5s that were built by them in an adjacent factory.

Birmingham (Elmdon), W. Midlands

It was officially opened as Birmingham's airport on 8 July 1939, although flying had been taking place since May 1936 when scheduled services commenced. An elementary flying school arrived in May 1939 with Magisters, Hinds, Audaxes, Tiger Moths, and Ansons and was resident until February 1946. The airfield was requisitioned by the Air Ministry on the outbreak of the Second World War and used for the test-flying of Stirlings and Lancasters built at the nearby Austin Longbridge works. It reopened for civil flying in July 1946, and scheduled services returned in April 1949. It is now Birmingham International Airport with a considerable number of scheduled and charter flights to long and short-haul destinations.

Bishops Court, NI

This RAF station opened in April 1943 and was used mainly by air observers, gunnery, navigation and advanced flying schools equipped with Ansons, Martinets, Wellingtons, and Oxfords until October 1947. It was also used regularly during the Second World War as a diversion airfield for Coastal Command aircraft. It was then placed on C&M until March 1952 when an ANS arrived, which operated Varsities and Valettas until April 1954. Flying then all but ceased, but the airfield was kept open for communication flights. A VGS was based from February 1987 to October 1990.

Bishops Tachbrook

See Leamington Spa.

Taylorcraft Plus D G-AHVP of the Midland Aero Club above its Birmingham base at Elmdon Airport on 26 June 1947. (*Eddie Riding*)

View of Birmingham (Elmdon) Airport taken from the Taylorcraft in the previous picture on the same day. Note the camouflaged hangars and airport buildings but the lack of aircraft, apart from two Miles Aerovans and a Taylorcraft Plus D. The terminal, which was in use for passengers from 1939 to 1984, was awarded Grade-II listed status in 2018. (*Eddie Riding*)

Bishopton, Yorks

This RFC third-class night LG, later to become a second-class day and night LG, opened in August 1916 and was used for home defence until closure in June 1919.

Bisterne, Hants

This ALG was used between March and July 1944 by USAAF P-47s.

Bitteswell, Leics

This RAF training station opened in June 1941 as a satellite for Bramcote until July 1946 when the RAF departed. Types operated included Wellingtons, Ansons, Oxfords, Hurricanes, Masters, and Dakotas. Armstrong Whitworth built a factory on the airfield in late 1943 for the assembly and test-flying of Lancasters. After the war, this role continued with Shackletons, Vulcans, Sea Hawks, Hunters, Meteors, Javelins, and Argosies. The airfield closed in March 1983.

Blackboys (Uckfield), Sussex

This RFC second-class night LG was used for home defence from December 1916 to August 1917.

Blackbushe (Hartford Bridge), Hants

Opened as a RAF station in November 1942, it was home to a variety of units operating an assortment of types, the most notable being Bostons and Mosquitoes. Others included Tomahawks, Mustangs, Spitfires, Venturas, Havocs, Oxfords, and Mitchells. In March 1945, it transferred to Transport Command, equipped with Warwicks, Dakotas, and Ansons until November 1946, when the airfield closed. It reopened as Blackbushe Airport in February 1947 and soon attracted numerous charter airlines, some of which were involved in the Berlin Airlift, as well as scheduled services. The RAF returned in December 1950 with a squadron of Valettas, which stayed until September 1953. The US Navy arrived in October 1956 and operated R4Ds, R5Ds, R6Ds, and P2Vs until May 1960, when the airport closed again. Part of the site reopened in 1962 for club and executive flying; today, it is a very active GA facility with around 100 based aircraft that operate from a single licensed hard runway.

Blackheath Common, Gt. London

This LG was used by the RFC during 1915.

Blackheath Common (Colchester), Essex

This RFC first-class night LG opened in February 1917 and was used for home defence until closure in August 1919. Be2s were the main type operated.

Black Isle (Blackstand Farm), Highland

This SLG was used for the storage of mostly Beaufighters, Defiants, and Warwicks from August 1941 to October 1945.

Blackpool (Squires Gate), Lancs

Flying started here in October 1909 but did not really get underway until 1933 when scheduled services commenced. These continued until 1937 when they transferred to nearby Stanley Park. The RAF arrived in April 1939 with Magisters and Tiger Moths and went on to operate Battles, Wellingtons, Bothas, Hurricanes, Ansons, and Defiants attached to numerous units until August 1945. Over 3,000 Wellingtons were produced during the Second World War in a shadow factory on the airfield; this went on to build Hunters between 1951 and 1958. It reverted to civil use in August 1946 and a number of scheduled and charter flights were operated until October 2014. It continues in use as a licensed GA airfield with two hard runways and over 100 residents.

Blackpool (Stanley Park), Lancs

This municipal aerodrome came into use in August 1929 but was not opened officially until June 1931. Scheduled services began in 1933 and continued until the outbreak of the Second World War when it was requisitioned by the Air Ministry. The CAG arrived in August 1938 and stayed until September 1939. A satellite assembly line for Wellingtons was set up during the Second World War and completed aircraft were flown to Squires Gate for testing. A CRO repaired Beaufighters on the site and Hurricanes and Seafires were scrapped towards the end of the war, but this activity had ceased by 1946. An ACGS operated from August 1943 to January 1947.

Blackpool Sands, Lancs

This manufacturer's aerodrome was used occasionally by the RFC during the First World War.

Blakehill Farm, Wilts

This RAF Transport Command station opened in February 1944 and was used mainly by Dakotas,

Spartan Cruiser G-ACZM in British Airway's livery outside the main hangar at Blackpool (Stanley Park) on 24 April 1936. The airfield closed around 1946. (*Eddie Riding*)

Horsas, Albermarles, and Hadrians until January 1946. A flight of Oxfords was based between April and July 1946 and it became a RLG for South Cerney for a brief period from April 1948.

Blandford (Cemetery Farm), Dorset
This AALG was in use from the 1920s until 1939.

Blaris (Lisburn), NI
This RLG for RAF Sydenham was used mostly by Battles during May and June 1941. An ACGS was based between May 1943 and April 1944.

Blaston (Uppingham), Leics
This RFC first-class night LG opened in October 1916 and was used for home defence until closure in June 1919.

Blidworth, Notts
This SLG opened in August 1941 and was used to store fighters, possibly Whirlwinds and Lightnings, until closure in 1945.

Blyborough, Lincs
This RFC first-class night LG was used for home defence from October 1916 to February 1918. A private grass airfield in the vicinity at Blyborough Hall was in use from the 1970s to 1990s, the Lincoln Aero Club being resident for a short period in 1967–68.

Blyth, Northumberland
This LG was used by RAF Walruses between March 1942 and June 1943.

Blyton, Lincs
This RAF heavy bomber station opened in September 1942. The first arrivals were Wellingtons followed by Lancasters and Halifaxes, but from February 1943, the role changed to training by a HCU until the end of the Second World War. The airfield closed at the end of 1945 but was used as a RLG for Finningley between October 1951 and January 1954. Types operated included Harvards, Oxfords, and Meteors.

Bobbington
See Halfpenny Green.

Bodmin, Cornwall
This unlicensed airfield with two grass runways opened in 1970 and is home to about forty aircraft, including those of the Cornwall Flying Club.

Bodney, Norfolk
This RAF station was opened as a satellite for Watton in March 1940, the first residents being Blenheims that were followed by Venturas. Masters, Hurricanes, and Oxfords until May 1943, when the base transferred to the USAAF. They operated P-47s, later replaced with P-51s until flying ceased in January 1945. It remained a grass airfield until final closure in November 1945.

Bodorgan (Aberffraw), Gwynedd
This aerodrome was opened by the AAC in September 1940 and was used initially by Queen Bees and later by Henlys, Lysanders, and Martinets during the Second World War. A SLG opened in April 1941 and stored mainly Hurricanes, Wellingtons, Lysanders, and

Swordfish until it closed in January 1945. Flying ceased in September 1945.

Bognor, Sussex

This ALG opened in June 1943 and was used briefly by RAF Spitfires for only a month. More Spitfires arrived in March 1944, which stayed until the following June. An RAF Group support unit was then based here, which operated Mosquitoes, Mustangs, Typhoons, Tempests, Austers, and Ansons until this temporary airfield closed in September 1944.

Bognor Regis, Sussex

This unlicensed airfield opened in 1946 for the use of Lec Refrigeration with one grass runway (which was tarmacked in 1980) and closed in May 1993. It reopened in around 2012 and now has three additional grass runways. The Bognor Regis GC commenced operations in October 2016.

Bogton (Dalmellington), Strathclyde

This RFC LG was used by a gunnery school flying mostly Be2s and Scouts from April 1917 to 1918.

Bolt Head (Salcombe), Devon

This RAF forward fighter station was opened in 1941, the first arrivals being Lysanders. These were followed by Spitfires, Typhoons, and Walruses until flying ceased in February 1945. The airfield closed in 1947 but partly reopened around 2002 and is now in use by light aircraft with six being based here, operating from an unlicensed grass strip.

Booker (Wycombe Air Park), Bucks

This RFC second-class night LG was known as High Wycombe and used briefly for home defence from January to July 1917. It reopened as a civil aerodrome just before the Second World War as Marlow Airport, but little use was made of it until an elementary flying school arrived in 1939 equipped with Tiger Moths, Audaxes, Hinds, Magisters, Oxfords, and Messengers. This stayed until February 1950, and a UAS arrived in the following October with Tiger Moths, Oxfords, Chipmunks, Harvards, and Prentices. This departed in January 1956, but before this, a FTS operated with Chipmunks until July 1953. A couple of communications flights were based here from January 1947 to March 1963, operating Dominies, Oxfords, Austers, Proctors, Valettas, Ansons, and Pembrokes. It reopened for civil flying around 1951 and is now known as Wycombe Air Park, with over 200 resident aircraft that operate from one hard and two grass runways, which are all licensed. The Booker GC is also based here.

Bopeep Hill (Firle Beacon), Sussex

This gliding site was used by the Southdown GC from 1955 to 1974.

Boreham, Essex

This short-lived USAAF station was used by B-26s from March to July 1944. It closed in 1945.

Boscombe Down, Wilts

This TDS was known as Red House Farm and opened in August 1917, operating Avro 504s, Be2s, Pups, DH4s, DH6s, Dolphins, and DH9s until closure in May 1919. The RAF arrived in November 1930 with Virginias, Hinaidis, Heyfords, and later Ansons and Battles. In September 1939, the A&AEE moved in from Martlesham Heath and used a wide assortment of types, both civil and military: in May 1945, 176 aircraft were on strength. The base has stayed in the experimental testing role to the present day, currently under QinetiQ but a couple of UAS/AEFs currently operate Tutors from the airfield.

Boston (Wyberton), Lincs

This unlicensed airfield opened in 1948 and is home to a dozen aircraft, mostly microlights including those of Boston Aero Club. One grass runway is in use.

Bottesford, Leics

This RAF bomber station opened in August 1941, although the first arrivals were Beauforts and Oxfords of a training flight. Bombers in the shape of Manchesters arrived in the following November, which were followed by Lancasters and Stirlings until November 1943. It was then transferred to the USAAF as a transport base between January and April 1944 when C-47s and CG-4s were operated. A HCU was formed in July 1944 and stayed until September 1945. It was equipped with Lancasters, Mosquitoes, Beaufighters, Hurricanes, and Spitfires. From September 1944, various communications and training flights were based using Oxfords, Dominies, Tiger Moths, and Magisters. Flying ceased in 1948, although latterly the airfield was only used as a RLG.

Bottisham, Cambs

This RAF station opened in May 1940 as a satellite for Waterbeach and was used initially for training

Above: Piper Tomahawks G-BMVL and G-BMXL (of the British Airways Flying Club) and Cessna 182 G-WACV on the apron in front of the control tower at Booker (now known as Wycombe Air Park) in August 1987. The tower has since been replaced by a new building. (*Grant Peerless*)

Below: The short-lived Boreham USAAF station in the 1950s showing the abandoned runways. (*Aerofilms*)

with Tiger Moths and Magisters. It was then taken over by an AACU, which operated Lysanders and later Tomahawks and Mustangs. The USAAF arrived in November 1943 with P-47s and P-51s and remained until September 1944 when flying ceased. The airfield closed in May 1946.

Boughrood, Powys

This AALG was in use during the 1930s.

Boulmer, Northumberland

This RAF station opened in November 1942 as a satellite for Eshott and was home to an OTU operating Spitfires, Masters, Martinets, and Oxfords until June 1945. It was then placed on C&M until September 1961 when it was used as a RLG by Jet Provosts from Acklington. A communications flight was based with Devons from March 1963 to April 1968 when fixed-wing flying ceased. An SAR flight was set up in the 1960s with Whirlwinds, Wessexes, and later Sea Kings, which departed in September 2015.

Bourn, Cambs

This RAF bomber station opened in April 1941 and was home to Wellingtons, Stirlings, and Lancasters from February 1942. It became a major Mosquito base from November 1943 to July 1945 and closed in 1948. Short Bros (SEBRO) operated a Stirling repair unit during the Second World War. It reopened for civil flying in 1967, and around fifteen aircraft are based here, operating from one hard/grass unlicensed runway.

Bourne End (Cockmarsh), Bucks

This AALG, which opened in 1933, was adjacent to the River Thames near the Quarry Hotel and was still in use as late as 1950.

Bournemouth (Ensbury Park/ Kinson), Dorset

This civil aerodrome replaced Winton/Talbot Village as Bournemouth's airport in 1917. It was operated by the Bournemouth Aviation Company with Avro 504s that ran a scheduled service to Weymouth during 1919 and 1920. Flying then declined and ceased altogether in 1932.

Bournemouth (Hurn), Dorset

This RAF station opened in July 1941 as a satellite for Ibsley and was home initially to various units involved with target towing and transport duties. Types operated included Whitleys, Lysanders, Albermarles, and Halifaxes. In March 1944, large numbers of Mosquitos and Typhoons arrived and stayed until the following August. USAAF B-26s were based during August, but with their departure, military flying ceased, and the airfield was handed over to BOAC in November 1944. They then commenced scheduled services but transferred to the new Heathrow airport in June 1946. In 1951, Vickers Armstrongs took over an old BOAC hangar and used the airfield to flight-test Valiants, as well as building Varsities, Viscounts, and 1-11s until the factory closed in 1982. Airwork set up a FRU for maintaining naval aircraft and worked on many types including Mosquitoes, Sea Hornets, Sea Furies, Scimitars, Hunters, and Canberras. This unit moved to Yeovilton in December 1972. An AEF and UAS arrived in December 1978 with Chipmunks and later Bulldogs, staying until September 1991. Scheduled services recommenced in the early 1950s and continue to this day along with charter flights. Hurn is now Bournemouth Airport.

Bournemouth (Winton/Talbot Village), Dorset

This civil aerodrome was opened by the Bournemouth Aviation Company in 1915 but closed in 1917 when they moved to Kinson/Ensbury Park. It was used briefly as an ALG by USAAF L-4s during May–June 1944.

Bourne Park (Hurstbourne Tarrant), Hants

This unlicensed airfield opened in the 1990s with a single grass runway, which is home to a helicopter restoration company and around twenty-five light aircraft.

Bournes Green (Shoeburyness), Essex

This RFC second-class day LG was used for gunnery training for a short period from April to June 1917.

Bovingdon, Herts

This RAF bomber station opened in June 1942 but soon transferred to the USAAF who arrived with B-17s two months later. They stayed until September 1944 when they were replaced by C-47s and C-53s of a transport unit. It was handed back to the RAF in April 1946 but soon taken over by the MTCA and used by commercial companies including BOAC for airliner maintenance as well as a number of charter airlines. Types involved included Yorks, Haltons, Vikings, Tudors, and Hermes. Many of these were employed on the Berlin Airlift. The USAF returned in May 1951 with transport aircraft, mostly C-47s, which departed in October 1962. Various communications flights used the airfield from July 1947 to January 1969,

Grumman American AA-5 G-PURR in front of the control tower at Bourn on 29 October 2013. (*Grant Peerless*)

Above: Aerospatiale Gazelle helicopters and light aircraft on the grass airfield at Bourne Park (Hurstbourne Tarrant) on 17 July 2012. (*Grant Peerless*)

Below: RAF Bovingdon in the 1950s. Most of the runways are still in place and are used for a weekend market. Part of the site is occupied by a prison. (*Aerofilms*)

using Ansons, Oxfords, Devons, Valettas, Pembrokes, and Bassetts. During 1955, Hunting Percival used Bovingdon's facilities for night flying trials of their new Jet Provost and also for the export of the company's other products. Film companies used the airfield for several feature films between 1962 and 1978, including *The War Lover*, *633 Squadron*, *Mosquito Squadron*, *Battle of Britain*, and *Hanover Street*. Flying ceased in January 1969 but an ACGS continued to operate until the following September. Today, part of the western end of the east–west runway is used by a couple of resident aircraft.

Boxted, Essex
This USAAF station opened in May 1943 and was home to B-26s, P-51s, and P-47s. After the war, RAF Mosquitoes and Meteors were based until the airfield closed in January 1947, although an ACGS continued flying until April 1948. Some private flying still takes place and regular fly-ins are held.

Bracebridge Heath, Lincs
This factory was built by Robey and Co. in May 1916 to build Gunbuses and Longhorns for the RFC and at the same time established an aerodrome on which to test-fly them. Camels and Triplanes built by other local manufacturers also used the facilities. It was used as a RFC home defence night LG from 1916 and as an AAP from 1918 until closure in April 1920. From 1941, part of the site was used by Avro's for the salvage and rebuilding of Lancasters; this work continued after the war with Lincolns and Yorks. The site finally closed in 1982.

Braceby (Grantham), Lincs
This RFC second-class night LG was used for home defence between October 1916 and June 1919.

Brackla, Highland
This RAF station opened in July 1941 and was used mainly as a RLG by Oxfords, Defiants, Lysanders, and Masters until 1945. An OTU equipped with Whitleys was resident from January 1942 to April 1944. It was used as a SLG from 1941 to September 1947 and stored mainly Halifaxes and Warwicks. A communications flight operating Ansons was based here from February 1944 to September 1947 when flying ceased.

Bradford
See Yeadon.

Bradford (Phoenix), Yorks
This manufacturer's aerodrome, also known as Thornbury, was in use from 1916 to 1919.

Brading, IoW
This second-class day LG opened in December 1917 and was used initially for home defence. DH6s of a coastal patrol flight were operated from June to August 1918 and flying ceased in January 1919.

Bradwell Bay, Essex
This aerodrome opened in 1930 to service off-shore gunnery ranges. It was used by the RAF as an ELG from 1939 and became a RAF station in November 1941. It was home to Bostons, Mosquitoes, Typhoons, and Spitfires. Flying ceased in November 1945, and the airfield closed in 1946. A private airfield known as Dengie about 3 miles to the south-west was in use from around 1974 to 1993.

Braintree, Essex
This RFC second-class night LG was used for home defence from January 1917 to October 1918. Be2s were the main type operated.

Bramcote, Warks
This RAF bomber station opened in July 1940, although some Wellingtons arrived in September 1939, before the airfield was completed. Battles and Wellingtons were operated until December 1940 when the role of the station changed to training. Various units then appeared operating Wellingtons, Oxfords, Hurricanes, Ansons, and Dakotas. The base passed to the FAA in August 1947 as HMS *Gamecock* and numerous types were operated including Seafires, Sea Furies, Sea Hornets, Fireflies, Firebrands, Avengers Sea Balliols, Sea Princes, and Dominies. Flying ceased in January 1958.

Brampton, Yorks
This RFC third-class night LG was used for home defence for a short period from April 1916 to March 1917.

Brattleby
See Scampton.

Bratton, Salop
This RLG for RAF Shawbury was in use between November 1940 and July 1944 mainly by Oxfords, Masters, and Hurricanes.

Brawdy, Pembrokeshire

This RAF station opened in February 1944 as a RLG for St Davids and was home initially to Halifaxes of a meteorological flight. It passed to the FAA in January 1946 as HMS *Goldcrest* and a wide variety of naval types were operated, including Sea Furies, Sea Hawks, Gannetts, and Hunters, as well as aircraft on 'shore leave' from carriers. A few scheduled services were operated from 1958 to 1961. The base returned to the RAF in February 1974 and was used by an OCU flying Meteors, Hunters, Jet Provosts, and Hawks until flying ceased in August 1992.

Bray, Berks

This RLG for White Waltham and later Fairoaks opened in July 1940 and was used mainly by Tiger Moths until 1944. An ACGS was resident from December 1943 until February 1948 when the grass airfield closed.

Brayton, Cumbria

This SLG opened in May 1942 and closed in January 1946. It was used mainly for storing Fortresses, Halifaxes, Wellingtons, Mitchells, and Vengeances.

Breighton, Yorks

This RAF bomber station opened in January 1942 as a satellite for Holme-on-Spalding Moor and was home to Wellingtons, Halifaxes, Manchesters and Lancasters until flying ceased in September 1945. It reopened as a RLG for Full Sutton in June 1951 and was used by Spitfires, Harvards, Vampires, and Meteors until its closure in June 1954. Thor missiles were deployed from August 1959 to January 1963 and Bloodhounds from November 1960 to March 1964. An unlicensed grass strip alongside part of the east–west runway reopened around 1990 for private flying and over sixty aircraft are based here.

Brentingby (Melton Mowbray), Leics

This RFC second-class night LG was used for home defence from April 1916 to May 1918. Types operated included Be2s, Be12s, and Fe2bs. It reopened as an AALG in 1932 and closed in 1937. It hosted various flying circuses and displays during this time.

Brent Tor (Burnford Common), Devon

This gliding site opened in 1983 and is home to the Dartmoor Gliding Society. Around thirty gliders are based here, and light aircraft are accepted on prior notice.

Brenzett, Kent

This ALG opened in September 1943 but was used only by RAF Spitfires for three days. RAF Mustangs arrived in July 1944 and stayed until this temporary airfield closed in October 1944. The Brenzett Aeronautical Museum opened in 1972 in one of the wartime buildings on the site.

The busy apron at the former RAF bomber airfield at Breighton on 23 May 2010 featuring some of the aircraft of the Real Aeroplane Company along with Grumman American AA-5 G-PURR. (*Grant Peerless*)

Bressay (Maryfield), Shetland

This civil aerodrome was in use during the 1930s for limited scheduled services until Sumburgh became the main airport for Shetland. It was used as an ELG by the FAA during the Second World War.

Bridgend, Glamorgan

This field was used by an ACGS from December 1944 to June 1945.

Bridleway Gate, Salop

This RLG for RAF Shawbury opened in September 1940 and closed in January 1944. It was used mainly by Oxfords, Ansons, and Harvards. A MU was based for the remainder of the war.

Bridlington (Speeton), Humberside

This short-lived civil airfield was in use from the spring of 1946 but was not opened officially until 14 August 1947 by the mayor of Bridlington. It was used by the East Riding Flying Club for training and pleasure flying, closing around the end of 1955.

Bridlington (East Leys Farm), Humberside

Another Bridlington aerodrome, it opened in 1932 and was used for private flying and by flying circuses before the Second World War. It is probably the same site as Grindale, which was used by the Hull Aero Club between 1969 and 1991 and is still in use today by, among others, Skydive GB, a parachuting operation that arrived in 1993.

Brighton

See Shoreham.

Brigmerston Down, Wilts

This LG was used by the RFC and RAF during the First World War. It became a bombing range and closed in April 1919.

Brimpton, Berks

This unlicensed airfield at Lower Wasing Farm with a single grass runway is home to around twenty aircraft. It was owned and operated in the 1950s by Sir William Mount, a director of Miles Aircraft.

Brims Mains, Highland

This RAF ELG was in operation from 1940 to 1945 and used mainly by fighters based at Castletown.

Brinklow (Bretford), Warks

This SLG was in use between October 1941 and November 1944. It was also used as a RLG by Oxfords and Tiger Moths between February 1942 and September 1943 and by an ACGS from October 1943 to October 1945. A lone Cessna is based on a private strip at Peter Hall Farm, which may be part of the old airfield.

Bristol (Filton/Patchway), Avon

The British and Colonial Aeroplane Company started construction of the Boxkite in 1910, and this aerodrome opened shortly afterwards. It was used by the RFC for training from December 1915 using Be2s, Fe2s, RE8s, DH4s, DH6s, and DH9s. An AAP was set up in October 1917, which handled mostly DH9s and F2bs until closure in October 1919. British and Colonial became the Bristol Aeroplane Company in 1920 and built numerous types of aircraft, the most notable being F2bs, Scouts, Bulldogs, Bombays, and Blenheims before the Second World War. Bristol Aeroplane Company operated a RFS for the RAF from May 1923 using a variety of types, and in June 1929, an elementary flying school arrived with Avro 504s, DH9s, Hinds, and (later) Hurricanes. Training continued with a reserve flying school from 1935 with Tiger Moths, Audaxes, and Harts until the outbreak of the Second World War.

A wide variety of units occupied Filton during and after the war, equipped with an assortment of types including Gladiators, Hurricanes, Whirlwinds, Blenheims, Lysanders, Ansons, Buckinghams, Tempests, Spitfires, and Vampires. The site was transferred to the MOS in August 1946, but the RAF still retained a presence. An RFS was formed in April 1948 with Tiger Moths, Chipmunks, Ansons, and Proctors and stayed until March 1953. An UAS/AEF arrived in December 1950 and operated Chipmunks and, later, Bulldogs until March 1992. The Bristol Aeroplane Company built Beaufighters and Beauforts during the war and afterwards, the Brabazon, Freighters, Britannias, and Concordes. This continued under the BAe banner when major assemblies for the Airbus range were produced. Between 1978 and 1992, BAe worked on over 300 F-111s for the USAF. The airfield closed in December 2012, but construction of Airbus components continues. Aerospace Bristol opened in October 2017 on part of the old airfield.

Bristol (Lulsgate Bottom), Avon

This RAF station opened in August 1940 as a RLG for Tiger Moths based at Weston-super-Mare.

Control tower at Bristol (Filton) on a quiet day in January 1992 with Bae 146 G-BMYE parked on the apron. It was home to Concorde production, but the airfield closed in 2012. (*Grant Peerless*)

Training continued until April 1946 with Oxfords, Harvards, Masters, and Martinets. Fighters in the shape of Hurricanes and Defiants were based here briefly between January and May 1942. The MTCA took over in 1947, and gliders of the Bristol and Gloucestershire GC were resident from 1946 to 1956. It eventually became Bristol Airport on 1 May 1957. Scheduled services then commenced and continue to this day, along with charter flights and GA operations.

Bristol (Whitchurch), Avon

The first Bristol airport opened on 31 May 1930 with scheduled services commencing in 1932. It was used as a RLG during the 1930s and an elementary flying school was formed in December 1938, equipped with Tiger Moths, Harts, and Ansons. This was disbanded on the outbreak of the Second World War when private flying ceased, and the airfield was requisitioned by the Air Ministry. From August 1939 to November 1944, it was used by Imperial Airways and British Airways (which merged to form BOAC on1 April 1940) to store their fleets of airliners, including HP42s, Ensigns, Albatrosses, and DC3s. Scheduled services continued to operate throughout the war when Whitchurch was the only available civil airport in the UK. Beaufighters were also assembled and test-flown during the Second World War. An ATA ferry pool operated from May 1940 to September 1945 using mostly Ansons and Arguses. Civil flying resumed in June 1945, and scheduled services commenced a year later. It closed in April 1957 when Lulsgate became the official airport for Bristol.

Brize Norton, Oxon

This RAF station opened in August 1937 and was home initially to an FTS operating Harts, Oxfords, and Harvards. An HGCU arrived in July 1942, and glider training was to be the mainstay of the station until December 1945. Types used included Horsas, Whitleys, Albermarles, and Halifaxes. A MU communications flight was based between October 1938 and January 1952, which operated a wide variety of types. Transport Command took over in December 1945 with Dakotas, Halifaxes, Liberators, Yorks, and Hastings until July 1949. Training then briefly returned with Harvards, Mosquitoes, and Oxfords until June 1950. It was then transferred to the USAF who operated C-47s followed by B-36s, B-29s, B-50s, B-47s, KC-97s, and B-52s. It returned to the RAF in April 1965 and became the UK's main military transport base, a role it still fulfils today. Types operated over the years include Belfasts, Britannias, Argosies, Tristars, and VC10s. Hercules, Globemasters, Atlases, and Voyagers are currently based here.

Broad Salts (Sandwich), Kent

This RFC second-class night LG was used for home defence from October 1916 to late 1918.

The airport buildings at Bristol (Whitchurch) on 9 August 1937. It closed in 1957 when the former RAF airfield at Lulsgate Bottom became the new airport for Bristol. (*Eddie Riding*)

Hangar and terminal building at Bristol (Whitchurch) on 9 August 1937 with a BA Swallow in front of the Norman Edgar premises. (*Eddie Riding*)

Opposite above: At Brooklands on 23 October 1936, a fire broke out under the engine shop of the Brooklands Aero Club, causing considerable damage to two hangars. Members and staff managed to save all but six of the aircraft therein. (*Eddie Riding*)

Opposite below: A 1930s view of the control tower and hangars at Brooklands. Flying ceased in 1970, but the site is now home to the Brooklands Museum, which features an extensive collection of aircraft and cars. (*The Aeroplane*)

Broadwell, Oxon

This RAF station opened for Transport Command in February 1944 and was home to Dakotas and Horsas used for glider towing and parachute dropping. Flying ceased in December 1946, and the airfield closed in March 1947.

Brockton, Salop

This SLG opened in July 1941 and closed in December 1945. It was used for storing Spitfires, Hurricanes, Wellingtons, and Beaufighters.

Brockworth (Hucclecote), Glos

This flight-test aerodrome opened in 1915 for the H. H. Martyn Aircraft Company. An AAP was set up in 1918, which handled aircraft produced by the resident Gloucestershire Aircraft Company (formerly H. H. Martyn) until closure in April 1920. This became the Gloster Aircraft Company in November 1926, which was subsequently taken over by the Hawker Aircraft Company in May 1934. The E28/39 prototype, Harts, Albemarles (over 600), Hurricanes, Typhoons, Meteors, and Javelins were built here until all flight-testing moved to Moreton Valence in April 1960. Flying then ceased and the factory closed in April 1964.

Brooklands (Weybridge), Surrey

This was one of the earliest aerodromes in the country, opening in 1908 inside the motor racing circuit. From May 1914, it became a RFC home defence second-class LG operating Shorthorns, Be2s, RE7s, and Avro 504s. From August 1917, an AAP was formed, which handled mostly SE5s and Snipes until April 1920. It was home to several aircraft factories from 1910, including Martynside, Sopwith and its successor Hawker, Shorts, and Vickers Armstrongs. The Brooklands Aero Club was formed in 1927 and remained active at the airfield

until private flying ceased at the outbreak of the Second World War. Hawker produced Harts, Hinds, and Furies until it moved out early in the war, the prototype Hurricane having made its maiden flight here. Vickers concentrated on building and test-flying Wellesleys, Wellingtons, and Warwicks during the Second World War. After the war, they went on to produce the Viking, Viscount, Vanguard, Valiant, BAC 1-11, VC10, and TSR2, latterly as BAC. Flying ceased in February 1970.

Broom (Hagley), Worcs

This RFC second-class night LG was used for home defence from April to October 1916.

Broomfield (Essex)

See Chelmsford.

Broomfield (Grampian)

See Montrose.

Broomfield (Herne Bay), Kent

This RFC third-class night LG was used for home defence from October 1916 to June 1919. It continued in civil use after the First World War until closure around 1922.

Broomhill (Wombwell), Yorks

This RFC second-class night LG was used for home defence from June 1916 to November 1918.

Brough, Humberside

This RFC night LG was used initially for home defence from 1916 and by a marine acceptance depot from April 1918 until closure in December 1919. The Blackburn Aircraft Company set up a factory in 1916 to manufacture Kangaroos. Design and construction continued during the 1930s, the most successful aircraft being the Bluebird and B2. An elementary flying school was formed in 1935 and operated the indigenous Bluebird and B2, then later the BA Swallow, Magister, Battle, Hind, Hart, and Tiger Moth until March 1948.

During the Second World War, the Blackburn factory produced Bothas and Barracudas and modified US Navy aircraft for service in the UK. After the war, they went on to build the Beverley and as Hawker Siddeley and BAe, the Buccaneer as well as Airbus wings and major components for the Harrier and Hawk. A UAS operated Tiger Moths and later, Chipmunks from December 1950 to March 1969. Scheduled services commenced in October 1966 and again for a brief period in 1970 when Islanders of Humber Airways connected Hull with Leavesden. When a new tall chimney blocked the approach to the airfield the service moved to RAF Leconfield. The site is still operated by BAE Systems, but the airfield closed in 2013.

Broughshane, NI

This RAF day LG was used for a short time by RE8s in late 1918. Just to the south-west, an ELG at Ballymena was used by the RAF during the Second World War, but they may have been one and the same site.

Broughton

See Hawarden.

Broxbourne, Herts

This civil aerodrome was licensed in November 1930, the Herts and Essex Aero Club being the first residents, although it was not officially opened until 14 June 1931. It continued to be used by other clubs and private owners until private flying ceased on the outbreak of the Second World War. It became part of the CAG scheme in 1938. During the war, it was home to a CRO, which dealt mainly with Hurricanes, Spitfires, Proctors, and Harvards. The airfield reopened in May 1946 but closed in 1953.

Broxted, Essex

This RFC night LG was used for home defence for a short period during 1916.

Bruntingthorpe, Leics

This RAF training station opened in November 1942 as a satellite for North Luffenham, the first residents being Wellingtons and later Tomahawks. Power Jets set up a facility in June 1943 and test-flew early jet engines, mainly in Meteors. It was placed on C&M in late 1945 before being allocated to the USAF in November 1953 although no aircraft were based until January 1959. These were B-47s and later RB-66s, which stayed until August 1962 when the Americans departed. An ACGS was resident from 1946 to 1948. Flying resumed in 1982 when classic jet aircraft started to arrive, and a good number are now based here, operating from a long unlicensed hard runway. A grass strip is also available.

Brunton, Northumberland

This RAF station was opened in August 1942 as a RLG for Milfield. It was home to OTUs with Hurricanes, Spitfires, Typhoons, Tempests, and Martinets until May 1945. A fighter leaders school used the airfield from February to October 1944, equipped with Spitfires, Typhoons, and Hurricanes. Flying ceased in May 1945, but part

Most of the fleet of the Herts and Essex Aeroplane Club lined up in front of the hangar at Broxbourne on 17 May 1947. DH Tiger Moths predominate but also Percival Proctors and a DH Hornet Moth. The airfield closed in 1953. (*Eddie Riding*)

of the wartime airfield reopened for private flying and parachuting around 1983; it had closed by August 2003.

Bryansford (Newcastle), NI
This civil LG opened in 1913 and was used later by the RFC.

Buckminster, Leics
This RFC home defence flight station opened in September 1916 and was used by Fe2s, Be2s, Be12s, and Avro 504s. It was later used by an AAP and closed in June 1919.

Bucknall (Horncastle), Lincs
This RFC third-class night LG was used for home defence from October 1916 to June 1919.

Buddon, Tayside
This temporary airstrip was constructed by the Army in 1966 and used initially by a Beverley and then AAC Beavers until 1976.

Bude, Cornwall
This was predominantly a RNAS airship station, but an associated LG and was used by the RAF for a short period from May to December 1918.

Bulphan, Essex
This decoy site was in use from about March 1940 to April 1944. It was used by an ACGS for a short time from June 1945.

Bungay (Flixton), Suffolk
This USAAF bomber station was home to B-24s between December 1942 and July 1945. On a site nearby is the Norfolk and Suffolk Aviation Museum, which opened in May 1976.

Burcott, Beds
This unlicensed airfield at Holmbeck Farm with a single grass runway opened in 1986 and is home to over a dozen residents.

Bures
See Wormingford.

Burford, Glos
This airstrip was in use during the 1930s by private civil aircraft. It was used as a RLG for RAF Little Rissington during the Second World War and continued in civil use after the war for charter and pleasure flying until closure around the end of 1950.

Burgh Castle, Norfolk
This RNAS home defence flight station and night LG opened in November 1916 as a RLG for Great Yarmouth. It was used by Be2s, Camels, DH4s, and DH9s until flying ceased in March 1919.

Burn, Yorks
This RAF bomber station opened in June 1942 and was home initially to Wellingtons. These were later replaced by Halifaxes, which became the mainstay of

the base until it closed in April 1945. An AOP flight of Austers was based briefly between December 1943 and March 1944. Part of the wartime airfield reopened for gliding in 1983, and gliders of the Burn GC are based here today. Visiting aircraft are welcome to use the three unlicensed hard runways that are available.

Burnaston
See Derby.

Burnfoot, Cumbria
This RLG for RAF Kingstown opened in July 1940 and closed in July 1945. It was used mainly by Magisters and Tiger Moths.

Burnham-on-Crouch, Essex
This RNAS opened in late 1914 with a couple of TB8s. It became a RFC second-class night LG in April 1916 and was used for home defence until August 1919, latterly as a first-class day and night LG. An AALG just to the south was opened by the Duchess of Bedford in August 1934 and survived until closure on the outbreak of the Second World War.

Burrow Head (Kidsdale), Dumfries and Galloway
This RAF station opened in May 1939, its only user being an AACU that operated Henleys, Queen Bees, and Austers until November 1943.

Burscough, Lancs
This FAA station HMS *Ringtail* opened in October 1943 and was used by over forty units, flying a wide variety of naval types including Seafires, Corsairs, Hellcats, Wildcats, Avengers, Swordfish, Barracudas, and Fireflies. Like most naval stations, it also acted as host to aircraft from carriers while on 'shore leave'. It closed to flying in May 1946, but some communications flights continued to use the airfield, as did crop sprayers in the 1960s.

Burton Constable (Hull), Humberside
This private grass airfield was in use from the 1970s to the 1990s.

Burton-on-the-Wolds (Loughborough), Leics
This RFC third-class night LG, later reclassified a day LG, was used for home defence from October 1916 to early 1919.

Burton upon Trent (Moat Hall), Staffs
This private grass airfield was in use from the 1980s to at least 1993.

Burtonwood, Cheshire
This RAF MU and associated airfield opened in April 1940. Types stored included Hampdens, Beauforts, Magisters, Oxfords, Marylands, Lysanders, Spitfires, and Fortresses. The USAAF took over in June 1942 and designated the site a base air depot, the main types dealt with being P-38s, B-26s, A-20s, B-17s, and C-47s. The RAF regained control in January 1946 and it reverted to a MU until September 1950. The USAF returned in 1948 and again used the site for storage of C-54s, B-47s, B-50s, B-36s, C-119s, C-124s, C-118s, and C-123s. By 1953, it was the largest US base in Europe and continued in operation until April 1959. During 1951 and 1952, Scottish Aviation operated a daily service to Northolt with DC3s, calling the airfield 'Warrington'. The US Army stored helicopters here from January 1967 until June 1976, and a VGS used the airfield between October 1959 and June 1984, when all flying ceased.

Bury
See Upwood.

Bury St Edmunds (Westley), Suffolk
This AALG opened in 1934 and was later considered as a possible airport for the town. This did not happen, and it was used for private flying until the outbreak of the Second World War, including by the West Suffolk Aero Club. It was taken over by the RAF in September 1940 as a satellite for Snailwell; Lysanders, Tiger Moths, Austers, and gliders were operated until flying ceased in June 1944.

Bush Barn, Berks
This SLG opened in September 1941 and closed in February 1943. It became a RLG for RAF Shellingford in 1944 and was used by mostly Tiger Moths until flying ceased in January 1945.

Butley, Suffolk
This short-lived RFC/RAF LG was in use from 1918 to January 1919 as an experimental station housing units detached from Felixstowe and Orfordness. Types flown included DH9s and Camels. Woodbridge airfield is half a mile to the south and Bentwaters 1.5 miles to the north.

Buttergask, Tayside

This RAF station opened in November 1941 and was used as a RLG by Tiger Moths and Magisters from Perth until its closure in November 1945.

Caernarfon (Llandwrog), Gwynedd

This RAF training station opened in January 1941 as a satellite for Penrhos. It was home to several units operating Whitleys, Ansons, Lysanders, Defiants, and Blenheims. It closed in June 1945 but reopened for civil use in 1969 and is home to around forty aircraft that operate from two licensed hard runways. A flight of S92s and AW189s is based here, providing SAR duties for the MCA.

Caerwent, Gwent

This AALG was in use during the 1930s.

Cairnbeg, Grampian

This RLG was used by Oxfords from RAF Montrose from 1943 to 1944.

Cairncross (Reston), Borders

This RFC second-class night LG opened in October 1916 and was used for home defence. A coastal patrol flight operating DH6s was also based here until closure in August 1919.

Caistor, Lincs

This RAF station opened in November 1940 as a satellite for Kirton-in-Lindsey for a detachment of Hurricanes and was used from June 1942 as a RLG for various nearby airfields, notably Cranwell. Types using the airfield included Oxfords, Spitfires, Masters, Harvards, and Ansons until flying ceased in February 1945. Thor missiles were deployed at the base from September 1960 to May 1963.

Calveley, Cheshire

This RAF station opened in January 1942 as a RLG for Tern Hill, the first occupants being Masters. They stayed until February 1944 and were replaced from the following December with Harvards, Hurricanes, Ansons, and Oxfords. Flying ceased in May 1946, and the airfield closed five months later.

Cambridge (Fen Ditton), Cambs

This civil aerodrome opened in April 1929 and was used predominantly by the Cambridge Aero Club and at times as a RLG by the RAF. It closed in 1937 when all operations transferred to the new aerodrome at Teversham, a short distance away.

Cambridge (Hardwick), Cambs

This private aerodrome was home to the Cambridge School of Flying but used by the RFC during 1911. It was again used for a short time after the First World War by the Cambridge School of Flying until closure in December 1920.

Cambridge (Teversham), Cambs

This airport was opened by Marshall's in 1937 to replace Fen Ditton. It boasted a terminal building, hotel, and hangars. A RFS commenced training in February 1938 with Tiger Moths and Harts, and a unit of the CAG opened in the following July. The airport was opened officially on 8 October 1938 by the air minister, Sir Kingsley Wood. Marshall's was designated as a CRO and received its first contract just before the outbreak of the Second World War, which covered the repair and modification of Whitleys and Oxfords. This went on to include Albermarles, Mosquitoes, Typhoons, and Dakotas.

Training for the RAF continued throughout the war, and at its peak, some 120 Tiger Moths were on strength. On 1 January 1946, the first post-war private flight in Britain by a civil aircraft took place from here. Marshall's repair and overhaul work continued after the war and many types received attention including Sea Hornets, Venoms, Canberras, Valiants, Britannias, Viscounts, and Hercules. The latter are still being worked on along with other types. RAF flying training continued until 1954 at which time Chipmunks were used. An UAS was formed in 1946 and used Tiger Moths, Chipmunks and Bulldogs until moving out in 1999. Limited scheduled services have operated from the airport and continue to this day. Teversham remains a busy airfield thanks mainly to Marshall's operations. One hard and two grass runways are available, all licensed.

Cammeringham

See Ingham.

Campbeltown (Machrihanish/Strabane), Strathclyde

This RFC aerodrome opened in 1917 as a sub-station of the airship base at Luce Bay. Home to a coastal patrol flight, it operated DH6s and Fairey 3Fs from July 1918 to March 1919. A new airfield 2 miles to the north-west opened for the FAA as HMS *Landrail* in June 1941 and was used by numerous aircraft, mostly those on 'shore leave' from carriers until March 1946. Types accommodated included Swordfish, Albacores, Fulmars, Sea Hurricanes, Seafires, Barracudas, and Wildcats. The Navy returned in December 1951 with Sea

Above: Art Deco terminal building at Cambridge (Teversham) on 11 May 2008. (*Grant Peerless*)

Left: Cessna CitationJet N511TC parked by the impressive control tower at Cambridge (Teversham) on 11 May 2008. (*Grant Peerless*)

Furies, Harvards, and Fireflies and stayed until September 1952 when flying ceased. It was redeveloped as a master diversion airfield in 1960–62. The Navy used the base for helicopter operations between 1962 and 1989. Scheduled services are operated, using one hard licensed runway.

Campbeltown (The Strath/Kintyre), Strathclyde

This civil aerodrome opened in 1933 with scheduled services to destinations in Scotland, which continued until the outbreak of the Second World War. It was requisitioned by the FAA in February 1940 and became HMS *Landrail* 2 in April 1941. Swordfish and Albacores were operated until July 1943 when it became a satellite of Machrihanish. It then became home to naval aircraft on 'shore leave' until flying ceased in mid-1945.

Camphill (Great Hucklow), Derbys

This gliding site was used by an ACGS from May 1945 to August 1950. It is currently home to the Derbyshire and Lancashire GC with around forty gliders based.

Canterbury

See Bekesbourne.

Cardiff (Ely Racecourse), Glamorgan

Joy-riding took place on the racecourse just after the First World War, and a scheduled service to Paris was introduced in October 1919. It continued to be used for pleasure flying at least until 1931.

Cardiff (Splott/Pengam Moors), Glamorgan

The first municipal airport for Cardiff was opened officially on 3 October 1931, and scheduled services commenced in January 1932. These continued until the outbreak of the Second World War when the airfield was requisitioned as RAF Cardiff. Before this, in June 1937, Hinds and Hectors arrived, followed by Ansons, Hurricanes, Dominies, Tiger Moths, Oxfords, and Austers belonging to various units. A major resident during the war was a MU that packed aircraft for use abroad. Types handled included Harts, Lysanders,

The massive airship sheds at the former Royal Airship Works at Cardington on 13 December 2014. The left hand one was built in 1916–17 and extended during 1924–26, while the one on the right was relocated from Pulham in 1928. (*Tony Yarnold*)

Hurricanes, Gladiators, Harvards, and Spitfires and continued until October 1945. Scheduled services resumed after the war, but in April 1954, civil flying transferred to Rhoose, the new airport for Cardiff. The RAF had ceased flying in July 1953.

Cardiff (Rhoose), Glamorgan

This RAF station opened as a satellite for Llandow in April 1942 and was used for training with Spitfires, Masters, Ansons, Martinets, Defiants, Lysanders, and Whitleys. This use continued until August 1944, and an ACGS operated from May 1944 to March 1947. On 1 April 1954, Rhoose became the airport for Cardiff, although scheduled services had commenced a couple of years earlier. British Airways opened a maintenance base in 1993. Today, the airport supports many scheduled and charter flights.

Cardiff (Wenvoe), Glamorgan

This civil aerodrome was opened a month before Splott by Cardiff Flying Club in August 1931. Limited scheduled services were operated, and the aerodrome was used whenever Splott was unserviceable. It had closed by the outbreak of the Second World War.

Cardington, Beds

Most famous for airship and balloon development, Shorts opened a factory here in 1915, which led to it being known locally as Shortstown. A limited amount of fixed-wing flying took place, but an air storage unit was based here from August 1932 to February 1938, and a training aids development unit operated Harvards between December 1944 and March 1946. The site is still used for airship development.

Cardross, Strathclyde

This was a flight-test aerodrome for Be2s built by William Denny and Bros at their Dumbarton factory. It was in use from 1916 to 1918.

Carew Cheriton, Pembrokeshire

This RFC aerodrome, known as Pembroke, was used predominantly during the First World War for airship operations. It was also used by DH6s of a coastal patrol flight from June 1918 to January 1919. It reopened as a RAF station in April 1939 and was home to numerous units flying Lysanders, Ansons, Wallaces, Henleys, Beauforts, Blenheims, Beaufighters, Hurricanes, Oxfords, and Hudsons. It closed in November 1945, but an ACGS operated here between June and December 1946.

Cark (Grange-over-Sands), Cumbria

This RAF training station opened in January 1942 and was home to various units operating an assortment of aircraft including Henleys, Lysanders, Defiants, Martinets, Hurricanes, Magisters, and Ansons. The airfield closed in December 1945, but an ACGS continued flying until May 1947. Part of the wartime airfield reopened for private flying before 1974, and it is now primarily a parachute centre with a couple of aircraft being based here. One hard unlicensed runway is in use.

Carlisle (Botcherley), Cumbria

Carlisle's first aerodrome was short-lived, probably because it was suitable only for the smallest aircraft and only operated during 1920.

Carlisle (Crosby-on-Eden), Cumbria

This RAF training station opened in March 1941 and operated Hurricanes, Oxfords, Beauforts, Beaufighters, Dakotas, and Halifaxes until closure in June 1946. It reopened for civil use in 1947 when scheduled services commenced, and these continued sporadically until 1993. However, they resumed in July 2019 with services by Loganair to Southend, Belfast, and Dublin. It became Carlisle Airport in 1957 and is now known as Carlisle Lake District Airport. Two hard licensed runways are currently in use, and around fifty aircraft are based here.

Carlisle (Kingstown), Cumbria

This AALG opened in around 1930, which later became Carlisle's airport. It was licensed in March 1934, although scheduled services had commenced a year earlier, which continued until the outbreak of the Second World War. An elementary flying school was formed in July 1939, which operated Tiger Moths, Audaxes, and Hinds. It became a RAF training station during the war with Ansons, Magisters, Tiger Moths, and Battles; this role continued until March 1953, latterly with Ansons and Chipmunks. Limited scheduled services started again after the war, but the airfield closed in 1957 when Crosby-on-Eden became the airport for Carlisle.

Carlton, Yorks

This RFC first-class night LG was used for home defence for a short period only from March to November 1916.

Carlton Moor, Tyne and Wear

This gliding site was used by the Carlton Moor GC from the early 1960s to December 2008.

Carmunnock (Cathcart), Strathclyde

This manufacturer's aerodrome was used to test-fly Fe2s, DH9s, and Be2s during the First World War.

Carnaby, Humberside

This RAF ELG opened in March 1944 for Bomber Command but without any based units. However, it had an extra-long runway to enable it to be used as an emergency diversion airfield, and many aircraft in difficulties made successful landings. This was one of three airfields designated for this purpose, the others being Manston and Woodbridge. It closed in March 1946 but reopened as a RLG in September 1949. It was used by Meteors, Vampires, Prentices, Tiger Moths, Oxfords, and Harvards until flying ceased in July 1954. It was reactivated in August 1959 as a Thor missile base until they departed in April 1963. It saw some civil use during the 1980s.

Carrickmore, NI

This unlicensed airfield opened in about 2012 with one hard runway and around a dozen residents.

Castle Bromwich, W. Midlands

This civil aerodrome opened in 1909 for private flying, which continued until the outbreak of the First World War. It was used by the RFC from May 1915 mainly for training purposes, but it later became a home defence flight station. Types operated included Be2s, RE7s, FK8s, Avro 504s, Fe2bs, DH4s, and Camels. An AAP was set up in July 1918 and handled mostly SE5s and 0/400s. The RAF departed in April 1920. Scheduled services commenced in September 1919 and continued until May 1939 when they transferred to the new airport at Elmdon. A RAuxAF squadron was formed in October 1926 equipped with Wapitis and DH9s and later Harts, Gladiators, and Hurricanes.

An elementary flying school arrived in July 1937 with Tiger Moths, Harts, Magisters, and Ansons and was disbanded in September 1939. A large factory was built in 1938–39 by Vickers Supermarine to build their Spitfire aircraft, which were test-flown from the airfield. Nearly 12,000 Spitfires and 300 Lancasters were produced by December 1945 when the factory closed. An AACU arrived in April 1940, which operated various types until December 1943, and a unit operating Oxfords, Hurricanes, Beaufighters, and Spitfires was then based here, which departed in June 1946. Training returned in November 1947 with Tiger Moths, Ansons, Prentices, and Chipmunks, staying until June 1954. An UAS was in residence from May 1941 to March 1958, initially with Tiger Moths and Oxfords, which were followed by Prentices and Chipmunks. The last military unit to be based was an AOP flight equipped with Austers and Chipmunks from March 1953 to March 1957. The airfield closed in April 1958.

Castle Camps, Cambs

This RAF fighter station opened in June 1940 as a satellite for Debden. It was used by Hurricanes, Spitfires, and Mosquitoes until flying ceased in January 1946.

Castle Combe, Wilts

This RAF training station opened in May 1941 as a RLG for Hullavington and, later, Babdown Farm. It was used by Harvards, Masters, Hurricanes, Swordfish, Albacores, and Oxfords until flying ceased in June 1945. It closed in September 1948.

Castle Donington (East Midlands Airport), Leics

This RFC second-class night and day LG opened in October 1916 and was used for home defence until closure in August 1918. The site was incorporated into a RAF station opened as a satellite for Wymeswold in January 1943 and was used mainly for training with Wellingtons, Masters, Oxfords, Dakotas, and Ansons until flying ceased in September 1946. After redevelopment, it was reopened as East Midlands Airport in April 1965 by the Duke of Edinburgh.

Castle Douglas, Dumfries and Galloway

This AALG was in use during the 1930s.

Castle Kennedy (Stranraer) Dumfries and Galloway

This civil aerodrome was in use before and during the First World War. An RAF station opened in June 1941 and was home to a gunnery school that operated Defiants, Lysanders, Ansons, and Martinets until June 1945. From December 1942 to September 1943, a torpedo training unit was based equipped with Beaufighters, Beauforts, Bothas, and Wellingtons. A storage sub-unit was set up in July 1945, which stored mainly Wellingtons and Mosquitoes until August 1947. It closed to flying after the war but was retained as an ELG. It reopened for civil flying in 1955 when Silver City Airways commenced a car ferry service to Northern Ireland, but this was suspended in 1957. It was then used occasionally by light aircraft and a couple are based here today. One hard unlicensed runway is in use.

Castletown, Highland

This RAF station opened in June 1940 as a satellite for Wick and was used mainly by Hurricanes and Spitfires until May 1944. An ASR flight equipped with Walruses and Ansons was based from January 1943 to April 1944; flying ceased in March 1945. Some private flying took place after the war but had ceased by 2003.

Catfoss, Yorks

This RAF station opened in May 1930 and was home to a variety of units operating Virginias, Heyfords, Fairey 3Fs, Henleys, Gordons, and Harts until the outbreak of the Second World War. A few Spitfires arrived in February 1940 but had departed by the following May. It then hosted an OTU that operated Blenheims, Beauforts, Beaufighters, Ansons, Oxfords, Lysanders, Battles, Martinets, and Tiger Moths until February 1944. This was replaced by the Central Gunnery School, which was equipped with Spitfires, Mustangs, and Thunderbolts until flying ceased in November 1945. It was used for the deployment of a few Thor missiles between August 1959 and April 1963.

Catley Hill (Trimdon), Co. Durham

This RFC second-class night LG was used for home defence from October 1916 to June 1919.

Catterick, Yorks

This RFC aerodrome opened in February 1915 as a training station but was also used as a home defence flight station. Numerous types were operated including Shorthorns, Martynsides, Avro 504s, Be2s, DH4s, RE8s, Fe2s, 0/400s, and DH9s until flying ceased in March 1919. Flying resumed in August 1924 and a variety of units operated an assortment of types until the outbreak of the Second World War. These included F2bs, Atlases, Audaxes, Hectors, Lysanders, Demons, and Furys. Spitfires arrived in September 1939 and were joined by Hurricanes, Mustangs, and Blenheims until they departed in February 1944. Flying then all but ceased, but the airfield remained in use for communications flights and a VGS, which arrived in March 1960 and left in 2002.

Caunton (Knapthorpe Lodge), Notts

This unlicensed microlight site opened before 2001, which is home to the Derby and Nottingham Microlight Club, with about twenty residents. Two grass runways are available.

Causeway (Rhee), NI

This unlicensed airfield opened before 2010 with two grass runways and around a dozen residents, including those of the Ulster Flying Club.

Caxton Gibbet, Cambs

This civil aerodrome opened in May 1935 and was used by the Cambridge University Gliding Club (CUGC) and then by the Ely Aero Club. In July 1940, it was requisitioned by the RAF and used as a RLG for training flights from Teversham using Tiger Moths, Magisters, and Masters. It was also used for

AOP training flights using Austers. It remained a grass airfield until it closed in July 1945. The CUGC returned in February 1946 but moved to Bourn the following May when all flying ceased.

Chailey, Sussex

This short-lived ALG was used by RAF Spitfires and Austers between April and June 1944.

Chalgrove, Oxon

This RAF station opened in 1942 and was used initially as a RLG by Wellingtons from Harwell until 1943. The USAAF arrived in February 1944 and operated various types until they departed in October 1945. These included P-38s, F-3s, F-5s, F-6s, P-51s, A-20s, L-4s, L-5s, P-61s, C-47s, C-53s, C-109s, Mosquitoes, and Spitfires. An OTU equipped with Spitfires returned in July 1946 but only stayed until the following October. Martin-Baker took over the site as their test airfield in 1946 and is still resident today. One licensed hard runway and two unlicensed grass strips are available.

Challock (Squids Gate), Kent

This unlicensed airfield with two grass runways opened in June 1963 and is used mainly for gliding by the Kent GC. It saw use by a RAF VGS from March 1995 to 1996. Around thirty-five types are based here.

Chalvey, Bucks

This small civil aerodrome opened in 1928, becoming an AALG in 1933. It closed in 1937.

Charlton Horethorne, Somerset

Planned originally as a satellite for RAF Exeter, it was opened instead as FAA station HMS *Heron 2* in May 1942 as a satellite for Yeovilton. It was home to a dozen or so units operating Fulmars, Oxfords, Wildcats, Sea Hurricanes, Ansons, Swordfish, Tiger Moths, Proctors, and Harvards. Flying ceased in April 1945 when it was handed back to the RAF, who set up a MU that closed in 1948.

Charlton Park

See Malmesbury.

Charmy Down, Avon

This RAF station opened in November 1940 as a satellite for Colerne. It was home to a variety of units operating Hurricanes, Defiants, Whirlwinds, Spitfires, Havocs, Bostons, Beaufighters, and Oxfords. The USAAF arrived in March 1944 with P-61s, P-70s, and F-3s, but they only stayed until the following June. The RAF then returned, and training resumed until flying ceased in December 1945. The base closed in October 1946, although an ACGS carried on flying until February 1948. A few microlights operate from part of the old airfield at a site known as St Catherines.

Charterhall, Borders

This RFC first-class night LG, known as Eccles Tofts or Greenlaw, was used for home defence from January 1917 to early 1918. A site just to the north-east opened as a RAF station in May 1942 and was home to an OTU operating Blenheims, Defiants, Beaufighters, Oxfords, Mosquitoes, Wellingtons, and Hurricanes until November 1945. Spitfires and Mustangs were then based briefly until departing in March 1946. An armament practice flight used Martinets, Masters, and Spitfires from November 1945 to March 1947 when flying ceased. Part of the wartime airfield reopened for private flying before 1974, and a few light aircraft are currently based here, operating from an unlicensed hard runway.

Chasetown (Lichfield), Staffs

This RFC third-class night and day LG was used for home defence from October 1916 to October 1917.

Chathill, Northumberland

This LG was used by the RAF during 1918 and 1919.

Chatteris, Cambs

This unlicensed airfield with five grass runways opened before 1998 and is primarily used for parachuting; it is also open to visiting light aircraft. About twenty aircraft are currently based here.

Chattis Hill (Stockbridge), Hants

This RFC aerodrome opened in September 1917 and was home to mostly training units, becoming a TDS in July 1918. Various types were operated including Be2s, FK8s, RE8s, Avro 504s, Pups, Camels, and SE5s until flying ceased in May 1919. In December 1940, Vickers established an assembly plant for Spitfires; these were test-flown from the airfield until 1945. It eventually closed in May 1948.

Chavenage, Glos

This private airfield at Orange Grove Barn opened before 1998 with one grass runway at which over six aircraft are based, mostly microlights.

Chedburgh, Suffolk

This RAF bomber station opened in September 1942 as a satellite for Stradishall. The first residents were Stirlings, followed by Lancasters, Wellingtons, Warwicks, and finally Halifaxes. Flying ceased in December 1946.

Cheddington, Bucks

This RFC first-class night LG was used for home defence from March to October 1917. Just to the west, a RAF station opened in March 1942 as a satellite for RAF Wing and was used by Wellingtons, Ansons, and Lysanders of an OTU until the following September. The USAAF then put in a brief appearance with B-24s until October but returned in full force in August 1943. They operated B-24s, B-17s, P-47s, A-20s, and B-26s until June 1945 when flying ceased. Private flying takes place from part of the wartime airfield and around six aircraft are based here.

Chedworth, Glos

This RAF station opened in April 1942 as a satellite for Aston Down. It was used as a RLG, mainly by training units operating Spitfires, Hurricanes, Oxfords, Mosquitoes, Mustangs, Masters, and Typhoons until it closed in May 1945. The CFS used it for an ELG in the 1950s and 1960s.

Chelmsford, Essex

RNAS LG used for home defence from July 1915 to February 1916. A RFC second-class night LG known as Broomfield Court, 4 miles to the north, opened in April 1916 and was used for home defence until mid-1919. It reopened for civil use in 1932, the official opening ceremony being performed by the lord lieutenant of Essex on 18 May. The Broomfield Flying Club was formed in 1934 and continued until the airfield closed at the outbreak of the Second World War.

Cheltenham

See Staverton.

Cheltenham, Glos

This civil aerodrome at Badgeworth was in use from around October 1916 to June 1920 by the Cheltenham and West of England Aviation Company, who used it for flying training with Ruffy-Baumann biplanes. Another small aerodrome at Uckington was in use during 1920, mostly for joy-riding with Avro 504-sized aircraft.

Chelveston, Northants

This RAF station opened in December 1941 and was used initially for glider training with Hotspurs and Hamilcars, using Stirlings as tugs. The USAAF arrived in June 1942 with C-47s and went on to operate B-17s until July 1945. It was then placed on C&M until the Americans returned in December 1952 with C-47s, which were followed by B-47s and B-66s. They stayed until August 1962, when flying ceased, but it was retained as a reserve airfield for some time afterwards.

Chepstow (Racecourse), Gwent

This SLG was used for storing Spitfires, Hurricanes, Whitleys, Wellingtons, Bostons, Beauforts, and Typhoons from May 1941 to May 1945.

Chertsey Meads, Surrey

This civil aerodrome opened in around April 1930. Walruses were test-flown by Saunders-Roe from 1942 to January 1944, after which it closed.

Chessington, Gt. London

This RFC second-class day and night LG was used for home defence from October 1916 to October 1917. A civil aerodrome about 2 miles south (known as Byhurst Farm) opened in February 1920 and was used by Leatherhead Aviation Service for joy-riding and charter work. This activity did not last long, and the aerodrome closed in 1922. A private airfield just to the west at Rushett Farm opened in the early 1970s and has a single grass runway and a few resident light aircraft.

Chetwynd, Salop

This RAF station opened in October 1940 as a RLG for Tern Hill and was used by Masters, Hurricanes, Harvards, Tiger Moths, Prentices, and Provosts until July 1961. It then became a RLG for Shawbury's helicopters and continues in this role today.

Chewton Mendip (Franklyns Field), Somerset

This private grass airfield was in use from the 1990s and possibly into the 2000s.

Chilbolton, Hants

This RAF station opened in September 1940 and was home to mostly fighters until its closure in June 1946. Types operated included Hurricanes, Spitfires, Mustangs, Tempests, and Vampires. Glider training with Masters, Hotspurs, and Tiger Moths took place between December 1942 and May 1943. The USAAF put in a brief appearance from March to September 1944 with P-47s, P-51s, C-47s, and C-53s. Vickers-Armstrongs arrived in February 1947 and test-flew Attackers and Swifts but departed in 1957, while Folland's test-flew Midges and Gnats from 1953 to 1961. Flying then ceased but part of the wartime airfield reopened for private flying in 1979, known as Stonefield Park, and around fifteen aircraft are currently based here, operating from a single unlicensed grass strip.

Chiltern Park (Ipsden), Oxon

This unlicensed microlight site opened in 1988; it is also open to light aircraft that fly from a single grass strip. Around twenty-five aircraft are based here.

Chilworth, Oxon

This AALG was in use during the 1930s and was home to several residents together with the Chilworth Flying Club.

Chingford (Hall Lane), Gt. London

This RNAS opened in April 1915 and was used initially for home defence. It became a RFC second-class night LG in October 1917, again for home defence; in April 1918, a TDS was set up, which operated Avro 504s, Camels, RE8s, DH6s, DH9s, Pups, and F2bs. It closed in February 1919. The eastern part of the site was reopened for civil flying in 1923 but was never very popular and closed finally in 1934.

Chipping, Lancs

This gliding site opened in 1973 and is home to the Bowland Forest GC. Around twenty-five gliders are based here.

Chipping Norton, Oxon

This RAF station was opened in June 1940 as a satellite for Little Rissington and used mainly as a RLG by Oxfords and Harvards until closure in July 1945. Some 3 miles to the north-east was a gliding site at Coldharbour Farm, which was home to the Altair GC in the 1980s and 1990s.

Chipping Ongar (Willingale), Essex

This USAAF bomber station was opened in June 1943 with B-26s that stayed for just over a year before departing. Their place was taken by Hadrian gliders awaiting transfer to the RAF. The airfield was returned to the RAF in April 1945 and closed soon afterwards. Civil flying commenced in 1946, and the airfield was licensed for a couple of years. This use continued on and off during the 1960s, '70s, and '80s, and around a dozen aircraft are currently based here.

Chipping Warden, Northants

This RAF station was opened in August 1941, its first residents being an OTU equipped with Wellingtons, Ansons, and Hurricanes. This unit stayed until June 1945, and at the same time, a BAT flight of Oxfords was based here. An ANS was resident for a brief spell between July and December 1945 with Wellingtons, Ansons, and Oxfords. A MU stored Horsas and a few Liberators from January 1946 to December 1949. Flying ceased in December 1945, but the airfield was re-activated as a RLG in November 1952 and used by Oxfords from Wellesbourne Mountford until October 1953.

Chirk, Clwyd

This unlicensed airfield at Ley Farm was opened before 1978 with two grass runways and around a dozen resident aircraft.

Chiseldon, Wilts

An unlicensed airfield at Draycott Farm was used by crop sprayers during the 1960s and other light aircraft from the 1970s. It has one grass runway and is home to over a dozen aircraft. Another private airfield at Lower Upham Farm (also known as Ogbourne) is just to the east of Draycott Farm strip, which opened before 1998 and is home to over twenty aircraft, mostly microlights.

Chivenor (Barnstaple), Devon

North Devon Airport, also known as Heanton Court, was officially opened on 13 June 1934, although pleasure flying had started in 1933. Scheduled services were operated to Lundy Island and other destinations until it was requisitioned by the RAF on the outbreak of the Second World War. The new military airfield was built just to the west of the pre-war aerodrome, and its first residents from November 1939 were an AACU with Queen Bees, Magisters, and Tutors. Their stay was short-lived and an OTU replaced them with Blenheims, Ansons, and Beauforts.

Next on the scene was an aircraft that became synonymous with Chivenor—the Wellington, many of which were equipped with Leigh lights. Various other units arrived operating Spitfires, Oxfords, and Martinets. A CRO specialising in Tiger Moths was also resident during the Second World War. Civil flying returned in 1950 and scheduled services resumed from a terminal known as Wrafton Gate but ceased in 1956, with civil flying continuing to 1960. In March 1951, an OCU was formed, which operated Meteors, Vampires, Sabres, and Hunters until September 1974. A TWU arrived in 1980 equipped with Hunters and later Hawks, staying until October 1995 when fixed-wing flying all but ceased. SAR has long been a feature at the airfield, and in June 1957, helicopters arrived in the shape of Sycamores; these were followed by Whirlwinds, Wessexes, and finally Sea Kings, which departed in October 2015. A VGS was based from September 1965 to 2016, and while the airfield is largely intact, only helicopters are allowed. However, it is to remain open indefinitely.

Chorley, Lancs

This LG was in use from 1937 to test-fly aircraft produced by Moss Bros Aircraft Ltd (Mosscraft) in an adjacent factory. It closed in 1939.

Christchurch (Somerford), Dorset

This AALG opened in 1933 and was soon used by scheduled services, which continued until the outbreak of the Second World War when it was known as Bournemouth Airport. The RAF took over in April 1940 and based various units on the airfield equipped with Battles, Blenheims, Ansons, Harrows, and Defiants.

Also in 1940, Airspeed set up a shadow factory to produce Oxfords and Horsas as well as converting Spitfires to Seafires. The USAAF arrived in April 1944 with P-47s but only stayed until the following July. The RAF departed in January 1946, but an ACGS/VGS continued flying until July 1963. After the war, the airfield was used mainly by Airspeed, and later de Havilland for the production of Ambassadors, Vampires, Venoms, and Sea Vixens. To assist with test-flying, a hard runway was constructed in 1950. Production ceased in October 1962 and the airfield closed in 1967.

Christleton, Cheshire

This private grass airfield opened in around 1945 but had closed by 1985.

Church Broughton, Derbys

This RAF training station opened in August 1942 as a satellite for Lichfield. Types operated included Wellingtons, Ansons, Lysanders, and Oxfords. From 1944 to 1946, experimental flights with Meteor jets took place and the airfield then closed.

Church Fenton, Yorks

This RAF station opened in June 1937 and was home to mostly fighter units until 1959. A wide variety of types were operated during this period, including Gladiators, Gauntlets, Demons, Spitfires, Hurricanes, Mosquitoes, Beaufighters, Meteors, Vampires, Hunters, and Javelins. A night fighting OTU was based here between November 1940 and May 1942, equipped with Blenheims, Defiants, Havocs, and Masters.

In June 1959, the station's role changed to training, and this continued until closure in September 1992. Types employed included Chipmunks, Jet Provosts, and Bulldogs. The airfield continued to be used as a RLG by Tucanos from Linton-on-Ouse until the RAF finally withdrew in 2013. It reopened for civil use in January 2015 and is now known as Leeds East Airport with two licensed hard runways. About ten aircraft are based here.

Church Lawford, Warks

This RAF station opened in June 1941 and was home to Tutors and Oxfords of the CFS until October 1942. Training by other units continued until April 1948 with Ansons, Hinds, Magisters, Harvards, and Tiger Moths. A BAT flight equipped with Oxfords was resident here from October 1942 to March 1943. Flying ceased in April 1948, but a MU continued until 1956.

Cirencester, Glos

This RFC LG was used for training from May 1917 to February 1918 with Be12s and Avro 504s. An AALG on the opposite side of the road opened in 1933 and closed in 1937.

Clacton (Earls Hall), Essex

This civil aerodrome opened in 1932 and was used by Hillman's Airways for a scheduled service to Maylands until 1934 when the airfield license was withdrawn. Private flying continued, and a service from Clacton to Ipswich was introduced by Southern Airways in June 1939; however, this ceased on the outbreak of the Second World War when the airfield closed. An airfield 2 miles to the south-east near Jaywick opened in 1958 and is operated by the Clacton Aero Club, which uses a single, unlicensed grass runway. Around a dozen aircraft are based here.

Cleadon (Sunderland/South Shields), Tyne and Wear

This RFC third-class night LG was used for home defence from April 1916 to December 1917.

Cleave, Cornwall

This RAF station opened in May 1939 and was used mainly by an AACU that operated Wallaces, Queen Bees, Henleys, and Magisters. It closed in April 1945.

Cleethorpes Beach, Humberside

This beach aerodrome was first used by a DH6 in 1920, but its heyday was the 1950s when Norfolk Airways operated pleasure flights with a couple of Austers. Flying ceased in around 1962.

Cliff End, IoW

This RAF third-class day LG was used mainly for home defence from May to November 1918.

Clipston (Market Harborough), Northants

This RFC second-class night and day LG was used for home defence from December 1916 to November 1918.

Cluntoe, NI

This RAF station opened in July 1942 for an OTU but was never taken up. Instead, the USAAF arrived in August 1943 and used the base for crew training with B-17s, B-24s, and A-35s until November 1944. It was then taken back by the RAF but not used again until February 1953 when a FTS took up residence with Prentices, Harvards, and Provosts. These stayed until June 1954 when flying ceased.

Clyffe Pypard, Wilts

This RAF station opened in August 1941 and was home to an elementary flying school equipped with Tiger Moths, Magisters, Oxfords, Ansons, and Austers. It closed in November 1947.

Coal Aston (Greenhill), Derbys

This RFC night LG opened in February 1916 and was used for home defence with Be2s and Be12s until the following October. It then became an ARD and handled types including RE8s, FKs, Be12s, Fe2s, Sopwiths, and AWs until closing in October 1919. It reopened for civil use in August 1930 when the Sheffield Aero Club took up residence here. It was also listed as an AALG but closed in around 1935. An unlicensed grass strip at Bentley Farm, Apperknowle, approximately 2 miles south-east of the First World War aerodrome, opened in 1961 and is home to a few light aircraft.

Cobham (Tartar Hill), Surrey

This civil aerodrome was in use from 1922. It was used by an AOP flight of Austers between April and June 1944.

Cobnor, Sussex

This private aerodrome was used by the Wells Aviation Company during 1918.

Cockerham, Lancs

There are three grass airfields in the vicinity. Rossall Field opened around 2014 with two unlicensed grass runways and fifty or so based aircraft. Patty's Farm has a couple of residents, and Moss Edge Farm has six or so, mostly microlights.

Cockthorne, (Market Rasen), Lincs

This RFC second-class night LG was used for home defence from October 1916 to June 1919.

Cofton Hackett

See Longbridge.

Colchester (Blue Barns), Essex

This civil aerodrome, also known as Ardleigh, opened in August 1931 and was used by the Eastern Counties Aeroplane Club. Redwing Aircraft Ltd arrived in January 1932 but moved to Croydon two years later, having only built four new aircraft and repaired a couple more. The airfield then closed.

Coldham (Wisbech), Cambs

This RFC third-class night LG was in use between January 1917 and June 1919.

Coleby Grange, Lincs

This RAF station opened in May 1940 as a RLG for Cranwell and was home to mainly fighter units. Types operated included Hurricanes, Defiants, Beaufighters, and Mosquitoes. The fighters stayed until May 1945 and were replaced with training types such as Oxfords and Harvards until January 1946. Flying then all but ceased, but an ACGS continued up to December 1946. Thor missiles were deployed from September 1959 to May 1963.

Coleraine, NI

Two LGs on opposite sides of the River Bann were used mainly by visiting flying circuses during the 1920s and '30s.

Colerne, Wilts

This RAF station opened in January 1940 with its first resident being a MU, but it later became a fighter base equipped with Blenheims, Beaufighters, Defiants, Spitfires, Hurricanes, and Mosquitoes. The fighters departed in September 1946 and the airfield was then little used apart from ferrying and test-flying for the next five years. During this time, war surplus aircraft were dismantled. A fighter OCU then arrived with

Brigands, Meteors, and Vampires and stayed until May 1957. It then passed to Transport Command, who operated Hastings and Hercules until February 1968. In 1941, BOAC set up a repair facility, but this was absorbed into a MU a year later. An AOP flight operated from February 1949 to March 1957 with Austers, and a MU continued until 1962. The airfield closed in March 1976 but reopened in November 1992 when a UAS/AEF arrived with Chipmunks, Bulldogs, and latterly Tutors, but these departed in 2018. Visiting aircraft are welcome, but none are based here. The airfield is due to close by 2025.

Colinton (Edinburgh), Lothian
This RFC LG was used for home defence for a short period from April to September 1916.

Coll, Hebrides
There are four sites on this island. Breachacha Beach was used by Scottish Airways for scheduled services between 1936 and 1939. Another strip at Ben Feall was in use from 1950 to 1958, and one at Totronald between the 1950s and 1975. The current airfield at Ballards Farm opened in 1975 and is available for visiting aircraft as well as scheduled services and air ambulance flights, which operate from a single licensed hard runway.

Collyweston, Northants
This RFC TDS, known as Easton-on-the-Hill, opened in 1916 and was used until December 1919. Types operated included DH6s, DH9s, Be2s, RE8s, Avro 504s, Camels, and F2bs. Following expansion, it reopened for the RAF in May 1940 and was home to a number of units operating Spitfires, Blenheims, Hurricanes, Masters, Oxfords, and Austers. Its most famous resident, from March 1943, was an enemy aircraft flight that flew an assortment of captured aircraft, mostly German, until November 1945. Flying then ceased and the airfield is now part of RAF Wittering.

Colmworth (Honeydon), Beds
This private grass airfield was in use from the 1970s to the 1990s.

Colonsay, Hebrides
A civil airfield was in use here from 1947 to 1951. An airfield at Machrins Farm just south of the earlier one opened in May 1974 and is used by scheduled services, visiting light aircraft and air ambulance flights. A single licensed hard runway is in use.

Coltishall, Norfolk
This RAF fighter station opened in May 1940 and played a major role in the Second World War. Spitfires and Hurricanes were the first residents, followed by many other types, including Defiants, Beaufighters, Whirlwinds, Typhoons, Mustangs, and Mosquitoes. Coltishall entered the jet age in 1950 with the arrival of Meteors followed by Vampires, Venoms, Javelins, Hunters, Lightnings, and finally Jaguars. These were retired in April 2006 and the base then closed. ASR flights were present during the Second World War, equipped with Walruses and Ansons and after the war with Whirlwind, Wessex, and Sea King helicopters. The latter departed in 1999.

Colyton, Devon
This private LG was available for visiting aircraft; it opened in around 1930 and closed in 1933.

Combermere, Salop
This AALG in Combermere Park was in use from 1931 to 1939 and possibly into the 1940s.

Compton Abbas, Dorset
This licensed airfield opened in May 1962 for the Shaftesbury Flying Club. It has a single grass runway and is home to around fifty aircraft.

Condover, Salop
This RLG for RAF Shawbury was in use between May 1942 and June 1945 by Oxfords, Harvards, Hurricanes, and Masters.

Coningsby, Lincs
This RAF bomber station opened in November 1940, but its first aircraft, Hampdens, did not arrive until February 1941. These were followed by Manchesters, Lancasters, Lincolns, Mosquitoes, and Washingtons, the latter staying until 1953. Jets then came on the scene in the shape of Canberras until July 1961, which were followed by Vulcans to November 1964. The station was then placed on C&M until it reopened as a fighter station in February 1968. Phantoms were the first type to be operated followed by Tornadoes and currently Typhoons, which arrived in April 2005. A detachment of Sea King helicopters was resident from November 1993 to May 1999. The Battle of Britain Memorial Flight moved to Coningsby in March 1976 and is still resident today.

Conington, Cambs
This civil aerodrome opened in the late 1920s. Scheduled services were introduced in November 1928 to Hadleigh

and Grantham by Ipswich and Cambridge Airways, but these were short-lived and the aerodrome closed in March 1929. The current airfield at Main Hall Farm is in the vicinity of the earlier one and is home to around ten aircraft. It has a single unlicensed grass runway.

Conington

See Glatton.

Coolham, Sussex

This ALG was in use by RAF Mustangs and Spitfires from April to July 1944.

Copmanthorpe, Yorks

This RFC LG opened in June 1916 and was used initially for training with Be2s and Avro 504s. It later became a home defence flight station until flying ceased in May 1919.

Corsham (Wadswick), Wilts

This unlicensed airfield at Manor Farm opened before 1987 with a single grass runway and is home to ten or so light aircraft.

Cosford, Staffs

This RAF station opened in July 1938 and was used mainly for training, a use which continues to the present day. A school of technical training was first on the scene, operating Magisters, Tiger Moths, Clevelands, Varsities, and Chipmunks until 1995. A MU was set up in March 1939; this dealt mainly with Spitfires, Battles, Wellingtons, and Horsas until disbanded in 1956. A ferry pilots pool operated from 1941–45 equipped with Ansons and Arguses. Various GSs, AEFs, and UASs were based here over the years, using Chipmunks, Bulldogs, and Vigilants. The last VGS departed in 2016 but Tutors of a UAS/AEF are still in operation, together with gliders of the Wrekin GC. The RAF Museum is a major attraction on the still active airfield.

Costessey (Norwich), Norfolk

This airstrip used by AOP Austers in 1943 and 1944. It was in use as a civil airfield from the late 1940s to the early 1950s and used for pleasure, charter, and taxi flights, including some by Norfolk Airways during 1950.

Cottam, Yorks

This RAF station opened in September 1939 as a satellite for Driffield and later developed into a bomber base. However, it was not found suitable for this purpose and no units were based. Whitleys, Lysanders, and Battles used the airfield briefly between August and October 1940, and other types visited on rare occasions. It was used for civil flying up to 1984.

Cottenham, Cambs

This RFC first- and second-class night LG was used for home defence with Fe2s and Be2s from April 1916 to April 1919.

Cottesmore, Leics

This RAF bomber station opened in March 1938 and was home to Wellesleys, Battles, and Hampdens. Its role changed to training in April 1940, and various types were operated including Hampdens, Herefords, and Ansons until October 1942 when the base closed for runway construction. On reopening in September 1943, the USAAF took up residence with C-47s, C-46s, C-53s, and CG-4s and stayed until May 1945. An HCU then arrived equipped with Lancasters, Mosquitoes, and Beaufighters but only stayed until March 1946. Trainers then returned in the shape of Mosquitoes, Tiger Moths, Harvards, Prentices, and Balliols, remaining until April 1954. Its role then changed again to bombing with the arrival of Canberras for a short period of nine months after which the station closed for major development. It reopened as a 'V' bomber base in April 1958, initially with Victors, which were replaced in November 1964 with Vulcans until December 1967. Yet another role change took place in April 1969 when Canberras returned, together with Argosies until February 1976 when it was placed on C&M. It was reactivated in January 1981 for Tornadoes and these were replaced with Harriers in March 1999. These stayed until flying ceased in January 2011 and the base closed in March 2012.

Covehithe, Suffolk

This RNAS night LG and later a home defence flight station was used as a RLG for Great Yarmouth between March 1915 and August 1918. It was then home to a coastal patrol flight operating DH4s and DH9s until flying ceased in March 1919.

Coventry (Baginton), Warks

This aerodrome opened in 1936 a mile south of Whitley as Coventry's new airport. Armstrong Whitworth opened a factory on the site in May of that year and started producing and test-flying Whitleys. These were followed by Lancasters, Lincolns, Meteors, Hunters, Sea Hawks, and finally Argosies until the

Miles Falcon G-AEEG parked on the grass in front of the modern control tower at Coventry during a classic air show on 31 May 2003. (*Grant Peerless*)

factory closed in July 1965. It served as a satellite for RAF Honiley during the Second World War but saw little action. A camouflage unit was based here from October 1939 to September 1940, operating various types, while Hurricanes, Spitfires, and Tomahawks were resident here from September 1940 to October 1943. Scheduled services commenced in 1952 but are no longer operated, cargo and GA flights being the main users of the airport. One licensed hard runway is in use. Over 100 aircraft are currently based along with the Midland Air Museum.

Coventry (Burton Green), Warks
This civil aerodrome was in use during 1936 by the Coventry Air Training Club.

Coventry (Whitley), Warks
This AAP, known as Radford, opened in March 1917 and handled aircraft from local manufacturers including RE8s, DH9s, Pups, and SE5s until July 1919. In the early 1920s, a civilian flying school was set up and training continued until 1938. In 1923, Armstrong Whitworth moved in and produced Siskins, Argosies, Atlases, Atalantas, Hawker Harts, and the prototype Whitley bomber. The company outgrew this facility and moved to nearby Baginton in 1936. An elementary flying school arrived in 1935 and operated Harts, Tiger Moths, Battles, Magisters, and Ansons until September 1939. Whitley closed on the outbreak of the Second World War.

Cowes (Somerton), IoW
This civil aerodrome opened in March 1916 for test-flying by J. Samuel White and Co. It was used as a RAF second-class LG from September 1918 to September 1919 by Be2s and DH9s when it was known as Wight. Civil use returned in 1920, but there was little activity until Saunders-Roe commenced test-flying in 1929. Spartan Aircraft Co. set up a facility in the old J.S. White factory in February 1931. Scheduled services started in 1933 and continued until 1936 when Ryde became the preferred airport for the island. During the Second World War, aircraft built by Saunders-Roe (including the Walrus) were test-flown from the airfield, and communication flights made use of it. In August 1946, Somerton Airways commenced scheduled services and they continued until April 1951. The airfield closed around 1953.

Cowick Hall (Snaith), Humberside
This civil airfield was in use from the 1960s to around 1984.

Cowley, Oxon
Part of the Morris Motors factory was used from September 1939 by a CRO that dealt mostly with Spitfires and Hurricanes, but also Magisters and Tiger Moths. These were test-flown from a couple of adjoining airstrips until flying ceased in 1946. Large numbers of crashed aircraft were salvaged, and Morris Motors also built over 3,000 Tiger Moths here during

the Second World War. An ACGS was based from October 1944 to November 1946.

Crail, Fife

This RAF station opened in May 1918 and was used mainly for training with RE8s, FK3s, Fe2s, F2bs, Avro 504s, DH6s, and Camels until June 1919. Following expansion, it reopened in October 1940 by the FAA as HMS *Jackdaw* and was home initially to a torpedo and bomber training unit equipped with Swordfish and Albacores. It was then used by a variety of units operating most naval types then in service until flying ceased in May 1947. An UAS was based from March 1953 to February 1958 with Chipmunks and Prentices and civil flying commenced in the 1960s. The airfield is still open to visiting aircraft, but none are currently based here. Two unlicensed hard runways are available.

Cramlington

See Newcastle.

Cranage, Cheshire

This RAF station opened in August 1940 as a satellite for Calveley and was home to a variety of training and fighter units flying Masters, Oxfords, Harts, Ansons, Hurricanes, Defiants, Beaufighters, and Blenheims. It was also used for the assembly and test-flying of Wellingtons during the Second World War. It closed in June 1945, but an ACGS continued flying until March 1947.

Cranfield, Beds

This RAF station opened in July 1937 and was home to a variety of units, mostly in the training role, operating an assortment of types before and during the Second World War. These included Hinds, Blenheims, Battles, Ansons, Oxfords, Havocs, Beaufighters, Beauforts, Wellingtons, and Mosquitoes. In October 1945, the Empire Test Pilots School arrived and used various types such as the Lancaster, Mosquito, Boston, Meteor, Spitfire, Tempest, Oxford, and Harvard before moving to Farnborough in August 1947. The College of Aeronautics took up residence in 1946 and is now Cranfield University. These bodies operated and continue to operate a number of unusual and rare types. A communications flight was based here from March 1950 to September 1959 equipped with Chipmunks, Provosts, and Prentices. Today, Cranfield is a busy GA airfield with around seventy-five based aircraft that operate from a single licensed hard runway.

Cranwell, Lincs

RNAS HMS *Daedalus* opened in April 1916, mostly for training. It transferred to the RAF on 1 April 1918 and was used as a TDS until March 1919. Types operated included Camels, Avro 504s, Scouts, Pups, DH4s, DH6s, DH9s, and 0/400s. The RAF College was set up in 1920 and commenced a training role that continues to the present day. Types used over the years have been many and varied and include Avro 504s, DH9s, F2bs, Atlases, Snipes, Siskins, Tutors, Harts, Wallaces, Valentias, Mentors, Harvards, Proctors, Dominies, Oxfords, Ansons, Wellingtons, Tiger Moths, Prentices, Provosts, Chipmunks, Meteors, Vampires, Jet Provosts, Tucanos, Jetstreams, and Hawks. It is still active today, with King Airs, Prefects, and Phenoms being the main type operated here, as well as Tutors of an AEF and UAS. A grass strip to the north of the airfield is used only by gliders, the Cranwell GC being the main user.

Creetown, Dumfries and Galloway

This AALG was operated by the Duchess of Bedford and was in use between about 1933 and 1939. It was used by an ACGS from June 1945 to March 1947 and by civilian gliders until 1951.

Cricklewood, Gt. London

This aerodrome was opened in September 1912 by the Handley Page Aircraft Co., with joy-riding over London commencing in April 1919, followed by international scheduled services in the following September but these were transferred to Croydon in May 1921. Handley Page commenced building 0/100s, 0/400s, and V/1500 during the First World War and went on to W8s, W9s, and W10s after the war. Flying ceased in February 1930 and transferred to a new site at Radlett. However, production carried on at Cricklewood, and large numbers of Hampden and Halifax bombers were completed. After the war, Victors were produced until the factory closed in 1965.

Croft (Darlington/Neasham), Yorks

This RAF bomber station opened in October 1941 as a satellite for Middleton St George. It was home to various units operating Whitleys, Wellingtons, Halifaxes, and Lancasters until June 1945. It was used as a RLG by Mosquitoes from September 1945 to June 1946 when the airfield closed. It reopened as a RLG for Middleton St George in February 1951 and was used by Meteors, Oxfords, Prentices, and Vampires until flying ceased in June 1956. Some civil flying took place by the Darlington and District Aero Club from 1947 to 1952.

Second World War hangars and control tower at Cranfield on 23 November 1999. A visual control room has been added on top of the wartime tower. Jetstream G-NFLC of the College of Aeronautics can be seen in the background. (*Grant Peerless*)

Handley Page 0/400 F5417 landing in front of Indian troops at Cricklewood, *c.* 1919. Flying ceased here in 1930 when Handley Page moved to Radlett. (*Richard Riding collection*)

Cromer (Northrepps), Norfolk

This unlicensed airfield at Winspurs Farm with two grass runways opened in 2007 to replace an earlier one two fields away at Manor Farm. Over twenty-five aircraft are based here, mostly microlights.

Crosby-on-Eden

See Carlisle.

Croughton, Northants

This RAF station opened in June 1940 as a RLG for Upper Heyford and was used by Hampdens, Herefords and Ansons of an OTU until July 1942. Glider training then took over with Hotspurs, Hectors, and Masters until June 1946. A BAT flight of Oxfords was based from May 1943 to October 1944. Flying ceased in June 1946.

Crowfield (Coddenham), Suffolk

This unlicensed airfield with two grass runways opened in 1989 and is home to around twenty aircraft.

Crowland (Spalding), Lincs

This unlicensed airfield opened in 1968 with two grass runways and is home to over thirty resident aircraft. The Perkins Engines GC was based from 1968 to 1980, and the Peterborough and Spalding GC is now in residence.

Croydon, Gt. London

This RFC second-class LG, known as Beddington, opened in December 1915 and was used for home defence and training until February 1920. Types used included DH9s and F2bs. In October 1917, National Aircraft Factory no. 1 was constructed on a site just north of the First World War aerodrome known as Waddon, which initially dealt with the salvage of surplus aircraft and went on to build DH9s until it closed down in late 1919.

Civil flying returned after the war, and following a major investment, Croydon airport was opened on 31 March 1921; it soon attracted many airlines that commenced scheduled services to European destinations. Further improvements took place including a new terminal building, which was officially opened on 2 May 1928. Croydon then became the first purpose-built international airport in the world. Scheduled services continued unabated up to the outbreak of the Second World War when the airport was taken over by the RAF. They operated Gladiators, Hurricanes, Blenheims and Spitfires and these stayed until December 1942. An AACU arrived in August 1941 with Lysanders, Tomahawks and Mustangs and were resident until July 1944. Transport aircraft in the shape of Dakotas and Ansons then took over and stayed until September 1946. Civil flying resumed in May 1945 but never reached the pre-war level of activity. The airport closed on 30 September 1959, the last flight out being by a Morton Air Services Heron.

Croydon (Top Farm), Cambs

This unlicensed airfield with a single grass runway opened in 1982. Its main use is as an aircraft sales facility, but it is also home to a few light aircraft.

Cruchfield Manor, Berks

This private grass airfield was used as a base by Air Pegasus from about 1972 to 1974 when the company moved to Preston Candover.

Culdrose, Cornwall

This FAA station opened in April 1947 as HMS *Seahawk* and was home at various times to almost every naval aircraft in service, including many on 'shore leave' from aircraft carriers. These included Sea Furies, Fireflies, Avengers, Skyraiders, Attackers, Gannets, Sea Venoms, Sea Princes, Jetstreams, and Sea Harriers. The station was designated as a main helicopter training base in January 1958, and this role continues to this day. Initially, Dragonflies, Whirlwinds, Wessexes were used, with Sea Kings joining later; these have now been replaced by Merlins. Fixed-wing Hawks and Avengers are also operated. The Seahawk GC is also based.

Culham, Oxon

This AALG, known as Clifton Hampden, opened in 1933. It was requisitioned by the FAA in November 1944 as HMS *Hornbill,* and the first resident unit was a ferry pool that operated Ansons, Fireflies, Reliants, Oxfords, and Seafires, which stayed until August 1950. In May 1947, a photographic trials unit was formed, which operated Sea Mosquitoes, Sea Furies, Sea Hornets, Ansons, and Dominies. This departed in July 1950, but before this, in July 1947, FAA reserve squadrons began to arrive. They used Seafires, Sea Furies, Fireflies, and Harvards until July 1953 when flying ceased.

Culmhead (Church Stanton), Somerset

This RAF station opened in August 1941 and was used as a fighter base during most of the Second World War

A typical view from Croydon's control tower on 15 August 1936 featuring a variety of aircraft types of the period. (*Eddie Riding*)

Hangars, apron, and terminal building at Croydon in the mid-1930s. Flying ceased in 1959. (*Eddie Riding*)

with mainly Spitfires and Hurricanes. They departed in September 1944 and were replaced briefly with a GTS until July 1945. This unit operated Hotspurs, Horsas, Albermarles, and Masters. A MU then took over until the airfield closed in August 1946.

Cumbernauld, Strathclyde
This licensed airfield opened in 1966 with a single grass runway, which was replaced with a hard one in 1988. It is home to around thirty aircraft.

Currock Hill (Chopwell), Northumberland
This RFC third-class night LG was used for home defence from April 1916 to March 1917. In 1973, a site nearby opened for the Northumbria GC, but it is also open to light aircraft which operate from a single unlicensed grass strip. Around twenty types are based here.

Cuxwold (Caistor), Lincs
This RFC second-class night LG was used for home defence from October 1916 to June 1919. It may have been the site of a civil airfield known as Grimsby, which was in use from the 1970s to 1990s.

Dagenham, Gt. London
This LG, known as 'The Dagenham Experimental Ground', was opened by the Royal Aeronautical Society in February 1910 and was used mostly for test-flying until closure later the same year.

Dalcross
See Inverness.

Dale, Pembrokeshire
This RAF station opened as a satellite for Brawdy in June 1942 and was home to ASR Wellingtons until September 1943. The FAA then took over as HMS *Goldcrest* and operated Defiants, Seafires, Martinets, Blenheims, Beaufighters, Mosquitoes, Corsairs, Hellcats, Fireflies, and Ansons. Flying ceased in December 1947.

Dallachy, Grampian
This short-lived RAF station opened in May 1943 as a satellite for Banff and was home to various units operating Oxfords, Beaufighters, Mosquitoes, and Hampdens until flying ceased in June 1945. It was used by the Highland GC from 1976 to 1994.

Dalmuir (Robertson's Field), Strathclyde
This airstrip was used by William Beardmore and Company to fly out aircraft assembled at their nearby factory to Inchinnan for test-flying. It was in use from 1915 to 1921 and types handled included Be2s, Nieuport 12s, V/1500s, and Pups, as well as their own designs.

Dalton, Yorks
This RAF bomber station opened in November 1941 and was home to Whitleys, Wellingtons, and Halifaxes until closure in April 1945. During the latter part of the war, gunnery training took place with a few Hurricanes, Spitfires, Martinets, and Oxfords. Part of the wartime airfield reopened for flying in the 1970s, and a few light aircraft are based on what is known as Croft Farm.

Damyns Hall (Upminster), Gt. London
This was the site of a private strip before the Second World War, which reopened in 1969 as an unlicensed airfield. It has one grass runway and is home to over forty aircraft, mostly microlights but also the Tiger Club.

Darley Moor, Derbys
This RAF station opened as a satellite for Ashbourne in June 1943 and closed in February 1945. Types operated included Whitleys, Albermarles, Horsas, Ansons, and Blenheims. When flying ceased, a MU took over and the airfield closed finally in 1954. Some private flying still takes place from part of the wartime runways, mostly by microlights, some fifty being based here.

Darlington, Co. Durham
This private grass airfield at Newton Ketton Farm was in use from the 1970s to 1990s.

Darlton, Notts
This gliding site at Kingshaugh Farm opened in 2007 and is operated by the Darlton GC with over twenty residents.

Daventry (Newnham Grounds), Northants
This AALG was in use between 1933 and 1939.

Davidstow Moor, Cornwall
This RAF Coastal Command station opened in October 1942 and was home to various units operating Liberators, Wellingtons, Warwicks, and Beaufighters. It was placed on C&M in September 1944 and closed in

December 1945. Parts of three of the wartime runways are used by private aircraft, mostly microlights, and around ten are based here.

Deal (Ripple), Kent
This AALG was in use between 1933 and 1939.

Deanland (Ripe), Sussex
This ALG was used by RAF Spitfires from April to October 1944. It reopened for civil use in 1963 and is home to over forty private aircraft, which operate from a single unlicensed grass runway.

Debach, Suffolk
This short-lived USAAF bomber station was home to B-17s from April 1944. They departed in August 1945 and the airfield then closed, but a few private aircraft operate from part of the wartime runways.

Debden, Essex
This RAF fighter station opened in April 1937 with Gladiators as the first residents. These were followed by Hurricanes, Blenheims, Defiants, and Spitfires during the Second World War. The USAAF was present from September 1942 to July 1945 and operated Spitfires, P-47s, and P-51s. After the war, Meteors were the mainstay at the airfield together with various aircraft operated by the Empire Radio School and RAF Technical College including Lincolns, Varsities, Ansons, and Oxfords. The Army was resident in the late 1950s operating mainly Austers. The airfield closed officially in April 1975, but gliders of an ACGS continued to operate until April 1981.

Deenethorpe, Northants
This USAAF station opened in November 1943 and was home to B-17s until June 1945 when flying ceased. Part of a wartime runway reopened for civil use before 1982, and today, around forty aircraft are based here.

Defford, Worcs
This RAF station opened in September 1941 as a satellite for Pershore, its first residents being Wellingtons, Ansons, and Lysanders. In May 1942, it became the Radar Research Establishment, which operated Lancasters, Mosquitoes, Mitchells, Hastings, Valettas, Meteors, Venoms, Hunters, and Canberras on radar and radio evaluation flights. It closed in September 1957 when the unit moved to Pershore. Just to the south-east of the old airfield is an unlicensed grass strip at the Croft Farm, which opened before 1982 and is home to over twenty light aircraft.

Delny House, Highland
This LG was used by the RFC/RNAS/RAF from 1917 to 1921.

Denbury, Devon
This aerodrome, known as Torbay Airport, opened on 6 April 1935, with a few scheduled services commencing soon afterwards. It closed in 1939.

Denham, Bucks
This First World War aerodrome, known as Owl's Oak, was in use between July 1917 and January 1918 for the ground instruction of pilots and observers. The Martin-Baker Aircraft Company arrived in August 1929; they built and test-flew various types from here. It became an AALG in 1933 and a RLG for Booker in October 1941. As such, it was used by Tiger Moths and Magisters until July 1945 while an ACGS carried on until 1947. Civil flying returned after the war, and today, Denham is a busy, licensed GA airfield with one hard and one grass runway. It is home to over 100 aircraft.

Denton, Northants
This RAF station opened in November 1940 as a RLG for Sywell and was used by Tiger Moths, Oxfords, and Ansons until closure in July 1945.

Deopham Green, Norfolk
This was another short-lived USAAF bomber station that operated B-17s from January 1944 to August 1945.

Derby (Burnaston), Derbys
Derby Airport officially opened on 17 June 1939, but flying had commenced in the previous September by Hinds, Audaxes, Magisters, and Tiger Moths of an elementary flying school. Training continued throughout the Second World War and carried on after the war with Ansons, Oxfords, Prentices, and finally Chipmunks until July 1953. Civil flying resumed in 1946 with Derby Aviation taking up residence in February 1949 and operating Rapides, Marathons, and Dakotas on scheduled services. This company became British Midland Airways in July 1964, at which time it was operating seven Dakotas and three Argonauts, but it moved its operations to the new East Midlands Airport when it opened in April 1965. Light aircraft continued to use the airfield, which retained its grass surface, until 1989, when it was closed to make way for a Toyota car factory.

The grass airfield at Denham in the 1950s. A hard runway was laid in the 1970s, and it is now a popular GA airfield. (*Aerofilms*)

Derby (Burnaston) in the 1950s. The airfield remained grass-surfaced until it closed in 1989 to make way for a Toyota car factory. (*Aerofilms*)

Derby (Egginton), Derbys

This licensed airfield opened in 1993 to replace Burnaston, with three grass runways and is home to the Derby Aero Club and around forty-five resident aircraft.

Desborough, Northants

This RAF station opened in September 1943 for an OTU equipped with mostly Wellingtons until June 1945. Training then continued, this time for Transport Command from November 1945 to January 1947 with Dakotas, Wellingtons, Oxfords, and Ansons. The airfield was reactivated briefly between May and November 1951 as a RLG for North Luffenham and was used by Meteors, Vampires, and Harvards.

Detling, Kent

This RNAS/RFC home defence station was in use between May 1915 and October 1919 with Be2s, Be12s, Avro 504s, Pups, Camels, Snipes, and SE5s. It was briefly used for gliding in 1930 and following expansion reopened for the RAF in October 1938 with Hinds and Ansons. These were followed by a plethora of units, most of which only stayed for short periods until it was placed on C&M in November 1946. The FAA was present from September 1939 to July 1941 with Swordfish, Skuas, Rocs, and Albacores. Types operated by the RAF units were numerous and included Blenheims, Spitfires, Hurricanes, Defiants, Mustangs, Tomahawks, Lysanders, and Austers. Gliding took over in July 1949 and continued until June 1962 when flying ceased.

Devils Dyke, Sussex

This gliding site was used by the Southdown GC from 1935 to 1939. It was opened officially in April 1936.

Digby, Lincs

This TDS, known as Scopwick, opened in October 1918 and closed in April 1920. Types handled included Avro 504s, DH9s, Fe2bs, Be2s, F2bs, and Camels. It was renamed RAF Digby in July 1920 and training continued mainly with F2bs until April 1922 when the station was placed on C&M. It was reactivated in June 1924, still in the training role with Avro 504s, F2bs, Snipes, Tutors, Harts, and Furies until September 1937. Fighter Command then took over and stayed until July 1946, operating Gauntlets, Hurricanes, Spitfires, Blenheims, Defiants, and Mustangs. Training returned in January 1946 with Harvards, Tiger Moths, Oxfords, and Ansons, often as a RLG for Cranwell; this continued until January 1951. A RAF grading school then arrived and operated Tiger Moths until March 1953 when flying ceased.

Dishforth, Yorks

This RAF bomber station opened in September 1936 and was home initially to Heyfords, which were followed by Whitleys, Wellingtons, Halifaxes, and Lancasters. They departed in June 1945, and Transport Command then took over for the next seventeen years, operating Liberators, Yorks, Halifaxes, Dakotas, Hastings, Valettas, Ansons Beverleys, Andovers, and Argosies. In March 1962, the airfield was used as a RLG by Jet Provosts; this continued until at least 1990. Chipmunks of a UAS also made use of it during the 1960s. The station was transferred to the Army in 1991 and has been the base for helicopters ever since, the main types operated being Lynxes, Gazelles, and Apaches. Between January 1995 and July 2003, the RAF again used it as a RLG, this time with Fireflies. The airfield is due to close by 2024.

Docking, Norfolk

This RAF station opened as a satellite for Bircham Newton in October 1941 and was home to a variety of units operating Gladiators, Hurricanes, Oxfords, Hudsons, Wellingtons, Lysanders, Martinets, Hampdens, and Avengers. It remained a grass airfield until closure in August 1945, but some private flying took place around 1957 by the Fakenham Flying Group.

Doncaster, Yorks

While the racecourse was the site of the first British aviation meeting in October 1909, it was not used by the RFC or RAF during the First World War. An RFC training station opened on a site nearby in January 1916, and from the following March, it served as a first-class night LG that was used for home defence for a short time. Training continued with Be2s, Avro 504s, RE8s, FK3s, SE5s, G3s, and Camels until February 1919 when flying ceased. It became Doncaster Airport in May 1934, and scheduled services commenced in the following March. A RAuxAF squadron arrived in November 1938 with Hinds, Gauntlets, and Battles but only stayed until October 1939. An elementary flying school was formed in July 1939, equipped with Tiger Moths, Hinds, and Audaxes, but it only stayed for a couple of months.

A communications flight then moved in and operated HP42s, Tri-Motors, Albatrosses, and DH86s, as well as Bombays, Harrows, and Hudsons until February

1944. From July 1941, various units were based here with Lysanders, Tomahawks, Wellingtons, Dakotas, and Austers, until flying all but ceased in November 1945. An ACGS continued flying until December 1949, but before this, in November 1947, the RAF returned with a RFS equipped with Tiger Moths, Prentices, Ansons, and Chipmunks, which departed in June 1954. The airfield reopened for civil use after the war and closed in December 1992. The South Yorkshire Aircraft Museum is based on the northern part of the Second World War airfield.

Doncaster (Armthorpe), Yorks

This civil aerodrome was opened by the mayor of Doncaster on 16 June 1932 but was short-lived, being replaced by the above site in May 1934.

Donibristle, Fife

This RNAS second-class night LG, known as Aberdour, was in use from January 1917. It later became a shore base as well as an ARD that became the main repair facility for naval aeroplanes. It was placed on C&M in 1921 and reopened in October 1925 for aircraft on 'shore leave', mostly Flycatchers. A torpedo flight was formed in October 1928 with Horsleys and, later, Vildebeests, which operated until September 1939. The station became HMS *Merlin* in May 1939 and carried on as a naval repair yard; this use continued until April 1959, when over 7,000 aircraft had been handled. A communications flight was formed in December 1940, which used Dominies, Harrows, Oxfords, Travellers, and Reliants, and later Sea Princes and Sea Devons until 1958. Several front-line units were based during and after the Second World War, which operated most types then in naval service, particularly Swordfish, Albacores, Fulmars, Wildcats, Martlets, Fireflies, and Sea Furies. Flying ceased in 1958 and the repair yard closed in April 1959.

Donna Nook, Lincs

This was a RLG for North Coates from 1936 to 1950. It was used mainly by Lysanders, Beauforts, and Beaufighters.

Dorchester, Dorset

This aerodrome at Middle Farm opened in 1928 for the Dorsetshire Aero Club. It was used by scheduled services during 1934 but closed in 1935.

Dornoch, Highland

This aerodrome opened on the golf course in July 1935 with a scheduled service that only operated for a few months. It became a SLG in August 1941 and stored Spitfires, Havocs, Whitleys, Beaufighters, and Lancasters until September 1945. It reopened for civil flying in 1967, and another unsuccessful attempt was made at a scheduled service in 1972. It is still open to visiting aircraft that use one unlicensed grass strip on the south-eastern edge of the golf course.

Dotterel (Reighton), Yorks

This AALG was open from May to September between 1934 and 1939.

Douglas, IoM

This AALG was in use between 1933 and 1939.

Dounreay, Highland

This RAF station opened in December 1942, but no permanent units were based here. It transferred to the FAA in May 1944 as HMS *Tern 2* but was not used. It reopened for civil use in July 1967 in support of the adjacent nuclear power station but closed in 1993.

Dover (Guston Road), Kent

This RNAS home defence aerodrome opened in December 1914 and was home to Bleriots, TB8s, Be2s, Scouts, JN3s, Avro 504s, and Camels. From August 1918, DH4s and DH9s operated coastal patrol flights, but this unit was disbanded in March 1919, and the aerodrome closed soon afterwards.

Dover (Swingate Down/St Margarets), Kent

This RFC aerodrome opened in July 1914 and was used for home defence and training by Be2s, Avro 504s, RE8s, FB19s, Fe2bs, and DH4s until January 1918. A TDS was based here between July and October 1918 equipped with Camels, Avro 504s, and DH9s. A marine pilots school operated DH6s, DH9s, DH10s, and Vimys here from March 1919 to February 1920. It saw use by Cobham's flying circus on a couple of occasions in the 1930s and by the Prince of Wales who landed in a Tomtit in 1930; it closed finally before the Second World War. Flying returned briefly in July 1964 when scenes for *Those Magnificent Men in their Flying Machines* were filmed using a replica Bristol Boxkite.

Dover (Whitfield) Kent

This was Dover's first aerodrome and one of the first in the country. Opened in 1910, it was operated by Air Stations (Dover) and saw several pioneering flights as well as use by the Dover Aero Club. Following a government decision to ban civilian flying near the coast, it closed in 1913, Swingate and Guston Road becoming the aerodromes for the town.

Down Ampney, Glos

This RAF transport command station opened in February 1944, which was home to Dakotas, Horsas, Hamilcars, and Hadrians. Its main role was glider towing and casualty evacuation from France, with many thousands of wounded troops being repatriated. It closed in April 1946.

Down Farm (Westonbirt), Glos

This SLG was used for storing Defiants, Hampdens, Stirlings, Wellingtons, and Venturas between May 1941 and February 1946. It was also used as a RLG for Oxfords from RAF Babdown Farm from October 1944 to March 1945.

Downham Market, Norfolk

This RAF station was opened as a satellite for Marham in July 1942. Stirlings were the first residents, followed by Lancasters and Mosquitoes until flying ceased in April 1946.

Doynton, Avon

This private grass strip at Rookery Farm is home to about nine aircraft, mostly microlights.

Drayton St Leonard, Oxon

This unlicensed airfield at Manor Farm opened in around 2001 with a single grass runway and around six residents.

Drem, Lothian

This RFC first-class night LG, known as Gullane or West Fenton, opened in January 1917 and was used initially for home defence. It became a TDS in April 1918 until flying ceased in November 1919. Types operated included Pups, Camels, Avro 504s, and SE5s. The RAF used the site for an exercise with Harts in September 1933, but following expansion, it did not reopen fully until March 1939. The first residents were trainers in the shape of Oxfords, Harts, and Audaxes, but these were replaced with fighters in the following October. Numerous units were based here, operating Spitfires, Hurricanes, Defiants, Whirlwinds, Typhoons, Beaufighters, and Mosquitoes. The FAA arrived in October 1942 with a night fighter school equipped with Chesapeakes, Fulmars, Ansons, Fireflies, and Hellcats, but it did not become a full naval base until April 1945 when it was named HMS *Nighthawk*. It was returned to the RAF in March 1946, but they made no use of the airfield and flying then ceased, although an ACGS carried on until September 1947.

Driffield, Humberside

This RFC home defence night LG, known as Eastburn, opened in October 1917, but it saw little activity until July 1918 when it became home to a TDS. Types operated included SE5s, DH4s, Pups, and Avro 504s until flying ceased in February 1920. Following expansion, it reopened in August 1936 as a RAF bomber base, equipped initially with Virginias, which were followed by Ansons, Heyfords, Wellesleys, and Whitleys. Fighter Command took over for a brief period of three months from January 1941 and operated Hurricanes and Spitfires. Bomber Command then returned and stayed until September 1945, operating mainly Wellingtons and Halifaxes. The base was then placed on C&M and in September 1946 an ANS arrived with Ansons, Wellingtons, and Oxfords.

The role changed to training in March 1948 and various types were operated including Mosquitoes, Meteors, and Vampires. Another change took place in September 1955 when Fighter Command returned, this time with Venoms, Sabres, and Hunters, and stayed until flying ceased in March 1958. Thor missiles were deployed on the airfield between August 1959 and April 1963, and BAe used the runway for flight-testing Buccaneers from September 1967 to March 1968. The base was taken over by the Army in January 1977.

Drumshade, Tayside

This gliding site opened around 2008 for the Angus GC.

Dumfries (Tinwald Downs), Dumfries and Galloway

Possibly the site of a LG during the First World War, this RAF station opened in March 1940, the first resident being a communications flight. It was then used by a bombing and gunnery school, which was the main user of the airfield until June 1945. Types operated included Harrows, Battles, Seals, Henleys, Whitleys, Bothas, and Ansons. A MU was based from June 1940 and dealt with the storage, preparation, and dispatch of over 4,500 aircraft of numerous types until it departed in 1957. Typhoons were test-flown during the war, and Blackburn Aircraft modified American aircraft. Powered flying ceased in July 1945, but an ACGS continued operating until January 1958. Some private flying took place from the 1950s to 1980s.

Dundee, Tayside

This civil airport opened in 1963 with scheduled services commencing in 1965, which continue to this day. A hard runway was constructed in 1978, and today, the airport is known as Riverside Airport and is home to about twenty-five aircraft.

Dundonald, Strathclyde

This RAF station opened in March 1940 and was used for a year as a RLG by Tiger Moths from Prestwick. Various units were then based, both RAF and FAA, which operated Mustangs, Hurricanes, Blenheims, Lysanders, Ansons, and Seafires until flying ceased in December 1944. It was then placed on C&M and used as an ELG until August 1945 when it finally closed.

Dungavel, Strathclyde

This civil aerodrome was used by private light aircraft during the 1930s and as a RAF ELG between 1939 and 1945. An ACGS operated in 1948 and 1949.

Dunholme Lodge, Lincs

This RAF bomber station opened in December 1942 as a satellite for Scampton and was home to Lancasters until flying ceased in December 1944. It was reactivated in April 1959 for the deployment of Bloodhound missiles; these departed in March 1964.

Dunino, Fife

This RAF station opened in November 1940, although the first residents were the FAA who used it as a RLG for Crail. This use continued until March 1946. An AACU arrived in November 1941 with Lysanders and Mustangs, which stayed until November 1942. It was then transferred to the FAA as HMS *Jackdaw 2* who operated mainly Swordfish, Barracudas, and Walruses until flying ceased in 1946. The airfield was also used for storage, mostly for Barracudas.

Dunkeswell, Devon

Opened as a RAF station, it was used initially by the US Navy from July 1943 to June 1945 with PB4Ys and, later, PBYs. A ferry unit was set up in August 1945, which ferried aircraft to the Middle East and to foreign air forces. This operated until April 1946 when the airfield was placed on C&M. From November 1951, it was used as a RLG by Vampires, Meteors, Oxfords, and Prentices. This continued until December 1954 when the RAF departed. A GC arrived in 1952 and in 1967 the airfield reopened for civil use. This continues today, and over 150 based aircraft operate from two hard runways, one licensed.

Dunkeswick, Yorks

This RFC second-class day and night LG was used for home defence from April 1916 to June 1919.

Dunsfold, Surrey

This RAF station opened in December 1942 and was home initially to an AACU operating Mustangs and Tomahawks until July 1943. Mitchells then arrived, which were followed by Mosquitoes that stayed until October 1944. It was then placed on C&M and declared inactive in August 1946. In the following November, it was leased to Skyways, who used it as their main base until 1952, employing Yorks and Lancastrians among other types. The lease then passed to the Hawker Aircraft Company, who used it for final assembly and test-flying of Sea Hawks and Hunters, then later, Gnats and Harriers. BAe, the successor to Hawkers, departed in 2000, but the airfield is still open for flying from a single unlicensed hard runway. It is currently home to the BBC TV programme *Top Gear*, which has used the main wartime runway and perimeter tracks since 2001.

Dunsley, Yorks

This AALG was in use between 1934 and 1939.

Dunstable (Lewsey Farm), Beds

This AALG was in use between 1932 and 1934.

Dunstable Downs, Beds

This gliding site opened in 1930 for the London GC and is home to around 100 gliders, which operate from three unlicensed grass runways. Powered aircraft are also accepted subject to certain conditions.

Dunster, Somerset

This AALG was operated by Dunster Castle in use in the 1930s.

Durham, Co. Durham

This field was used by an ACGS from November 1944 to May 1946.

Durley, Hants

This private grass airfield at Hill Farm opened around 1992; it is home to about fifteen aircraft. Restoration work is also carried out here.

Duxford, Cambs

This RFC aerodrome opened in March 1918 and was home to DH4s, DH6s, DH9s, Avro 504s, and RE8s during the First World War. After the war, various fighter aircraft were based here, including Snipes, Grebes, Siskins, Bulldogs, Tutors, Harts, and Gauntlets. In July 1938, the first Spitfire squadron was formed; these aircraft went on to operate from the airfield throughout the Second World War, together with Hurricanes, Typhoons, and Airacobras, along with P-47s and P-51s of the USAAF. The first jet aircraft arrived in February 1947 in the shape of the Meteor; these were followed by Javelins and Hunters.

The airfield had remained grass surfaced throughout the war, albeit with the addition of steel mesh; however, to facilitate jet operations, a concrete runway was laid in 1951. The RAF departed in July 1961, but military aircraft graced the skies over Duxford again in the summer of 1968 when scenes for the *Battle of Britain* film were shot. The Imperial War Museum took over in the early 1970s, their first aircraft, a Sea Vixen, being flown in in 1973. Today, Duxford is a major museum and restoration centre and hosts regular flying displays although the type of aircraft able to participate was curtailed when the M11 motorway reduced the length of the eastern end of the main runway. Two licensed runways are in use, one hard and one grass.

Dymchurch (Hythe/Palmarsh), Kent

This RFC aerodrome opened in November 1915 and was home to a gunnery school operating RE7s, Be2s, FB5s, FK3s, Avro 504s, Pups, and 0/400s until November 1918. It was then used as an ELG but closed in 1920.

Dysart, Tayside

This RLG for RAF Montrose was in use from March 1936 to July 1945. Types operated included Audaxes, Harts, Oxfords, Tiger Moths, Masters, and Magisters.

Eaglescott, Devon

This unlicensed airfield opened in 1983 with two grass runways and is home to over forty aircraft. It is operated by Devon Airsports and the North Devon GC is also based here.

Earls Barton, Northants

This RLG was used by Sywell-based training aircraft, mostly Tiger Moths from late 1941.

Earls Colne, Essex

This USAAF bomber station opened in May 1943, the first occupants being B-17s. These were followed by B-26s until the Americans moved out in July 1944. Their place was taken by Albermarles, Halifaxes, and Horsas of the RAF in September 1944, which stayed until the airfield closed in May 1946. It reopened for civil flying before 1974 on a limited basis, but

DH Dragon Rapide G-AIYR parked on the grass in front of the control tower at Duxford on 2 July 1994. The Rapide was busy giving pleasure flights over the local area. (*Grant Peerless*)

its use intensified in 1983. A licensed hard and grass runway is available and around forty aircraft are based here.

Earls Farm Down, Wilts

This possible day LG was used by the RFC and RAF during the First World War but could have been on the site of RAF Boscombe Down. It may also have been used as a RLG by Netheravon and Upavon.

Earnley, Sussex

This RAF second-class night LG was used for home defence from May 1918 to August 1919.

Earsham, Suffolk

This RFC third-class night LG was used for home defence from April 1916 to June 1919.

Easington (Seaham Harbour), Co. Durham

This RFC second-class night LG was used for home defence from April 1916 to June 1919. It was reclassified as a third-class night LG and second-class day LG in July 1917.

East Boldre

See Beaulieu.

East Fingask, Grampian

This field was used as a dispersal site for RAF Dyce during the Second World War.

East Fortune, Lothian

This RNAS aerodrome opened in September 1915 and was used initially for home defence as well as being an airship station. It was later used for training and by a gunnery school until mid-1920. Types operated included Cuckoos, Camels, Pups, 1½ Strutters, and F2bs. Following expansion, it reopened in June 1940 as a satellite for Drem, but no aircraft arrived until a year later. The main user was an OTU that operated Defiants, Blenheims, Masters, Oxfords, Beaufighters, Mosquitoes, and Buckmasters, until May 1946 when flying ceased. It reopened briefly in 1961 as the airport for Edinburgh while runway works were carried out at Turnhouse. Today, East Fortune is home to the National Museum of Flight (opened in July 1975) as well as a large number of microlights that fly from the western end of the Second World War airfield.

East Grinstead (Hammerwood House), Sussex

This LG was used by RAF AOP Austers from November 1943 to June 1944.

East Hanney, Oxon

This civil aerodrome opened in 1919 and was home to the Berkshire Aviation Company, which operated pleasure flights all over the country during the 1920s. It moved to Witney in 1926 and East Hanney then closed.

East Hanningfield, Essex

This RFC third-class night LG was used for home defence between April and November 1916.

East Haven, Tayside

FAA station HMS *Peewit* opened in May 1943, its main user being a deck landing school equipped with Swordfish, Sea Hurricanes, Barracudas, Seafires, and Fireflies. It closed in August 1946.

East Heslerton

See Scarborough.

East Kirkby (Hagnaby), Lincs

This RAF heavy bomber station opened in August 1943, home to Lancasters and later Lincolns until October 1945. The base then closed, but it was reactivated for a short period between August 1947 and February 1948 for a detachment of Mosquitoes. It was later used as a USAF reserve airfield from August 1954 to 1958 and used mainly by C-47s. Today, it is home to the Lincolnshire Aviation Heritage Centre, which opened in 1988 and taxi-runs a Lancaster and flies a Dakota. It is open to visiting aircraft with use of two unlicensed hard/grass runways.

East Medina, IoW

This aerodrome was used for flight-testing Avro 504s built by the Saunders Company at nearby Osborne. It was in use during 1917 and 1918.

East Midlands Airport

See Castle Donington.

East Moor, Yorks

This RAF bomber station opened in June 1942 and was home to Halifaxes, Wellingtons, and Lancasters until May 1945. An OTU arrived in November 1945 and operated Mosquitoes, Wellingtons, Spitfires, and Vengeances until November 1946 when flying ceased. It was used towards the end as a RLG for Leeming.

Restored Second World War control tower at the former RAF bomber station at East Kirkby, now home to the Avro Lancaster bomber of the Lincolnshire Aviation Heritage Centre. The photo was taken on 24 June 2014. (*Tony Yarnold*)

East Retford, Notts

This RFC first-class night LG opened in April 1916 and was used initially for home defence with Be2s, Be12s, and Scouts. In June 1917, its role changed to training; this continued until flying ceased in May 1919. Training types operated included Fe2s, Farmans, DH1s, Avro 504s, Pups, FB9s, DH6s, and Elephants.

East Winch, Norfolk

This unlicensed airfield with a single grass runway opened in the 1980s and is home to around six aircraft.

East Wretham, Norfolk

This RAF station opened as a satellite for Honington in September 1940, the first residents being Wellingtons followed by Lancasters. The station was transferred to the USAAF in October 1943, P-47s and P-51s being based until November 1945 when flying ceased.

Eastbach (English Bicknor), Glos

This unlicensed airfield, also known as Spence, opened before 1974 with two grass strips but is only available to microlights and STOL aircraft. It is home to a dozen or so light aircraft.

Eastbourne, Sussex

An aerodrome at Willingdon was used by Bleriots of the Eastbourne Flying School from December 1911 to August 1914. The RNAS then opened a training school known as St Anthony's Hill, equipped with Avro 504s, Bleriots, JN3s, Be2s, and Caudrons. A factory on the aerodrome produced Be2s and Avro 504s. The RAF took over in April 1918 with a TDS that operated Avro 504s, DH6s, DH9s, Camels, and Pups until October 1919. Civil flying then resumed but ceased in December 1920. A short-lived aerodrome known as Frowds Field opened nearby in April 1932 and closed in August 1933.

Eastburn

See Driffield.

Eastchurch, Kent

This aerodrome was first used in November 1909, and in February 1910, the Royal Aero Club arrived. Shorts built a factory on the site in October 1910, and training for naval pilots commenced in March 1911. In 1913, it became HMS *Pembroke 2* and the RNAS and RAF continued training throughout the war. In April 1918, a TDS was formed, staying until March 1919. Flying, gunnery, observer, and wireless training continued until 1932. Numerous diverse units operating a wide variety of types were based here, some for only short periods, including DH9s, Fawns, Snipes, Horsleys, Wallaces, Blenheims, and Ansons. The first Spitfires arrived in July 1940 and were joined by Hurricanes and Typhoons until the fighters departed in November 1945. It was then placed on C&M and closed in December 1948.

A peaceful scene at Eastchurch on the Isle of Sheppey on 22 August 2019. (*Grant Peerless*)

Just to the west of the wartime airfield, at Parsonage Farm, is an unlicensed grass strip opened in the 1980s with a few residents.

Easterton, Grampian

This unlicensed airfield opened in 1995 and is home to mostly gliders operated by the Highland GC. Around thirty are based here and a single grass runway is in use.

Easthorpe, Essex

This RFC second-class night LG was used for home defence from April 1916 to December 1919.

Eastleigh

See Southampton.

Eaton Bray, Beds

A 'Model Sportsdrome' was developed in the late 1930s for model aircraft flying, motor racing, and private flying, but the war intervened, and it did not open until April 1946. It was an extremely popular venue for motor racing during its brief life, and several air displays were held in 1949. It closed around 1952 and may have been the same site as Mead Farm, Leighton Buzzard, which was used by the Bedford School of Flying. A private airfield at nearby Park Farm opened in the 1970s with a single grass runway, and it is home to about a dozen light aircraft.

Ecclesfield, Yorks

This RFC night LG was used for home defence for only a short time from April to October 1916.

Eccles Tofts

See Charterhall.

Eday, Orkney

This licensed airfield opened in 1971 with one grass and one hard runway. It is served by scheduled services.

Edburton, Sussex

This unlicensed grass airfield at Truleigh Farm opened in the 1960s with a single runway and is home to about six aircraft.

Eddsfield, Yorks

This unlicensed airfield opened in the early 1990s with a single grass runway and is home to about six light aircraft.

Edge Hill (Shenington), Oxon

This RAF station opened in October 1941 as a satellite for Moreton-in-Marsh and was used mainly by Wellingtons of an OTU until June 1945. It was also used between February 1942 and May 1943 to test-fly the Gloster E28/39 prototype. It reopened in July 1952 as a RLG for Moreton-in-Marsh and was used

Derelict Second World War control tower at RAF Edge Hill on 18 October 2011. Now known as Shenington, it is home to the Shenington Gliding Club and some light aircraft. (*Grant Peerless*)

by Harvards and Prentices until November 1954 when flying ceased. Part of the wartime airfield reopened for gliding in 1984, and it is now home to the Shenington GC and also some powered aircraft—about fifty in all. Two hard and two grass runways are available, all unlicensed.

Edgware

See Stag Lane.

Edinburgh (Turnhouse), Lothian

This RFC flight station opened in 1915 and was used mostly for home defence and training until flying ceased in June 1919. It was also used as a repair depot. Types operated included Farmans, Be2s, JN4s, Camels, Avro 504s, and DH9s. Following expansion, it reopened as a RAF station in October 1925 with DH9s and Wapitis while Hinds of Bomber Command were based here from August 1936 to March 1938. It transferred to Fighter Command in October 1939, and Gladiators, Hurricanes, Spitfires, and Defiants were operated until August 1945. Many other units were based for short periods during the Second World War, including some FAA ones, and it was also used extensively by visiting aircraft, particularly American ones. This use continued after the war.

A RAuxF squadron arrived in January 1946 with Spitfires; these were later replaced by Vampires until it was disbanded in March 1957. An AOP flight of Austers was present between May 1949 and March 1957, and communication flights operated from September 1946 to May 1960. An UAS/AEF was formed in October 1946 and operated Tiger Moths, followed by Harvards, Prentices, Chipmunks, Bulldogs, and Tutors until departing in February 1996. It reopened for civil use after the war, and scheduled services recommenced in 1947. Today, it is a busy Edinburgh Airport.

Edzell (Bridgend), Tayside

This RAF aerodrome opened in July 1918 and was home to a TDS equipped with RE8s, Fe2s, Avro 504s, SE5s, and Camels until flying ceased in April 1919. It became an AALG in the 1930s. A new RAF station just south of the First World War aerodrome opened in August 1940 and was used initially as a RLG for Montrose. It was then occupied by various units, the main one being an aircraft storage unit. This handled Hurricanes, Oxfords, Wellingtons, Proctors, Hampdens, Ansons, Albacores, Beauforts, Defiants, Horsas, Magisters, Mosquitoes, and Dakotas until closure in July 1956. Spitfires followed by Vampires were based here from October 1951 to November 1952, and it was used again as a RLG between May 1952 and December 1953. Flying then ceased although an ACGS continued operating until May 1958.

Eggesford, Devon
This unlicensed airfield at Trenchard Farm opened in 1972 with one grass runway and is home to around twenty-five aircraft, many being Auster types.

Egilsay, Orkney
This grass strip opened in February 1979 and is used mainly by air ambulance flights.

Eglinton
See Londonderry.

Elgin, Grampian
This civil aerodrome was in use during the 1920s. It reopened as a RAF station in June 1940 as a satellite for Lossiemouth and was home to an OTU equipped with Wellingtons and Ansons until June 1945. Blenheims arrived in August 1940 and Hurricanes the following December, staying until September 1941. It was used as a RLG by Oxfords from Dalcross for a brief period from May to July 1943, and in July 1945, a sub storage unit was set up. This handled mainly Lancasters and Harvards until closure in December 1947.

Elmdon
See Birmingham.

Elmsett, Suffolk
This unlicensed airfield at Poplar Hall opened in 1970 with one grass runway and is home to nearly twenty light aircraft.

Elmswell
See Great Ashfield.

Elsham Wolds, Lincs
This RFC home defence flight station, known as Elsham, was in use from October 1916 to August 1918, Fe2s and Be2s being the main types operated. A site just to the west was opened as a RAF heavy bomber base in July 1941 and was home to Wellingtons, Halifaxes, and Lancasters until December 1945. An HGCU then took over and operated Halifaxes, Whitleys, Albermarles, and Horsas until December 1946 when flying ceased.

Elstree (Aldenham), Herts
This civil aerodrome opened in conjunction with a country club and was first licensed in July 1934, although it may have been used as early as 1930. It opened officially on 20 April 1935 and became home to sales, training, and joy-riding companies. It was also used by the RAF as an ELG for Hendon and Northolt and closed in November 1939. Redwing Aircraft Company, a CRO, moved in in August 1940 and overhauled numerous types but mainly Lysanders and Wellingtons. They dealt with nearly 500 and 1,200 respectively until they departed in October 1945. The MAP constructed three hangars and laid down a short concrete runway in 1942.

An ACGS operated here from August 1943 to October 1947, and an Allied Expeditionary Air Force communication flight from August 1944 to July 1945. It reopened for civil use as Elstree Aerodrome in January 1946, and its first resident was London Aero and Motor Services (LAMS), which operated air taxi, charter, and training services. It even used Halifax freighters for a short period from April to December 1946. LAMS ceased trading in 1950, but the aerodrome went on to host numerous GA companies that continues to this day, some 140 aircraft being based here, operating from one licensed hard runway.

Elvington, Yorks
This RAF bomber station opened in October 1942 and was home to Halifaxes until October 1945 when it was placed on C&M. From 1954, major works were carried out in preparation for the arrival of B-66s of the USAF, but they did not materialise and the Americans departed in December 1958. In June 1962, it began to be used as a RLG by Jet Provosts from Linton-on-Ouse and Church Fenton, and this continued until 1992. Today, Elvington is occupied by the Yorkshire Air Museum, which opened in 1986 and is an important tourist attraction, with visiting aircraft welcome to use the long unlicensed hard runway.

Ely (Westfield Farm), Cambs
This AALG opened in 1933 and was used by the Ely Aero Club until the outbreak of the Second World War when the aerodrome closed.

Enniskillen (St Angelo), NI
Opened for a SLG in June 1941, it was not used as such. It saw many arrivals of diverted aircraft during the Second World War, and an OTU was based here from July 1942 to June 1945 equipped with Martinets, Hurricanes, Ansons, and Oxfords. A flying instructor's school was set up in May 1944 and operated Wellingtons, Beauforts, and Mosquitoes until disbanded in June 1945. A MU then took over, storing mostly Ansons until February 1947, and the Army based a few Austers here from November

Aerial view of Elstree in 2002. It features a rare MAP 'R' type hangar (the big black one) and short concrete runway laid during the Second World War for Wellington test flying. (*Pete Stevens*)

Right: 'New' control tower at Elstree on 24 June 2018, which was brought into use in 2013. It is in fact based on the earlier one built in 1960 but extended in height and re-clad. (*Richard Riding*)

Below: View of Elstree taken during an air display on 27 July 1947 featuring the short-lived blister hangar and the mortal remains of Handley Page Halifax G-AHZM behind the main hangar. Most of the foreground area this side of the lane is now part of Hilfield Reservoir. (*Aerofilms*)

1959 to March 1960. Civil flying returned in the 1960s, and today, Enniskillen is a busy GA airfield with a single licensed hard runway and over a dozen resident aircraft.

English Bicknor
See Eastbach.

Enstone, Oxon
This RAF station opened in September 1942 as a satellite for Moreton-in-Marsh and was home to Wellingtons and Ansons of an OTU until December 1945. A bomber defence training flight was based here briefly between February and August 1944 with Tomahawks and Hurricanes. It was used as a RLG for Little Rissington from May 1946 until the 1950s. Part of the site reopened for civil flying before 1982, and today, over 120 aircraft are based here, including those of the Oxfordshire Sport GC. The airfield is unlicensed and has one hard and two grass runways.

Errol, Tayside
This RAF station opened in August 1942, its main user being an AFU operating types including Masters, Hurricanes, Swordfish, Albermarles, Mosquitoes, and Harvards. Flying ceased in June 1945, but an ACGS continued to operate until November 1945. Limited scheduled services were operated by Scottish Airways during 1951, and part of the wartime airfield is still used for private flying.

Eshott (Felton), Northumberland
This RAF station opened in November 1942 and was home to an OTU equipped with Spitfires, Masters, Martinets, Battles, Hurricanes, Dominies, and Oxfords until June 1945 when flying ceased. Part of the western side of the airfield reopened for civil flying in 1987, and today, over eighty aircraft are based here, mostly microlights that operate from two hard and one grass unlicensed runways.

Etchilhampton (Lydeway Field), Wilts
This unlicensed airfield opened before 2010 with a single grass runway and around six residents.

Evanton (Novar), Highland
FAA station HMS *Fieldfare* opened in September 1923 and was used mainly by aircraft on 'shore leave' from carriers. The main types accommodated included Walruses, Fairey 3D/Fs, and Blackburn 2s. The RAF arrived in 1937 and shared the station with the Navy, numerous units being based here, some for only short periods. Gunnery training began in September 1937 and lasted until August 1944, various types being used including Audaxes, Gordons, Henleys, Bothas, Harrows, Wallaces, Battles, and Ansons. Flying ceased in December 1944 but returned in 1951 when Oxfords from Dalcross used it as a RLG until September 1953. It saw occasional use by light aircraft in the 1980s.

Everleigh, Wilts
This RLG was used by Masters of the CFS in 1940 and 1941. In December 1941, it became a SLG and stored Blenheims, Hurricanes, Lysanders, Oxfords, Spitfires, Wellingtons, Hotspurs, and Stirlings until November 1945.

Exeter (Bypass), Devon
This grass airfield with two runways replaced an earlier strip at nearby Hele School, which was in use from May 1938 to September 1939. It opened in the late 1940s and was used by the Devonshire Flying Club until closure in the late 1950s.

Exeter (Clyst Honiton), Devon
This civil aerodrome opened officially on 30 June 1938, although scheduled services had commenced in May 1937. An elementary flying school arrived in July 1939 with Tiger Moths but was disbanded on the outbreak of the Second World War. Fighters began to arrive in June 1940 and were present until April 1944. Types operated included Hurricanes, Spitfires, Whirlwinds, Typhoons, and Beaufighters. When these departed, the USAAF took over for a few months with C-47s and CG-4s, but they left in the following September.

The RAF then returned with various units that stayed for brief periods until the station closed in October 1946. It was transferred to the MTCA in January 1947 when civil flying resumed. The RAF returned in April 1949 with a RFS operating Tiger Moths, Chipmunks, and Ansons that stayed until June 1954. Before this, in March 1951, a CAACU arrived and used Mosquitoes, Vampires, Meteors, Jet Provosts, and Hunters until December 1971. Between September 1958 and December 1995, an AEF was based with Chipmunks, as well as an ACGS. Scheduled services resumed in 1952, and today, Exeter Airport is busy with these together with charter flights and regular GA activity.

Eye (Brome), Suffolk
This short-lived USAAF bomber station was in use from April 1944 to August 1945 by B-24s and B-17s.

Eynsford, Kent

This LG was used by the RFC during the First World War.

Eyres Field, Dorset

This gliding site just east of Bovington Camp opened in 1984, at which twenty or so gliders are operated by the Dorset GC.

Fadmoor, Yorks

This unlicensed airfield at Boon Hill Farm opened in 1989 with two grass runways and is home to a few resident aircraft.

Fairford, Glos

This RAF Bomber Command station opened as a satellite for Keevil in November 1943, but its first residents were Oxfords of an AFU. They departed in March 1944 and were replaced with Stirlings but only for a few months until the following October when it became a RLG for an HGCU. It operated Albermarles, Horsas, and Hadrians until October 1945. Oxfords of a BAT flight then appeared but only stayed for a year when they were replaced by Halifaxes until October 1948. Mosquitoes of an AFU used the airfield as a RLG between August 1949 and June 1950; the RAF then departed.

The USAF arrived in February 1953 and operated B-36s, B-47s, and C-47s until June 1964. The RAF then returned, and it was used as a RLG for Little Rissington, the Red Arrows being based with their Gnats from March 1965 to August 1966. Transport Command arrived in November 1965 and employed Belfasts, VC10s, and Hercules until April 1971. It was then designated as a reserve airfield until the USAF returned in September 1979 with KC-135s. They stayed until 1990 when the airfield was again relegated to reserve status—a condition that remains today. It is home to the annual Royal International Air Tattoo as well as being open to visiting private aircraft. Fairford will be best remembered as the test airfield for Concordes between April 1969 and January 1977.

Fair Isle, Shetland

This ELG was used by Highland Airways from May 1937 and by the RAF from 1939 to 1946. A licensed airfield with one hard runway operated by the National Trust opened nearby in 1969 from which scheduled services are operated.

Fairlop, Gt. London

There have been five flying sites in close proximity to each other in the Fairlop area. The first was a civil aerodrome used by Handley Page for test-flying in 1911 for about a year. In April 1916, it reopened as a RNAS LG and was used for training until April 1918 with Be2s and Camels. It then became a TDS equipped with Avro 504s, RE8s, Camels, Pups, Scouts, DH6s, and DH9s until July 1919. Just to the south-west was RFC Hainault Farm, the fifth site (see separate entry).

Some civil flying took place after the war from the western side of the aerodrome from a second site known as Forest Farm or Barkingside. Just over half a mile to the east was the third site, another civil aerodrome known as Chigwell. This was opened at an official ceremony by Mrs F. G. Miles on 24 September 1938, although flying had commenced in the previous July. It was used by the Romford Flying Club, who trained pilots for the CAG and the Midland Bank Flying Club. Scheduled services were briefly operated to Margate and Ramsgate for a short period before the aerodrome closed at the outbreak of the Second World War. The fourth site, just to the south of the First World War Fairlop aerodrome, was a RAF station opened in November 1941 as a satellite for Hornchurch and was used as a fighter base until March 1944. It was home to numerous squadrons employing mostly Spitfires but also Hurricanes and Typhoons. An ACGS continued flying until August 1946 when the airfield closed.

Fairoaks, Surrey

This civil aerodrome, known as Dolley's Farm, opened in 1931 and was used by an elementary flying school from 1936 with Tiger Moths, Harts, and Battles. Training continued until July 1953, latterly by an RFS operating Tiger Moths, Ansons, and Chipmunks. An ACGS was based from 1945 to 1948 and a UAS from December 1947 to October 1950 equipped with Tiger Moths, Chipmunks, Oxfords, Ansons, and Prentices. It reopened for civil use in the spring of 1946 for the Fairoaks Aero Club, and a hard runway was laid in 1978. Today, it is a busy GA licensed airfield with around eighty resident aircraft.

Fairwood Common

See Swansea.

Faldingworth, Lincs

This RAF bomber station opened in August 1943 and was home to Halifaxes and Lancasters, some belonging to a HCU until January 1947. It was also used by a BAT flight of Oxfords from May 1944 to January 1945 and by a detachment of Mosquitoes between October 1946 and January 1947 when flying ceased.

Messerschmitt Bf 108 Taifun G-AFZO pictured in front of the control tower at Fairoaks on 10 July 1948. (*Eddie Riding*)

It was placed on C&M in October 1948 but reopened for a MU in 1957.

Falgunzeon, Dumfries and Galloway
This gliding site opened in around 1975 and is operated by Dumfries and District GC.

Fambridge, Essex
This rudimentary aerodrome was used for flying training and test-flying from February to November 1909.

Farley Chamberlain, Hants
This private airfield at Farley Farm opened in around 1992 with a single grass runway and is home to over twenty light aircraft.

Farnborough, Hants
This is the site of an airship factory built in 1905. The first powered flight of an aeroplane in the British Isles took place here on 16 October 1908. In May 1912, the RFC arrived, and in October 1917, an ARD was set up that handled Fe2s, FK8s, RE8s, DH4s, DH9s, DH10s, F3s, SE5s, and Dolphins. This continued until November 1918, but before this, in 1916, the Royal Aircraft Factory was established, building Fe2s, RE8s, and SE5s. Following the formation of the RAF, the factory was renamed the RAE in July 1918 and was to remain on the airfield until March 1994, being responsible for dealing with most types of military aircraft.

An AACU arrived in April 1920 and stayed until November 1943 using F2bs, Atlases, Audaxes, Henlys, Queen Bees, Lysanders, and Austers. Research and development was the main activity during the Second World War, and in July 1947, the Empire Test Pilots School was formed, which was to remain until January 1968. The first of many SBAC shows took place in September 1948, and in September 1964, the Army returned with Sioux, Scouts, Gazelles, and Lynxes that stayed until March 1982.

Before this, in September 1946, a meteorological research flight was formed, which flew numerous types during its long stay such as Halifaxes, Mosquitoes, Hastings, Camberras, Hunters, Varsities, and Hercules until it departed in 1994. Today, Farnborough is a busy GA airport that deals with mostly corporate jet movements as well as hosting the famous bi-annual flying display and trade show. Flying takes place from one licensed hard runway.

Farningham, Kent
This RFC home defence flight station opened in October 1915 and became a second-class night LG used by Be2s. It was then used as a RLG for Joyce Green until the end of the First World War.

Farsley, Yorks
This RFC third-class night LG was used for home defence from April 1916 to March 1917.

Farthing Corner, Kent

This unlicensed airfield at Stoneacre Farm opened in 1991 with one short grass runway and is home to around a dozen aircraft.

Fearn, Highland

This RAF station opened in late 1941 as a satellite for Tain but was little used. It was transferred to the FAA in July 1942 as HMS *Owl* and was used by a variety of units, notably for torpedo training until flying ceased in May 1946. The main types operated were Swordfish, Barracudas, and Fireflies. Flying returned in May 1952 when Oxfords from Dalcross used it as a RLG until September 1953. Parts of the old airfield are used by light aircraft, with some being based to the north of the Second World War site and a few more on the south side from an unlicensed grass runway known as Easter.

Felixkirk, Yorks

This unlicensed grass airfield opened before 1982 with a single grass runway and is home to around six light aircraft.

Felixstowe (Landguard Common), Suffolk

This RNAS home defence flight station opened in September 1915 and was used as such until August 1916. It then became a day LG for use by land-based aircraft visiting the adjacent seaplane base until closure in 1917.

Feltham

See Hanworth.

Felthorpe, Norfolk

This unlicensed airfield with two grass runways opened around 1964 and is home to nearly twenty private aircraft.

Felton

See Eshott.

Feltwell, Norfolk

This RFC aerodrome opened in November 1917 and was used mostly for training with Be2s, SE5s, DH4s, DH9s, Avro 504s, and Pups until March 1920. Following expansion, it reopened as a RAF bomber station in April 1937 and was home to numerous units operating Harrows, Wellingtons, Venturas, and Lancasters. In April 1946, its role changed to training and Harvards, Tiger Moths, Magisters, Prentices, and Provosts were operated until May 1958. The last residents were AAC Austers, which departed in July 1959, after which flying ceased. It was used as a Thor missile base between September 1958 and July 1963.

Fenland (Holbeach St Johns), Lincs

This licensed airfield opened in 1972 with some fifty residents, operating from two grass runways.

Fersfield, Suffolk

This USAAF bomber station opened in July 1944 and was home to B-17s, which only stayed until the following December. The RAF then took over and operated Mitchells and Mosquitoes until flying ceased in December 1945.

Control tower and clubhouse at Fenland on 21 August 2012. (*Grant Peerless*)

Feshiebridge (Kincraig/Aviemore), Highland

This unlicensed airfield opened in 1967, which is primarily used for gliding by the Cairngorm GC. Over twenty gliders are based here. Powered aircraft are welcome to use the single grass runway.

Fetlar, Shetland

This unlicensed airfield opened in 1972 with one hard runway. Scheduled services operated here in the 1970s.

Fife (Glenrothes), Fife

This unlicensed airfield with a single hard runway opened in 1964 and is home to nearly twenty aircraft.

Filton

See Bristol.

Findo Gask, Tayside

This SLG opened in June 1941 but was not used and was eventually abandoned in November 1942. RAF Mustangs then arrived and stayed until April 1943, after which it was used as a RLG by Masters from Errol until November 1944. Flying ceased in 1945, but the airfield was used as a FLG by Air Service Training from Perth during the 1960s.

Finedon, Northants

This RFC second-class night LG was used for home defence for a short period only from January to July 1917.

Finmere, Bucks

An AALG at Tingewick (Gawcott) was in use in the 1930s. Just to the west, a RAF station opened in 1941 and was used initially as a RLG for Bicester by Blenheims of an OTU. These were followed by an assortment of types from various units including Bostons, Mitchells, Havocs, and Mosquitoes until July 1945. A communications flight operated from December 1942 to September 1943 equipped with Wellingtons, Ansons, and Leopard Moths. Flying ceased in July 1945, but part of the wartime airfield reopened for private flying before 1974. Today, around twenty aircraft are based here, operating from one unlicensed hard runway.

Finningley (Doncaster Sheffield Airport), Yorks

This RFC second-class night LG, known as Brancroft, opened in December 1916 and was used mainly by Avro 504s for home defence until closure in June 1919. Land approximately 1 mile to the north was later developed into RAF Finningley, a bomber station opened in August 1936. It was home initially to Heyfords, followed by Wellesleys, Audaxes, Whitleys, Hampdens, Ansons, Wellingtons, Manchesters, Halifaxes, Lancasters, and Lincolns until March 1947. Some of these were operated in the training role. A BAT flight equipped with mainly Oxfords and Blenheims operated between January 1941 and March 1943, and various other units were based here during the war. A squadron of Mosquitoes arrived in May 1946; they were replaced with Meteors until they departed in May 1955.

The station's role changed to training in March 1947, which continued until May 1954. Types operated included Oxfords, Harvards, Spitfires, Wellingtons, and Meteors. After a runway extension, 'V' bombers arrived in October 1957 in the shape of Vulcans, followed by Valiants; these stayed until December 1969. Training resumed in May 1970 with Varsities, Dominies, Jetstreams, Jet Provosts, Hawks, and Tucanos, continuing until March 1996. An UAS/AEF was based here with Chipmunks and Bulldogs from August 1975 to October 1995, and a SAR helicopter flight operated here between January 1976 and October 1992 with Whirlwinds, Wessexes, and Sea Kings. A flight of Jetstreams was based here from July 1992 to October 1995. The RAF departed in March 1996, but in April 2005, the airfield reopened as Robin Hood Airport and is now known as Doncaster Sheffield Airport.

Firbeck, Yorks

This civil aerodrome opened in 1935 in conjunction with a nearby country club and was later used by Sheffield Aero Club. It was taken over by the RAF in October 1940 and was home to Lysanders until July 1941. It was then used as a RLG for Hucknall until November 1945, mainly by Tiger Moths. It was used by a flight of Austers from September 1942 to August 1943 and by an ACGS until February 1948 when flying ceased.

Fishburn (Morganfield), Co. Durham

This unlicensed airfield was opened by Tony Blair MP on 30 June 1995. Over fifty aircraft based here operate from a single grass runway.

Fiskerton, Lincs

This RAF bomber station opened in January 1943 and was home to Lancasters until October 1945.

A BAT flight of Oxfords operated from January 1944 to January 1945, and a detachment of Mosquitoes was a brief resident between September 1944 and June 1945. Flying ceased in October 1945.

Flimston Down, Pembrokeshire

This LG was used by AACU Wallaces from May 1937 to September 1938.

Flitwick (Ampthill), Beds

This RFC night LG was used from October 1916 to July 1917.

Flotta, Orkney

A LG at Rotten Gutter was in use from 1975 to 1977, which was then replaced with the current unlicensed airfield. It has one hard runway and is used predominantly by helicopters, although it is open to fixed-wing ambulance and emergency flights.

Folkingham, Lincs

Originally intended for use by RAF Bomber Command, this airfield was instead used by the USAAF as a transport base from February 1944. Types operated included C-46s, C-47s, C-53s, and CG-4s until they departed in February 1945. It then closed to flying but was reactivated as a RLG for Cranwell between September 1957 and August 1959. Thor missiles were deployed on the site from December 1959 to August 1963. Some civil flying took place in the 1980s.

Ford, Sussex

This RFC aerodrome, known as Yapton, opened in March 1918 and was used initially for training by Fe2s and F2bs until the following June. The USAAS arrived in September 1918 and operated F20s, Be2s, and DH4s but only stayed for a couple of months. The RAF returned in February 1919 with DH10s, Avro 504s, and F2bs and was resident until the following December when flying ceased. It reopened for civil flying in 1928 and was used by the Ford Motor Company from 1931 to 1934 to sell and maintain Ford Tri-Motors. Alan Cobham then used the airfield as a base for his National Aviation Day fleet until the end of the 1935 season. His company, Flight Refuelling Ltd, arrived in 1936 and stayed until May 1940 (they returned in 1946 and moved out in 1948).

Following expansion, it reopened as a RAF station in December 1937 and was used for training by Coastal Command Sharks and Swordfish. It transferred to the FAA as HMS *Peregrine* in May 1939 and Sharks, Walruses, Rocs, Swordfish, and Albacores were operated until August 1940. The RAF then returned and employed Blenheims, Havocs, Bostons, Hurricanes, Mosquitoes, Mustangs, and Spitfires. The Navy returned in July 1945 and stayed until September 1958 when flying ceased. During their stay, they operated almost every type of naval aircraft then in service from Fireflies to Seahawks. Part of the wartime airfield reopened for civil flying in 1964, which continued sporadically until final closure in the early 1980s.

Fordoun, Grampian

This RAF station opened in November 1942 as a satellite for Peterhead but was used mainly as a RLG for Montrose. Oxfords and Masters were the main types operated here, and flying ceased in September 1944, although an ACGS continued flying until May 1946. Part of the old airfield reopened for civil flying in May 1965 but closed in the mid-1980s.

Foreland (New Bembridge), IoW

This aerodrome was used by DH6s of a RAF coastal patrol flight from June 1918 to May 1919.

Fornham All Saints (Bury St Edmunds), Suffolk

This aerodrome was first used by the RFC in October 1914 and later became a night LG for home defence between April and October 1916.

Forres, Grampian

This RAF station opened in April 1940 as a satellite for Kinloss and was used by a bomber OTU equipped with Whitleys, Wellingtons, Ansons, and Lysanders until October 1944. An AFU operating Oxfords, Ansons, and Masters was also based here between May and November 1943. Flying ceased in October 1944, but in 1959, a short concrete airstrip was constructed on part of one of the former wartime runways. This was known as Mundole and was used by executive aircraft until about 1985.

Foula, Shetland

This unlicensed airfield with one hard runway opened in 1969 and is used occasionally by air ambulance flights.

Foulsham, Norfolk

This RAF bomber station opened in May 1942, but the first aircraft, Mitchells, did not arrive until the October of that year. These were followed by

Lancasters, Wellingtons, Halifaxes, and Mosquitoes until the airfield closed in October 1945. Some private flying took place after the war, but this had ceased by the early 1990s.

Fowlmere, Cambs

This RFC first-class night LG opened in August 1916 and was used for home defence until December 1917. It then became a training station and operated DH4s, DH9s, and RE8s until it closed in April 1920. An RAF fighter airfield was established on a nearby site in June 1940 as a satellite for Duxford and was home to Spitfires and Hurricanes until July 1943. It then transferred to the USAAF who operated P-51s until October 1945 when the airfield closed. Part of the site reopened for private flying in 1990 using one of the wartime hangars and is now home to a dozen or so light aircraft that operate from a single unlicensed grass runway.

Framlingham (Parham), Suffolk

This USAAF bomber station was used between May 1943 and August 1945 by B-17s. Some private flying still takes place from part of the old airfield and a few microlights are based here.

Fraserburgh, Grampian

This RAF station opened in December 1941 as a satellite for Peterhead but was used initially by FAA Swordfish and Sea Hurricanes until February 1942. An OTU then arrived with Spitfires, Mosquitoes, and Masters, staying until February 1943. An AFU was next on the scene, and its Oxfords and Ansons stayed until September 1944. The last occupants were ASR Warwicks from December 1944 to June 1945, when flying ceased. The Aberdeen GC used part of the site during the 1950s.

Freethorpe, Norfolk

This RFC first-class night LG was used for home defence from April 1916 to June 1919.

Freiston, Lincs

This RNAS second-class LG opened in late 1916 and was used mainly for gunnery training. Types operated included Be2s, DH5s, SE5s, Avro 504s, Camels, and Snipes. It closed in March 1920.

Frensham, Surrey

This unlicensed airfield at New Farm (Wishanger Farm) opened before 1986 with a single grass runway and has around ten resident light aircraft.

Frettenham, Norfolk

This RFC second-class night LG was used for home defence from August 1916 to June 1919.

Frinstead (Harrietsham), Kent

This RFC second-class LG was in use for home defence from October 1916 to June 1919 by Be2s, FB19s, RE8s, FK8s, Pups, and SE5s.

Friston, Sussex

A private LG was in use before the Second World War and was used by RAF Audaxes during the summer of 1936 and as an ELG by Fighter Command in 1940. A flight of ASR Walruses was based here between July and October 1941. Fighter Command took over in June 1942 and operated Hurricanes, Spitfires, and Mustangs until May 1945. The Southdown GC arrived in 1946 and stayed until March 1955 when flying ceased.

Frome, Somerset

This AALG was in use between 1933 and 1934.

Frost Hill Farm, Hants

This FLG was used by RAF Magisters and Lysanders during 1940 and 1941. It was prepared as an ALG in 1943, but no aircraft were handled here. It was used by helicopters from Middle Wallop for training during the 1980s.

Fulbeck, Lincs

This RAF station opened as a RLG for Cranwell in 1940 and was used by Oxfords and Tutors. In June 1942, training commenced with Lancasters and continued with Manchesters, Martinets, Defiants, Oxfords, and Lysanders until August 1943. It was then transferred to the USAAF as a transport base and was home to C-47s, C-53s, and CG-4s, which stayed until June 1944. Lancasters returned in October 1944 and were later joined by Mosquitoes until flying ceased in April 1945. The airfield was reactivated in February 1956, again as a RLG for Cranwell and was used by Vampires and other types until closure in July 1977.

Full Sutton, Humberside

This RAF bomber station opened in May 1944, but this use was short-lived, with its Halifaxes departing in August 1945. These were replaced with a training unit operating Lancastrians and later Oxfords until October 1946. The base was then placed on C&M until May 1951 when training resumed, this time with Meteors,

Vampires, Harvards, and Spitfires, which stayed until August 1954. It then became a RLG and was used by Vampires, Meteors, and Jet Provosts until July 1959. A few Thor missiles were then deployed, departing in April 1963, and the airfield closed. Part of the wartime airfield reopened for private flying in 1992, and around forty aircraft are currently based, which operate from a single unlicensed grass runway.

Funtington, Sussex

This ALG was used by RAF Mustangs from September to October 1943 and by RAF Hurricanes, Typhoons, Spitfires, and Mustangs from April to August 1944.

Fyfield (Ongar), Essex

This RFC third-class night LG was used for home defence from October 1916 to December 1919.

Gainsborough, Notts

This RFC third- and second-class night LG was used for home defence, and later training from October 1916 to April 1919. Types based included Fe2s.

Gamston (Retford), Notts

This RAF training station opened in December 1942 and was home to several units operating Oxfords, Ansons, Wellingtons, Hurricanes, and Masters until June 1945 when flying ceased. It was reactivated in September 1952 as a RLG for Worksop and was used by Meteors, Oxfords, and Prentices up to 1954. Flying then ceased again, and the RAF departed in 1957. Civil flying then took over, and today, Retford Airport is a busy GA airfield with over eighty residents. Two hard runways—one licensed and one unlicensed—are available.

Gatwick, Sussex

This civil aerodrome opened as Cotland Farm in March 1929 and was licensed on 1 August 1930. It was owned by the Redwing Aircraft Company from July 1932 to January 1934. Scheduled services commenced in May 1936, and the rebuilt Gatwick Airport was officially opened on 6 June 1936. An elementary flying school arrived in October 1937 with Tiger Moths, Harts, and Magisters, which stayed until the outbreak of the Second World War. The RAF then took over and a wide variety of units were operated but the main function was Army co-operation. An assortment of types were based here, including Blenheims, Spitfires, Lysanders, Defiants, Tomahawks, Mustangs, Hurricanes, Typhoons, Ansons, Oxfords, and Mosquitoes. The RAF departed in August 1946, but an ACGS continued flying until June 1949. Civil flying resumed in August 1946 when several maintenance companies were set up, one of which repaired Sea Hornets and Seafires until the airfield closed in March 1956. It reopened as Gatwick Airport on 9 June 1958 and is now London's second main airport.

Grumman American AA-5 G-PURR parked in front of a hangar at Gamston (Retford) with a Beech King Air by the control tower on 27 October 2005. (*Grant Peerless*)

British Airways DH86 G-ADEB in front of the 'Beehive' at Gatwick in June 1936. (*Flight*)

Gaydon, Warks
This RAF station opened in June 1942 as a satellite for Wellesbourne Mountford and was used by Wellingtons, Ansons, Masters, and Hurricanes of an OTU until July 1945. It was then used for glider training with Masters, Hotspurs, and Tiger Moths before being placed on C&M in June 1946. It again reopened briefly as a RLG for Wellesbourne Mountford between September 1952 and October 1953, Oxfords being the main user. In January 1955, 'V' bombers arrived in the shape of the Valiant, and these were followed by Victors until the 'V' force departed in June 1965. An ANS then arrived and operated Valettas and Varsities until May 1970. Flying then ceased but a VGS that had been formed in April 1966 continued flying until November 1977.

Gifford (Townhead/Haddington), Lothian
This RFC third-class night LG was used for home defence from February 1917 to November 1918. Lennoxlove SLG was fewer than 2 miles to the north-west.

Gigha Island, Hebrides
This unlicensed airfield opened in 1991 with a single grass runway.

Gilling (New Malton), Yorks
This RFC second-class day and third-class night LG was used for home defence from December 1916 to June 1919.

Gilmerton (Edinburgh), Lothian
This RFC second-class night LG was used for home defence from December 1916 to the end of 1918.

Girvan
See Turnberry.

Glasgow (Abbotsinch), Strathclyde
This RAF bomber station opened in January 1933 with Wapitis, later replaced by Hinds and Hectors. It transferred to Coastal Command in January 1937, who operated Ansons and Tiger Moths. The FAA arrived in December 1939 and used Swordfish, Henleys, and Walruses. Blackburn set up an assembly facility in 1939 and flight-tested Bothas, Sharks, etc. until the end of the Second World War. A torpedo training unit was set up in March 1940 and operated mainly Beauforts until November 1942. An aircraft assembly unit handled American types between 1940 and 1943.

The base was taken over by FAA in August 1943 as HMS *Sanderling* and was subsequently used by many and varied units operating most types then in service until the Navy departed in October 1963. In the late 1950s and early 1960s, an aircraft holding unit was set up, which scrapped hundreds of surplus naval aircraft including Avengers, Skyraiders, Sea Venoms, and Seahawks. It was also a receiving point for American aircraft shipped up the Clyde as well as an overflow site for Lockheeds at Renfrew. When the Navy departed in 1963, it was developed as

Glasgow Airport and was officially opened by HM the Queen on 27 June 1966, replacing Renfrew. An AEF and UAS currently operate Tutors from the airport.

Glasgow (Renfrew), Strathclyde

This aerodrome was used for test-flying locally built Fe2s and DH9s from 1915 as well as housing the Beardmore Flying School until 1918. It became a RFC aerodrome known as Moorpark, and an AAP opened in March 1918. This dealt with Camels, DH9s, Fe2s, Fairey 3s, and Cuckoos until its closure in March 1920. An ARD also operated from the end of 1918. Civil flying then recommenced, and in December 1925, a RAuxAF unit arrived equipped with DH9s, Fawns, and Wapitis. This was resident until January 1933 when the Scottish Flying Club took over civil operations.

Scheduled services were flown from April 1933 until the outbreak of the Second World War, but strategic routes continued throughout the war. The RAF returned in December 1940 and operated Lysanders until May 1941, and a UAS equipped with Tiger Moths was based here from February 1943 to December 1945. During the war, Lockheed assembled imported American aircraft, mostly Lightnings and Mustangs. A RAuxAF squadron arrived in July 1949 with Spitfires and departed in April 1951 by which time it was flying Vampires. Civil flying resumed after the Second World War and a new terminal was constructed in 1954. Scottish Aviation overhauled CF-100s and F-86s between 1954 and 1960. Renfrew closed as Glasgow's airport in May 1966 when operations relocated to Abbotsinch only 1 mile away.

Glatton (Conington), Cambs

This USAAF bomber station opened in January 1944 and was home to B-17s until June 1945. It was then used by a flight of RAF Oxfords until April 1946 when flying ceased. In 1965, Peterborough and Spalding Aviation moved in from Westwood with their blister hangar. It was renamed Conington in 1974 and is also known as Peterborough Business Airport. It is a thriving GA airfield with over thirty residents operating from two hard runways—one licensed and one unlicensed.

Gleneagles, Tayside

This AALG was opened in 1920 and closed in 1939.

Glenforsa (Isle of Mull), Hebrides

This unlicensed airfield opened in 1966 with scheduled services, which continued until 1976. It has a single grass runway and is used by air ambulance flights as well as light aircraft.

Blister hangar at Glatton (Conington) believed to have been moved from Westwood Airfield after it closed in 1965. The photo was taken on 18 October 2011. (*Grant Peerless*)

Control tower at Glatton (Conington) on 18 October 2011. (*Grant Peerless*)

Glenrothes
See Fife.

Gloucester Airport
See Staverton.

Gloucester (Churchdown/Hatherley), Glos
This AALG opened in September 1932 and was home to the Cotswold Aero Club until May 1937. It then closed but moved to a new site on the opposite side of the road, which became Staverton Airport.

Godmersham Park, Kent
This LG was in use by the RAF during 1918.

Goldhanger (Gardeners Farm), Essex
This night LG was used by the RNAS from August 1915 to June 1916 and then by the RFC as a home defence station. Various types were operated including Be2s and Be12s until flying ceased in March 1919.

Goldington (Bedford), Beds
This RFC third-class night LG (later to become a second-class and a day LG) was used for home defence from October 1916 to September 1917, mainly by Be2s and Be12s. It may have been the site of a civil aerodrome opened in August 1930 by the Bedfordshire Aero Club, but it closed again in 1935.

Golspie (Kirkton), Highland
This ELG opened for Highland Airways in March 1933 and was later used for limited scheduled services. It reopened as a SLG in August 1941 and was used to store Whitleys, Spitfires, Wellingtons, Havocs, and Bostons until February 1945.

Gooderstone Warren, Norfolk
This RFC second-class night LG was used for home defence from August 1916 to June 1919. A civil airfield about 2 miles north-west at Gooderstone was in use during the 1970s and 1980s.

Goodwood, Sussex
A RFC first-class night LG, known as Shopwhyke, was used for home defence during 1917, mostly with Be2s. Following expansion, it reopened as RAF Westhampnett in July 1940 as a satellite for Tangmere and was home initially to fighters, mostly Spitfires but also Hurricanes and Typhoons until September 1944. USAAF Spitfires were based for a short period from July to October 1942. The naval air fighting development unit moved in in July 1945 and flew Hellcats and Ansons until departing the following November. The airfield was

used as a RLG for Tangmere during 1945 and closed in May 1946. The Goodwood motor racing circuit, which utilised the Second World War perimeter track, opened in September 1948 and closed in 1965. Civil flying resumed in 1958, and today, Goodwood is a busy GA airfield with over 125 resident aircraft that have the use of three licensed grass runways.

Gosberton (Spalding), Lincs

This RFC second-class night LG was used for home defence from October 1916 to June 1919.

Gosfield, Essex

This USAAF station opened in December 1943 with P-47s followed by B-26s and A-20s until the Americans departed under a year later in September 1944. It was used by RAF Stirlings for a short while in January 1945 and closed in July of that year. A few light aircraft operate from part of the old airfield.

Gosport (Fort George/Fort Rowner), Hants

This aerodrome opened in November 1909, and in April 1910, the Hampshire Aero Club arrived and stayed until early 1914. The RFC took over in July 1914 with Farmans and Avro 504s; these were replaced by Scouts, Tabloids and Avro 504s of the RNAS in the following October. It became an RFC first-class night LG in August 1916 and was used for home defence until the end of the war. Training also continued with Fe2s, DH2s, F2bs, Longhorns, Shorthorns, and Camels.

After the First World War, numerous units equipped with a wide variety of types were based here, including Cuckoos, Vildebeests, Horsleys, Darts, Flycatchers, Bisons, Fairey 3Fs, Sharks, and Swordfish. During the Second World War, the RAF operated Battles, Defiants, Hurricanes, Barracudas, Hudsons, and Beaufighters. It transferred to the FAA in August 1945 as HMS *Siskin*; they operated Sea Otters, Barracudas, Seafires, Firebrands, Avengers, Hellcats, and Mosquitoes until March 1947. It then became a helicopter training unit that employed R4s, S51s, HTE2s, and S55s until flying ceased in May 1956.

Goxhill, Humberside

This RFC night LG was in use for home defence for a short period between April and autumn 1916. Following expansion, it reopened as a RAF station in June 1941 and was home briefly to a Lysander flight before being used during January 1942 by a Spitfire squadron. The USAAF arrived the following June with P-38s, Spitfires, P-47s, P-39s, and P-51s and stayed until December 1944. It was then returned to the RAF and flying ceased.

Grafton Underwood, Northants

This USAAF station opened in May 1942, its first residents being A-20s, but these only stayed for a

Piper Tomahawk G-BGRK taxiing past the then new control tower at Goodwood in April 1988. (*Grant Peerless*)

month. They were replaced by B-17s, which remained until flying ceased in June 1945.

Grain (Port Victoria), Kent

This RNAS flying boat base opened in December 1912 and was used as a naval repair depot in 1915. It became a marine experimental station in October 1918, which operated various types including Avro 504s until closure in June 1924.

Grangemouth, Central Region

Although opened as Central Scotland Airport on 1 July 1939, flying had commenced the previous April. It saw little use until civil flying ceased on the outbreak of the Second World War. An elementary flying school was formed in May 1939 with Tiger Moths, Hinds, Audaxes, and Ansons, but this was disbanded in the following September. Fighters then arrived in the shape of Spitfires, Blenheims, Gladiators, and Hurricanes, and in December 1940, an OTU was formed. This operated Spitfires, Masters, Hurricanes, Battles, and Dominies until it departed in June 1944. A RFS equipped with Tiger Moths and Ansons was based here from April 1948 to April 1949 and flying then ceased, although an ACGS continued operating until 1965.

Gransden Lodge, Cambs

This RAF bomber station opened as a satellite for Tempsford in April 1942 and was home to Halifaxes, Wellingtons, Lancasters, and Mosquitoes. It closed in February 1946, but part of the site reopened in 1990 for gliding by the Cambridge GC and is now home to around seventy gliders.

Grantham (Sudbrook House), Lincs

This private grass airfield was in use during the 1980s.

Graveley, Cambs

This was another RAF bomber station used as a satellite for Tempsford and opened in March 1942. Its first residents were Lysanders and Whitleys, but they soon departed and their place was taken by Halifaxes, Lancasters, and Mosquitoes until September 1946. It was then placed on C&M until December 1950 when it came into use as a RLG for Harvards, Meteors, and Vampires from Oakington until closure in July 1964.

Graveley, Herts

This unlicensed airfield at Graveley Hall Farm opened before 1993 with a single grass runway and is used mainly by microlights but is also open to light aircraft. About twenty types are based here.

Gravesend (Chalk), Kent

This civil aerodrome opened on 12 October 1932 and while it was available as a diversion airport for Croydon, scheduled services never materialised. Percival Aircraft Ltd set up a factory in 1934 and built Gulls and Mew Gulls before relocating to Luton in October 1936. An elementary flying school arrived in October 1937, equipped with Hinds, Harts, Tiger Moths, and Ansons and was resident here until the outbreak of the Second World War. It then became a satellite for Biggin Hill and hosted mainly fighter operations until June 1944. Spitfires were mostly operated here, but Hurricanes, Blenheims, Defiants, Typhoons, Mustangs, and Mosquitoes were also used. It was placed on C&M after the war, and an ACGS was based here until December 1945. It reopened for civil flying after the war, mainly by Essex Aero and closed in March 1956.

Great Ashfield, Suffolk

This RFC first-class night LG, later a home defence flight station, was also known as Elmswell and was used for home defence from April 1916 to May 1919. Types operated included Be2s and Be12s. Following expansion, it reopened as a USAAF bomber base in March 1943, but the first aircraft to use it were RAF Stirlings that carried out circuit training. The Americans arrived in June 1943 with B-17s and stayed until August 1945, after which flying ceased. A few light aircraft operated from part of the old airfield until it closed at the end of 2017.

Great Barr

See Walsall.

Great Bookham, Surrey

This civil aerodrome at Phoenice Farm was in use between September 1926 and September 1935.

Great Dunmow (Easton Lodge) Essex

This USAAF bomber station opened in May 1943, but the first residents were RAF Stirlings and Halifaxes that used the airfield until the following June. In September 1943, B-26s of the USAAF arrived; these were resident until October 1944. The RAF then returned with Stirlings and Halifaxes and stayed until January 1946 when flying ceased.

Percival Mew Gull ZS-AHO photographed in front of the hangars at Gravesend, *c.* 1936. The airfield closed in 1956. (*Flight*)

Great Hucklow

See Camphill.

Great Massingham, Norfolk

This RAF station opened in September 1940 as a satellite for West Raynham and was home to various units operating Blenheims, Bostons, Mosquitoes, Beaufighters, Wellingtons, Oxfords, and Ansons during the Second World War. It closed in July 1945 but was used as a RLG for West Raynham from December 1945 to November 1950. Private flying returned to part of the wartime airfield before 1974 and now about six aircraft are based here, operating from three unlicensed hard runways.

Great Oakley, Essex

This unlicensed airfield opened in 1993 with two grass runways and is home to over twenty aircraft.

Great Orton, Cumbria

This RAF station opened in June 1943 as a satellite for Silloth, home to various units operating Wellingtons, Hurricanes, Masters, Martinets, and Warwicks. It was placed on C&M in April 1945 and closed in 1952. Part of the wartime airfield reopened for microlight flying around 1989, but this had ceased by 2001.

Great Sampford, Essex

This RAF fighter station opened in April 1942 and was home to Spitfires until March 1943; however, from September 1942, these were operated by the USAAF along with P-47s. Flying then ceased and the airfield closed in August 1944.

Great Shefford, Berks

This site was used as a dispersal aerodrome for Woodley during 1940 and as a RLG for Little Rissington later that year. It then became an ELG until the end of the war.

Great Yarmouth (South Denes), Norfolk

This RNAS LG opened in 1913 and was used mostly for coastal patrol duties until flying ceased in June 1919. Various types were operated including Be2s, DH4s, DH9s, and Camels. It may have seen civil use during 1920.

Great Yarmouth (North Denes), Norfolk

This civil airfield opened in 1953 and was used mostly by helicopters from 1965. It closed to fixed-wing aircraft in 2011 and helicopters in 2015.

Great Yarmouth (Wheatcroft), Norfolk

This AALG opened in 1932 and was visited by Cobham's Flying Circus on several occasions until closure in 1939.

Greencastle (Kilkeel), NI

This RAF station was planned as a bomber OTU when it opened in July 1942 but was instead taken over by the USAAF in August 1943. They used it as a satellite air depot for Langford Lodge and dealt mainly with B-17s and B-24s until May 1945. It was then handed back to the RAF, but no more flying took place.

A private grass strip at Derryogue is possibly on the site of the Second World War airfield and is home to around eight residents, mostly microlights.

Greenham Common, Berks

This RAF station opened in December 1942 and was used initially as a RLG by Oxfords until September 1943. The USAAF arrived in November 1943 and operated P-51s, P-47s, C-47s, and CG-4s until February 1945 when flying ceased. The Americans returned in March 1954 with B-47s, C-47s, and KC-97s, staying until April 1964. Only occasional use was then made of the airfield, particularly a detachment of F-111s from March to September 1976 until May 1983 when Tomahawk cruise missiles arrived. These departed in September 1990, and the base closed in 1992.

Greenland Top (Stallingborough), Lincs

This RFC first-class night LG was used for home defence from December 1916 and by a coastal patrol flight operating DH6s from May to November 1918. Flying ceased in May 1919.

Grimsetter

See Kirkwall.

Grove, Oxon

This RAF station opened in August 1942 as a satellite for Harwell and was used initially as a RLG by Wellingtons and Oxfords until July 1943. From February to May 1943, it served briefly as an HGCU with Whitleys and Horsas. The USAAF arrived in November 1943 and operated C-47s, C-46s, C-53s, and C-64s until December 1945. The RAF then returned, and the airfield was used briefly as a RLG for Brize Norton, as well as by a MU disposing of surplus aircraft. It closed in 1958.

Grove Park, Gt. London

This RFC second-class night LG near Bromley was used for home defence from June 1917 to May 1919.

Grove Park, Notts

This SLG was in use between 1942 and April 1944.

Guernsey, CI

An aerodrome at L'Eree was opened for the Guernsey Aero Club in September 1934. Scheduled services were operated for a brief period from May to October 1935, but the aerodrome then closed. A new airport was opened on 5 May 1939, and scheduled services commenced, which continued until the outbreak of the Second World War. The RAF then arrived and based a few Ansons and Hurricanes here until the Germans invaded in June 1940. Civil flying resumed after the war, and a hard runway was laid in 1961. Regular scheduled services continue to operate.

Guilton (Ash), Kent

This RFC second-class night LG was used for home defence from May 1918 to June 1919.

Gullane

See Drem.

Hackney Marshes, Gt. London

This RFC first-class night LG was used for home defence from April 1916 to October 1917. It continued to be used by the RAF until 1935.

Aurigny Airlines Britten-Norman Trislander G-BBYO taxies past the control tower at Guernsey Airport in August 1983. (*Grant Peerless*)

Hadleigh, Suffolk

This RFC first-class night LG, known as Hintlesham, opened in April 1916 and was later upgraded to a home defence flight station. Types operated included Be2s, Be12s, and Avro 504s until flying ceased in November 1918. About 2.5 miles to the north-west, a civil aerodrome opened in 1927, and in November 1928, a scheduled service was operated to Conington but was short-lived. The aerodrome closed in 1931 but may be the site of a civil airfield known as Whatfield, which was in use between 1965 and 1990 by the Essex and Suffolk GC and later by light aircraft. Another grass airfield in the vicinity, known as Harvest Farm, was in use during the 1990s.

Hainault Farm, Gt. London

This RNAS day LG opened in October 1914 but was only in use until February 1915. It became a RFC third-class night LG in April 1916 and was used for home defence until July 1919. Types operated included Be2s, 1½ Strutters, and Camels. It was used as an ELG for Hornchurch during the Second World War. RFC Fairlop was just to the north-west and RAF Fairlop just to the west.

Haldon (Teignmouth), Devon

This civil aerodrome opened officially in September 1929, although flying had commenced in June 1928. Scheduled services started in April 1933 but moved to Exeter in 1937. It was requisitioned by the Air Ministry at start of the Second World War, and in August 1941, it became an FAA station HMS *Heron 2*, a satellite to RNAS Yeovilton. It was used mainly by Skuas and Masters on target towing duties until placed on C&M in May 1943. An ACGS operated here from August 1944 to June 1946. Sporadic civil flying took place from the 1950s until at least 1974.

Halesland, Somerset

This RAF gliding site opened in July 1946 and was home to an ACGS until September 1955. It was also used by civilian gliding clubs and is still active today, the Mendip GC being the main user with a dozen gliders.

Halesworth (Holton), Suffolk

This USAAF station opened in July 1943 with P-47s the first residents. These were replaced with B-24s in May 1944; these stayed until the following November. An emergency rescue squadron then arrived and operated P-47s, OA-10s, and B-17s. The base passed to the RAF in June 1945 but was soon taken over by the FAA as HMS *Sparrowhawk*, who operated Barracudas, Fireflies, Harvards, Oxfords, Beauforts, and Mosquitoes until the airfield closed in January 1946.

Halfpenny Green (Bobbington), Staffs

This RAF training station opened in February 1941 and was home to several units flying Bothas, Ansons, and Oxfords. Flying ceased in November 1945, and the site was placed on C&M in January 1946. It was reactivated at the time of the Korean War and training took place with Ansons and Prentices between May 1952 and September 1953. It reopened as a civil airfield in March 1961 and is now a thriving GA site with around 100 based aircraft that have the use of three licensed hard runways. It is now known as Wolverhampton Airport.

Halkirk, Highland

This civil aerodrome at Georgemas Junction was used intermittently from late 1933 by Highland Airways.

Halton (Wendover), Bucks

Flying commenced here in September 1913 but was short-lived and took place some way away from the present airfield. RFC Bleriots and Farmans were used for army manoeuvres in September of that year but soon moved on. The RFC returned in 1916 with a TDS, and from March 1920, it became a RAF school of technical training. The current aerodrome, known as Halton Park, was established in 1921. Types dealt with by the school over the years were numerous, starting with Avro 504s and Snipes and finishing in September 1993 with Jet Provosts and Canberras. Other types handled included Gnats, Jaguars, Comets, and a Vulcan, all of which were flown into this grass airfield. Various other units were based from February 1940 including a communications flight equipped with Wellingtons, Ansons, C30s, Tiger Moths, Hornet Moths, Dominies, and Oxfords, which stayed here until 1948. Gliding has been an important part of the Halton scene since September 1947 and is still going strong by the Halton GC. A VGS operated Vigilants until 2016 and over fifty aircraft including gliders are based here. They operate from two licensed grass runways. The airfield is due to close by 2025.

Halwell, Devon

This unlicensed grass strip opened in around 1995 and is operated by the South Hams Flying Club. It is home to about ten aircraft, mostly microlights.

Restored Second World War control tower at Halfpenny Green (formerly RAF Bobbington) still in use on 16 January 2016. (*Grant Peerless*)

Hamble, Hants

There were two main sites at Hamble: North and South.

Hamble South

Hamble South opened as a LG in 1913 and was used during the First World War as an AAP that handled mostly flying boats. Fairey Aviation took over an existing factory on the site in 1915 and constructed Campanias, 3Fs, Seafoxes and Fireflies. Another manufacturer, A. V. Roe and Co., opened a factory in 1916 that built 504s and Avians. They continued to make use of the airfield until 1926 when they moved to the adjacent North site. However, production continued for several years by the Cierva Autogyro Co., and in 1937, Avro built eleven Ensign airliners in their old factory.

Hamble North

Hamble North was opened in 1926 and used by A. V. Roe and Co. for testing their aircraft but only until 1928 when Armstrong Whitworth took over the facility. In 1931, Air Service Training was formed and operated a flying school to train RAF reserve officers using a fleet of Avians, Tutors, Atlases, Siskins, and DH9s. This was formalised as an elementary flying school in April 1933 although with civilian aircraft, but by 1938, RAF Harts, Hinds, and Battles were used. As well as the eleven Ensigns, Armstrong Whitworth built the prototype Albermarles here.

Folland Aircraft arrived in 1936, and during the war, they produced components for Blenheims, Beauforts, Mosquitoes, Wellingtons, Sunderlands, Spitfires, and, later, Midges. In June 1940, an ATA ferry pilot's pool was formed, using mainly Argus and Anson taxi aircraft until September 1945. An RFS was established in August 1947 equipped with Tiger Moths, Ansons, and Chipmunks; this stayed until August 1953. A naval air signals school moved in in November 1949 with Ansons and was resident until November 1953. An UAS, and later an AEF, operated Chipmunks until December 1978. On the civil side, the College of Air Training took over the former Air Service Training facility in 1960 and went on to train airline pilots until the airfield closed in the summer of 1984.

Hampstead Norris, Berks

This RAF station opened in September 1940 as a satellite for Harwell. Its first residents were Wellingtons and Ansons of an OTU that stayed until March 1944. From December 1942, a BAT flight of Oxfords was based here, and Stirlings from Harwell used the airfield as a RLG between March and October 1944. Glider training took place from March 1944 with Albermarles, Stirlings, Halifaxes, and Horsas until February 1945. It continued as Harwell's RLG until the following July when flying ceased. Part of the wartime airfield reopened for private flying in 1984 from a grass strip known as Haw Farm, and six aircraft are based here.

Hamsey Green (Warlingham), Surrey

This civil aerodrome opened in 1933 and was in use up to the outbreak of the Second World War. It was used by

ACGSs from October 1942 to June 1946 and by US Army communications light aircraft during 1943 and 1944.

Hanslope (Newport Pagnell), Bucks

This RFC first-class night and day LG was used for home defence from December 1916 to November 1918.

Hanworth (Feltham), Gt. London

This civil aerodrome opened for the Whitehead Flying School in 1915, operated by the Whitehead Aircraft Company, who went on to build Be2s, Pups, SE5s, and DH9s. An AAP was formed in April 1918 that handled the types built by Whiteheads as well as 0/400s until it closed in March 1919; however, it was retained as an ELG. It reopened for civil use as London Air Park on 1 September 1929 and soon became a busy aviation centre. Two manufacturers set up factories in 1934: British Aircraft Mfg Co., which built Swallows and Eagles; and General Aircraft, which produced Monospars as well as Hawker Furies and components for other companies, including sub-assemblies for Whitleys. An elementary flying school arrived in June 1935 with Blackburn B2s, Harts, Ansons, Battles, and Magisters and departed in June 1940. General Aircraft then became a CRO and repaired many aircraft during the war, particularly Hamilcar and Hotspur gliders, until the airfield closed in 1948.

Hardwick, Norfolk

This USAAF bomber station opened in October 1942, the first arrivals being B-25s, but these only stayed for a month. Their place was taken by B-24s, which remained for the duration and left in June 1945 when the airfield closed. Private flying resumed before 1977 from part of the wartime runways, and a dozen or so aircraft are now based here. Just to the east, a few aircraft are based on a grass strip at Airfield Farm.

Hardwick Park, Notts

This SLG was used to store mostly Defiants between September 1941 and September 1943.

Harlaxton, Lincs

This RFC first-class night LG opened in November 1916 and was used initially for home defence. It later became a TDS and closed in May 1919. A variety of types were operated including RE7s, DH4s, Avro 504s, DH5s, DH6s, RE8s, Nieuports, and Shorthorns. It was reactivated as a RLG for Spitalgate in October 1939 and used by Harts, Battles, Ansons, Blenheims, and Oxfords until closure in February 1945.

Harling Road (Roudham), Norfolk

This RFC home defence flight station opened in September 1916 and was home to Be2s, Be12s, Fe2s, Camels, SE5s, and F2bs. Its role changed to training in September 1917, and it later became a TDS that operated DH4s, DH9s, Dolphins, Camels, Avro 504s, and RE8s until flying ceased in March 1920. It may have been used by USAAF C-47s during the Second World War.

Harpswell

See Hemswell.

Harrington, Northants

This RAF station opened in November 1943 as a satellite for Desborough and was used initially by Wellingtons of an OTU. This only lasted until March 1944 when the USAAF arrived. They operated B-24s, B-17s, C-47s, A-26s, and Mosquitoes until August 1945 when flying ceased. It was reactivated in December 1959 for the deployment of Thor missiles, which stayed until August 1963, after which the base closed.

Harringworth

See Spanhoe.

Harris (Northton), Hebrides

This civil aerodrome opened in October 1935 as a request stop for scheduled services but closed at the end of 1938. It was used after the Second World War by air ambulance flights.

Harrogate (The Stray), Yorks

Flying took place from here before 1914 to the 1930s. The Kings Cup Air Race started here in 1925.

Harrowbeer, Devon

This RAF station opened in August 1941 as a satellite for Exeter and was used as a fighter base operating mainly Spitfires, Hurricanes, and Typhoons until August 1944. Various short-lived units then took over until it was transferred to the MTCA in May 1946. A communications flight with Dominies, Ansons, Proctors, and Oxfords operated from December 1947 to July 1948 and an ACGS until August 1950. In 1947, the Ministry planned to use Harrowbeer as the airport for Plymouth, but this proposal was dropped in 1950 due to strong local opposition. It came to a head again in 1960 when Plymouth Council proposed its use as the city's airport, but this was rejected by the House of Lords.

Two Avro 504s outside Aircraft Exchange and Mart's hangar at Hanworth on 12 August 1939. (*Eddie Riding*)

Hanworth (London Air Park) in the 1930s. It closed in 1948. (*Aerofilms*)

Harty, Kent

This RFC third-class night LG was used for home defence from December 1917 to October 1919.

Harwell, Oxon

This site was used as a RAF LG between 1920 and 1936. Following expansion, it reopened as a RAF bomber station in April 1937 and was home to an OTU operating Audaxes, Hinds, Ansons, Battles, Blenheims, and Wellingtons until March 1944. It then became an airborne forces base used by Albermarles, Stirlings, and Horsas until July 1945. The next resident was a transport command development unit, which operated various types for a short period to December 1945. Flying then ceased and the base was transferred to the Atomic Energy Research Establishment, who still operate the site.

Hassocks, Sussex

This gliding site was used by an ACGS during the Second World War.

Hastings (Pebsham), Sussex

Hastings Council purchased land for a municipal airport in 1933, although some flying took place from the site as early as 1930, mostly pleasure flights by Kent Aircraft Services. Little progress was made before the Second World War, and the grass airfield finally opened in July 1948. A few aircraft were based, air displays were held, and joy-rides were provided by Hastings and East Sussex Air Services. It was never developed into a proper airport and flying ceased around 1959.

Hatfield, Herts

A RFC night LG, known as Bishops Hatfield, was used for home defence for a short period from April to October 1916. Just over 1 mile to the south-west, an aerodrome was opened by de Havillands in June 1930 to replace Stag Lane, which soon attracted flying schools, residents, and visiting aircraft. The London Aeroplane Club moved in from Stag Lane in September 1933. The factory was completed in September 1934 and started producing Moths, Dragons, DH86s, and Rapides/Dominies (and later Flamingoes, Oxfords, and Mosquitoes). Over 3,000 Tiger Moths were built at Hatfield. The DH School of Flying became an elementary flying school in August 1935 and operated Hinds, Tiger Moths, Battles, and Ansons until departing in September 1942. The annual SBAC display was held here in 1936 and 1937 with military types being prominent. An ATA ferry pilot's pool was based from January 1940 to April 1942, which operated various types of communications aircraft. After the war, DH built Vampires, Doves, Chipmunks, Comets, Tridents, 146s, and various missiles. A hard runway was laid in 1947. The airfield was popular for corporate use and business jets were regular visitors until flying ceased in March 1993.

Hatston

See Kirkwall.

Haverfordwest (Withybush), Pembrokeshire

An AALG on a disused racecourse at Portfield was in use between 1922 and 1939. Nearby a RAF station opened in October 1942, but the first aircraft did not arrive until June 1943. These included Whitleys, Wellingtons, Ansons, Liberators, Halifaxes, Mosquitoes, and Spitfires, which were attached to the various training units based at the airfield. Flying ceased in June 1945 and it closed in the following November. It reopened as a civil airport in 1952 and a few scheduled services were operated. Today, it is a busy GA airfield with around forty resident aircraft using two licensed hard runways.

Hawarden (Broughton/Chester), Clwyd

This RAF aerodrome, known as Bretton, was used as a RLG in May 1937 but opened officially in 1939 to test-fly Wellingtons and, later, Lancasters produced in a shadow factory on the airfield. It became a RLG for Sealand in 1939 and was used mainly by Oxfords. It was then predominantly a training station and supported numerous units operating Spitfires, Hurricanes, Masters, Mustangs, and Dominies. An ATA ferry pilot's pool was also based from November 1940 to November 1945. Towards the end of the war, it became a sub-storage unit and large numbers of aircraft were stored, mainly Halifaxes, Wellingtons, Vengeances, Martinets, Hotspurs, and Ansons. Aircraft production returned in 1948 when de Havilland took over the factory and built Doves, Vampires, Hornets, Mosquitoes, Chipmunks, Herons, Comet 4s, 125s, and 146s, latterly as BAe. The RAF moved out in March 1959, but an ACGS continued flying until September 1955 and a VGS departed in May 1963. Some scheduled services were operated in the 1960s and '70s but were short-lived. Today, the factory is a major supplier of Airbus wings, and the airfield is open to visiting aircraft. A single licensed hard runway is in use and about forty aircraft are based here.

Above: DH Dragonfly G-AEDT in front of the flight test hangar and control tower at Hatfield during a charity air day on 23 September 1990. (*Grant Peerless*)

Left: DH Hornet Moth G-ADIS flying over the clubhouse and other de Havilland buildings at Hatfield in the late 1930s. The airfield closed to flying in 1993. (*The Aeroplane*)

Below: Piper Navajo G-UMMI parked in front of the modern control tower at Haverfordwest, formerly RAF Withybush on 15 June 2010. (*Grant Peerless*)

Hawkinge (Folkestone), Kent

This RFC aerodrome opened in February 1915, which in August 1917 became an AAP handling mostly Fe2s and DH9s until October 1919. It became a RAF fighter station in February 1920 and was home to various types until the outbreak of the Second World War, predominantly Snipes but also Grebes, Siskins, Furies, Gladiators, and Blenheims. During the war, it was used mainly by Spitfires but also Hurricanes as well as an ASR flight equipped with Lysanders, Walruses, Warwicks, and Sea Otters. It was placed on C&M in November 1945, but an ACGS operated until December 1961 when flying finally ceased, although scenes for the *Battle of Britain* film were shot here in June 1968. A gliding site at Dane Farm, just to the south-west of the airfield was used by the Channel GC during the 1930s.

Haydock Park, Merseyside

This unlicensed grass strip situated inside the racecourse has been in use since before 1974 and is available to visiting aircraft normally on race days only. It was used by USAAC L-4s during 1944 and was probably the site of a British Empire Air Display in August 1936.

Hayle (Polkinghorne), Cornwall

This AALG opened in 1933 and was used for limited scheduled services until closure in 1939.

Hayling Island, Hants

This civil aerodrome opened in 1929 and was used mainly for joy-riding and flying instruction until closure in September 1939.

Haywood, Herefs

This unlicensed microlight site at Broadmeadow Farm opened in 1993 with about twenty residents, which have the use of a single grass strip.

Headcorn

See Lashenden.

Headon, Notts

This microlight site at Headon Farm opened in 2000 by the Microflight Aviation School; it is home to about twenty-five aircraft.

Heathrow, Gt. London

This civil aerodrome was opened in June 1930 as the Great West Aerodrome by Fairey Aviation. Types test-flown by the company from the site included Fairey 3Fs, Hendons, Gordons, Seals, Swordfish, and Albacores. It was used by Magisters from Hanworth as a RLG from December 1939 to June 1940 and by FAA Swordfish and Proctors between February 1944 and April 1945. It was then developed and intended to be a base for B-29s, but the war finished before this could be realised, and it became a civil airport instead. The first official flight from the new airport took place on 1 January 1946 and civil operations commenced on 31 May 1946. 'London Airport' was officially opened by the Queen on 16 December 1955 and is now one of the world's major international airports.

Heaton Chapel (Stockport), Gt. Manchester

A shadow factory opened here in October 1917, producing DH9s and DH10s that were test-flown from an adjacent airstrip. It was also in use by the RAF and civil operators from 1918 to 1919.

Hells Mouth, Gwynedd

This aerodrome opened in 1937 in connection with a nearby gunnery range but was little used. It became a RLG for RAF Penrhos between May 1942 and May 1944 with Ansons and Blenheims being the main users. Its main claim to fame was as a haven to lost aircraft making landfall on this remote part of the country.

Helperby (Brafferton), Yorks

This RFC first-class night LG opened in March 1916, later becoming a home defence flight station. Various types were based here, including Be2s, Avro 504s, and F2bs until closure in March 1919.

Hemswell, Lincs

This RAF first-class night LG, known as Harpswell, was used for home defence and later training from December 1916 to June 1919. Types based included Fe2s, Farmans, Avro 504s, DH1s, and 1½ Strutters. It was reactivated and expanded as a bomber base in February 1937 and was home to Audaxes, Blenheims, Hampdens, Wellingtons, and Lancasters until the end of the Second World War. Mosquitoes and Lincolns then arrived followed by Canberras in 1952 and Varsities in 1957. Flying ceased in July 1958, but Thor missiles were deployed between December 1959 and May 1963. Some civil flying took place in the 1960s and '70s, the Lincoln Aero Club being based from 1968 to 1975 and an ACGS operated from October 1965 to April 1974.

Hendon, Gt. London

This site opened in October 1910 as 'The London Aerodrome,' although flying in the area had been taking place since 1909. It was used initially by Claude Grahame-White for aircraft production and pleasure flying until requisitioned by the RNAS for home defence on the outbreak of the First World War. It became an RFC first-class night LG in 1916 and an AAP in March 1917. This handled types from local manufacturers including DH4s, DH5s, DH6s, DH9s, Avro 504s, Camels, Dolphins, and 0/400s until closure in January 1919. Civil flying resumed in May 1919 but ceased when the RAF took over in 1926. Between July 1919 and the mid-1920s, another aerodrome on an adjacent site was used by Grahame-White for flying instruction known as Hendon South. The RAF used mostly DH9s, Wapitis, Harts, Demons and Blenheims until the outbreak of the Second World War. The Kings Flight was based from July 1936 to September 1939 and operated Envoys, Flamingoes, Dominies, and Hudsons. Fighters—mainly Hurricanes, Spitfires, and Blenheims—were then based together with numerous other units operating a wide assortment of types during the war. Spitfires returned in May 1946 and stayed until March 1949. A plethora of units, some American, were based post-war including a communications flight that had been formed in October 1942 and continued operations until flying ceased in November 1957, although an ACGS carried on flying until March 1968. One last movement took place in 1968 when a Beverley flew in for the RAF Museum, which is now based on part of the old aerodrome and was opened by HM the Queen in 1973.

Henley-on-Thames (Crazies Farm), Oxon

This RLG for White Waltham and later Woodley from July 1940 until 1944 was used mainly by Tiger Moths and Magisters. Some Spitfire assembly and test-flying took place on the site during the Second World War. In August 1944, a radar calibration unit arrived equipped with Rotas, Hornet Moths, Oxfords, and Hoverflies that stayed until the grass airfield closed in November 1945.

Henlow, Beds

This ARD opened in February 1918, dealing with F2bs and DH4s. This role was to continue for the next forty years, and during this time, thousands of types passed through its workshops, including Snipes, Fawns, Flycatchers, Ansons, Magisters, and Mosquitoes. During the Second World War, a MU assembled and test-flew Hurricanes, along with Mosquitoes and Typhoons. Numerous other units have been based over the years operating Gamecocks, Vimys, Virginias, Gauntlets, Gladiators, Queen Bees, Halifaxes, Ansons, Austers, and Chipmunks. A VGS was formed in June 1958 and departed in 2016. Today, Henlow is an active RAF station with around forty civilian aircraft based here, which operate from four licensed grass runways. It is due to close by 2024.

Hendon in about 1920 when the aerodrome extended on both sides of Aerodrome Road. The RAF ceased flying from Hendon in 1957. (*Flight*)

Henstridge, Somerset

This FAA station HMS *Dipper* opened in April 1943 and was used mainly for training with Seafires until January 1946. It was then little used until August 1949 when training recommenced with Fireflies and Sea Furies up to September 1952. It reopened as a satellite for Yeovilton in 1954, mainly for deck landing practice, and closed as a naval base in June 1957. Bristow Helicopters set up a base in 1953 and light aircraft then began to return. Today, over eighty are based here, operating from a single unlicensed hard runway.

Hereford, Herefs

An AALG, known as Kings Acre, was in use during the 1930s. Flying commenced from another site on the city's racecourse in 1932 but the official opening was not until September 1936. It was used during November 1940 by an AACU and by an ACGS until January 1946. It reopened for civil use after the war and was used mainly for charter flying until closure in 1952.

Heronfield (High Tree Farm), W. Midlands

This LG was used during the Second World War as a dispersal site for Spitfires built at Castle Bromwich.

Hertford (Ware), Herts

This RFC second-class night LG was used for home defence from October 1916 to mid-1918.

Heston, Gt. London

This civil aerodrome was opened on 6 July 1929 by the Minister of Aviation, soon attracting flying schools and sales agents. In 1932, it was designated as a diversion airfield for Croydon, and scheduled services commenced in January 1934. Comper Aircraft arrived in 1933 to build their Swift but ceased trading a year later, their assets being taken over by Heston Aircraft Co., (producer of the Phoenix). Heston became a very busy and popular airport, but this came to an end on the outbreak of the Second World War when private flying stopped. The first resident during the war was a photographic development unit that operated Spitfires, Blenheims, and Hudsons until December 1940. Training then took over until fighters arrived in April 1942, mostly Spitfires but also Defiants and Mustangs that stayed until April 1944. Several communications flights were then based including American and FAA units and the last of these departed in January 1947. The airfield passed to the MAP in January 1945 for use by Fairey Aviation, but they moved to White Waltham in November 1947. An ACGS operated here until March 1948, and the airfield closed in the following October.

Hethel, Norfolk

This USAAF bomber station opened in September 1942 with B-26s that stayed only a month. These were replaced with B-24s in June 1943, remaining until May 1945. The station then passed to RAF Fighter Command in the following September, operating Mustangs and Spitfires until January 1947 when the airfield closed. In 1966, Lotus Cars established a base on the airfield, and the runways are now used as a race and test track. Fixed-wing flying ceased in 1999.

Hethersett, Norfolk

An ACGS operated from the racecourse here from June 1943 to August 1945. A private grass strip opened nearby in 1991.

Heysham, Lancs

This LG on the beach was used for pleasure flights from about 1921 to 1961.

Hibaldstow, Humberside

This RAF station opened in May 1941 as a satellite for Kirton-in-Lindsey and was home to various units operating Defiants, Hurricanes, Beaufighters, Bostons, Havocs, Typhoons, and Spitfires until flying ceased in May 1945. Part of the wartime runway is now used by a parachuting club that arrived around 1992, and around six aircraft are based here.

High Ercall, Salop

This RAF fighter station opened in October 1940, operating mainly Beaufighters, Spitfires, and Hurricanes. This role changed to training in May 1943 when an OTU arrived that operated mostly Mosquitoes until March 1945. The USAAF had a brief presence in 1942 with Spitfires, P-38s, P-39s, and P-40s. It became a RLG for Tern Hill in May 1951 and was used by Harvards, Tiger Moths, and Provosts until 1961. After the war, it was used to store large numbers of surplus aircraft, mostly Halifaxes and Spitfires, then later Prentices. The airfield closed in February 1962.

High Halden, Kent

This ALG was used by USAAF P-47s from April to July 1944 and briefly by RAF Meteors in August that year.

Imperial Airways' Handley Page HP42 G-AAXC *Heracles* and some light aircraft, mostly foreign, registered in front of the impressive terminal building at Heston in the mid-1930s. The airfield closed in around 1948. (*Aerofilms*)

Shell Mex and BP's DH Leopard Moth G-ACLY during a visit to Heston, *c.* 1935 (*Eddie Riding*)

High Post, Wilts

This civil aerodrome opened in October 1931 for the Wiltshire School of Flying, although the official opening was not until 19 April 1932. The school used Redwings, Taylorcrafts, and Piper Cubs until the airfield closed on the outbreak of the Second World War. In June 1940, some RAF Lysanders arrived, and between April 1940 and June 1941, it was used as a RLG for Upavon and Netheravon by Masters, Battles, and Oxfords. It was then taken over by Vickers Supermarine for the assembly and test-flying of Spitfires; this activity continued after the war with the prototype Attacker until the company moved to Chilbolton in February 1947. The Wiltshire School of Flying resumed flying in April 1946 but ceased when High Post closed in June 1947.

High Wycombe

See Booker.

Highnam, Glos

This microlight site at Over Farm opened around 2007; it is home to Over Farm Microlights and around twenty aircraft.

Hildenborough (Old Barn), Kent

This civil aerodrome was in use between 1931 and 1933, mostly by visitors to the adjacent tea rooms.

Hill Head, Hants

This RLG for Hamble, Watchfield, and Shellingford was in use from September 1939 to March 1948. Tiger Moths and Magisters were the main types used.

Hingham, Norfolk

This RFC LG was used for home defence from September 1916 to September 1917, by Be2s, Be12s, and Fe2s.

Hinstock (Ollerton), Salop

This SLG opened in October 1941 and was used to store Wellingtons, Battles, Masters, and Magisters. This use continued until August 1942 when the FAA arrived and it became HMS *Godwit*. Several units were resident here, operating Oxfords, Ansons, Swordfish, Harvards, Lancasters, Mosquitoes, and Seafires. The airfield closed in March 1947.

Hinton-in-the-Hedges, Northants

This RAF station opened in November 1940 and was used initially as a RLG by an OTU operating Ansons, Blenheims, and Wellingtons. This continued until April 1943 when a Signals Development Unit arrived with Whitleys, Ansons, Beaufighters, Oxfords, and Mosquitoes. This unit stayed until July 1944, when flying ceased. Part of the wartime airfield reopened for private flying around 1963 and is used primarily for parachuting. Gliding by the Banbury GC and Motor Glider Club also takes place here, and light aircraft are also in evidence. Over fifty types are based here, flying from a single unlicensed hard runway.

Hitchin, Herts

This AALG was in use during the 1930s.

Hixon, Staffs

This RAF training station opened in June 1942 and was home to Wellingtons, Hurricanes, Masters, Tomahawks, Beauforts, and Oxfords until June 1945. It was then used by a MU until closure in November 1957.

Hoar Cross, Staffs

This SLG was used to store Whitleys, Hellcats, and Typhoons between July 1941 and June 1945. A gliding site at Cross Hayes Field opened nearby in 1980, which is operated by the Needwood Forest GC; around a dozen gliders are based here.

Hockley Heath, W. Midlands

This RAF station opened in August 1941 and was used as a RLG for Elmdon by Tiger Moths, Oxfords, and Harvards until 1945. Between December 1943 and February 1945, it was also used for glider training by Masters and Hotspurs. An ACGS continued flying until June 1947, and the RAF departed in 1948.

Hodnet, Salop

This RLG for RAF Sealand was used briefly in November and December 1940 by Masters before becoming an SLG. This stored Blenheims, Hurricanes, Swordfish, Masters, and Martinets between June 1941 and February 1945.

Holme-on-Spalding Moor, Humberside

This RAF bomber station opened in August 1941 and was home to Wellingtons, Halifaxes, and Lancasters until August 1945. Oxfords of a BAT flight were based here from October 1941 to June 1944. It was placed on C&M in October 1945 but reopened for training in March 1952 with Prentices and Harvards until January 1953. Jet Provosts from Linton-on-Ouse used it as a RLG between June 1962 and June 1966. Blackburn Aircraft moved in in 1957 and used the airfield for flight-testing Buccaneers and Phantoms. Blackburn's successor (BAe) continued this operation until they departed in December 1983 and flying then ceased.

Holmsley South, Hants

This RAF station opened in September 1942 initially as a bomber base, operating Wellingtons, Halifaxes, and Whitleys. In March 1944, its role changed to fighting and Spitfires, Typhoons, Mosquitoes, and Mustangs came on the scene. These stayed until the following July when the USAAF arrived with B-26s for a brief stay of one month. Transport Command then took over and operated Warwicks, Liberators, Skymasters, and Yorks until the airfield closed in October 1946.

Holt (Bayfield), Norfolk

This RNAS night LG was used as a RLG for Great Yarmouth from August 1915 and by a coastal patrol flight from August 1918 with DH9s. It closed in March 1919 but could have been in use as late as 1920.

Honeybourne, Worcs

This RAF station opened in November 1941 and was used mainly for ferry training until March 1942. Types operated included Hudsons, Beauforts, Liberators, Wellingtons, and Venturas. An OTU then arrived with Whitleys, Ansons, and Wellingtons, staying until flying ceased in July 1945. The base then passed to a MU that stored Wellingtons and Hamilcars until closure in July 1948.

Honiley, Warks

This RAF fighter station opened in May 1941 and was home to Defiants, Hurricanes, Havocs, Beaufighters, and Spitfires until September 1943. Its role then changed to training, and an OTU operated various types here, including Beauforts, Wellingtons, and Mosquitoes, until March 1944. A signals flying unit was next on the scene with Ansons, Beaufighters, Wellingtons, and Oxfords until September 1946. A RAuxAF squadron then arrived with Mosquitoes (and later, Vampires and Meteors), staying until March 1957. From June 1949 to June 1952, an instrument training flight was based with Harvards, Oxfords, and Chipmunks. The FAA put in an appearance in July 1955 and operated Sea Vampires and Attackers until March 1957. Flying then ceased, and the airfield closed in March 1958.

Honington, Suffolk

This RAF station opened in June 1937 and was home to bombers until September 1942. These included Audaxes, Wellesleys, Heyfords, Harrows, and Wellingtons. The USAAF arrived in February 1944 and operated P-38s and P-51s until November 1945. It was transferred to Transport Command in April 1946, and Dakotas, Yorks, and Hastings were based here until May 1950. It was then placed on C&M until February 1955 when jets arrived in the shape of Canberras; they were followed by Valiants, Victors, Buccaneers, and Tornadoes. Flying ceased in February 1994 when the site was handed over to the RAF Regiment, but a VGS operated Vigilants here until 2016, and some limited flying still takes place.

Hooe (Bexhill), Sussex

This RFC third-class day and night LG was used for home defence from December 1916 to February 1918.

Hook (Ace of Spades), Gt. London

This civil aerodrome opened in June 1933 and was used by the Thames Valley Aero Club until closure in 1937.

Hooton Park, Cheshire

This RFC TDS opened in September 1917 with Avro 504s, Pups, Camels, DH10s, and F2bs. It closed in May 1919 but reopened in 1927 for the Liverpool and District Aero Club. This was followed by the construction of a factory for Compers, which built Swifts and assembled some Ford Tri-motors. It became Liverpool's airport in 1930 and scheduled services were operated until 1933 when most transferred to the new airport at Speke. The RAF arrived in February 1936, and various units operated Harts, Hinds, Spitfires, Ansons, Tiger Moths, Lysanders, Beauforts, Oxfords, Proctors, Walruses, Bothas, Austers, Chipmunks, Prentices, and Meteors. An SLG was set up in November 1944 and stored mostly Halifaxes up to 1947. During the war, an aircraft assembly unit was formed, which assembled and maintained Bostons, Harvards, Hampdens, Halifaxes, Mosquitoes, Sabres, and T-33s, and built various gliders. This operation continued after the war and into the 1950s. Flying ceased in March 1957.

Hoprig Mains

See Macmerry.

Horham, Suffolk

This USAAF bomber station opened in May 1943, and like several others in the area, its first arrivals were B-26s that stayed for only a month. B-17s then arrived and stayed until August 1945 when the station reverted to the RAF for use by MUs. This continued until October 1948 when the airfield closed. It later saw use by Bloodhound missiles, but they had departed by 1961. A couple of private light aircraft are based on part of the wartime airfield and operate from an unlicensed grass strip.

Hornby Hall, Cumbria

This SLG was used to store Battles, Blenheims, Bothas, Hudsons, Wellingtons, Mustangs, and Hurricanes between March 1941 and July 1945.

Hornchurch, Gt. London

This RFC home defence station, known as Suttons Farm, opened in October 1915 and was used by Be2s, Be12s, SE5s, Pups, Camels, and Snipes until December 1919. Following expansion, it reopened as RAF Hornchurch in April 1928 and was home to fighter units operating Siskins, Bulldogs, Gauntlets, Gladiators, and Spitfires until the outbreak of the Second World War. It remained a fighter station during the war when the Spitfire was the main type operated, along with Blenheims, Defiants, and Mustangs. Various units were based here after the war, and in July 1948, a RFS was formed with Tiger Moths, Ansons, Oxfords, and Chipmunks, staying until July 1953. In December 1950, a CAACU arrived and operated Beaufighters, Mosquitoes, Spitfires, and Ansons until December 1956. The last RAF unit to be based here was an aircrew selection unit, which used Chipmunks from April 1952 to April 1962. Flying then ceased and the station closed in July 1962.

Horndean

See Winfield.

Horndon-on-the-Hill (Woodcock Field) Essex

This RFC night LG was used for home defence from April to September 1916.

Horne, Surrey

This ALG was used by RAF Spitfires for only two months from April to June 1944.

Horsegate, Tyne and Wear

This RFC third-class night LG was used for home defence between May 1917 and May 1919.

Horseheath, Cambs

This RFC second-class night LG was used for home defence from April 1916 to April 1919.

Horsey Toll, Northants

This AALG, also known as Peterborough, opened in May 1930 and was used by various flying clubs until the outbreak of the Second World War when it became a CRO specialising in Hurricanes. It was used from February 1944 as a RLG by Masters and Hurricanes from RAF Westwood. Flying may have continued until around 1952.

Horsham St Faith (Norwich Airport), Norfolk

This RAF airfield was built during 1939, but the first units did not arrive until February 1940. Spitfires, Blenheims, Hudsons, and Mosquitoes were operated here until October 1942 when the USAAF arrived. They initially used P-47s followed by B-24s until they moved out in July 1945. The RAF then returned and numerous units operated Hornets, Spitfires, Mustangs, Meteors, Hunters, Vampires, Venoms, and Javelins. A SAR flight of Sycamores was based here from September 1955 and continued until April 1963, latterly with Whirlwinds. The Battle of Britain Memorial Flight was also resident from November 1961 to April 1963 when flying ceased. The site became Norwich Airport on 30 May 1970 but had been used for civil flying since about 1967. Scheduled and charter services are operated to numerous destinations at home and abroad.

Horton Kirby, Kent

This aerodrome was used from 1931 by joy-riding operators and by the RAF as an ELG. The Horton Kirby Flying Club was established in January 1939 to train pilots for the CAG, but this was disbanded on the outbreak of the Second World War, when the airfield closed.

Hounslow Heath, Gt. London

This civil aerodrome opened in 1909 and was requisitioned by the RFC on the outbreak of the First World War. It was used for home defence and training, later becoming a TDS. Types based here included Farmans, Be2s, FB5s, DH2s, Avro 504s, SE5s, RE8s, M1cs, Snipes, and Camels until closure in August 1919. It then returned to civil use and became Britain's first terminal airport, scheduled services commencing soon afterwards. Its use was short-lived, however, and services were transferred to Croydon in 1921. It was used by an ACGS from 1943 to May 1945.

Hove

See Brighton.

Above left: Britain's first terminal airport at Hounslow Heath in about 1920. Scheduled services transferred to the new Croydon Airport in 1921 when this aerodrome closed. (*Richard Riding collection*)

Above right: The view from inside the control tower at Hucknall with Pitts Special G-OODI and Grumman American AA-5 G-PURR parked on the grass outside. This photo was taken on 6 July 2014, nine months before the airfield closed in March 2015. (*Tony Yarnold*)

Howden, Humberside

This RFC night LG opened in March 1916 for home defence but was predominantly an airship base. It was used occasionally by aircraft and closed around 1930.

Hoy, Orkney

Three aerodromes have been in use on this island. There are no details of the first, Brims Ness but Snellsetter was used by Highland Airways between 1934 and 1936. It was reactivated for the RAF in 1939 and used as an ELG until 1945. Longhope opened in August 1936 and was used by charter flights until the outbreak of the Second World War. It was used again from 1972 to 1993, mostly by air ambulance flights.

Hucknall, Notts

This RAF TDS opened in April 1918 and was used by DH6s, DH9s, Avro 504s, Pups, RE8s, and F2bs until closure in January 1920. It reopened for civil use by the Nottingham Flying Club in 1926; they stayed until 1929. A RAuxAF squadron arrived in March 1928 and was equipped with Horsleys, Wallaces, and Hinds. In December 1934, Rolls-Royce set up a factory on the aerodrome and went on to test run engines as well as repairing Hurricanes and Spitfires as a CRO. Training was the major role during the Second World War, and various units operated Battles, Ansons, Tiger Moths, and Magisters, followed by Harvards after the war. Fighters in the shape of Mosquitoes and Spitfires appeared in November 1946 and stayed until April 1949. An AOP flight with Austers was resident here from September 1949 to March 1957 when the RAF finally departed. Rolls-Royce continued testing its engines until 1971, and the Merlin Flying Club was set up in 1963 but flying ceased in March 2015 when the airfield closed.

Huddersfield (Crossland Moor), Yorks

This unlicensed airfield opened in 1947 with one hard runway and is home to around twenty aircraft.

Hull (Hedon), Humberside

Flying started here from an old racecourse as early as 1909. It became a RFC first-class night LG in April 1916 and was used for home defence until early 1919, mainly with Be2s. It was opened as Hull's municipal airport on 10 October 1929, with scheduled services commencing in July 1933. It closed on the outbreak of the Second World War but was used by an ACGS from September 1943 to February 1946. It did not reopen for civil flying after the War and was abandoned in 1951.

Hull (Paull), Humberside
This grass airfield opened in mid-1968 and was licensed from 1 January 1969. A Beverley was flown in during March 1974 but moved out in 1983. It closed in the spring of the same year.

Hullavington, Wilts
This RAF station opened in June 1937 and was used mostly for training until September 1965. Numerous units operated an assortment of types over the years including Harts, Ansons, Masters, Hurricanes, Harvards, Oxfords, Valettas, Varsities, Marathons, Provosts, and Jet Provosts. A MU opened at the start of the war and continued in operation until December 1959. It dealt with storing and scrapping large numbers of aircraft, including Defiants, Stirlings, and Mosquitoes. The airfield reopened for limited flying in June 1989 when an AEF arrived, followed in March 1992 by a UAS, both operating Chipmunks and Bulldogs. These had departed by 1993 and were replaced by a VGS that flew Vikings until flying ceased in December 2016.

Humbleton (Moorlands), Yorks
This private grass airfield was in use from the 1970s to 2000s.

Hunsdon, Herts
This RAF station opened in May 1941, with the main type operated being the Mosquito. Hurricanes, Havocs, Beaufighters, Mustangs, Tempests, and Oxfords were also used until flying ceased in May 1945.
Microlights arrived in 1993; they use three unlicensed grass strips on part of the wartime airfield, where over thirty are based.

Hunstanton, Norfolk
This civil aerodrome was used during the summer months from 1929 to 1931 for scheduled services to Skegness. It was then used for joy-riding and closed at the end of 1935.

Hunton (Maidstone), Kent
This RFC third-class night LG was used for home defence from August 1916 to October 1917.

Hurn
See Bournemouth.

Hursley Park, Hants
This LG was used by USAAS DH4s from December 1917 to September 1918 and by US Army communications aircraft during the Second World War.

Hurst Park, Gt. London
This RFC aircraft park was established on the racecourse in May 1916, which was occupied by Be2s and DH5s. It closed to flying in December 1917 but continued to be used as a stores depot until the RAF departed in 1919.

Husbands Bosworth (Cote Hill), Leics
This AALG was in use from 1931 to 1939. The RAF used it as a RLG for Wellingtons from Market Harborough from July 1943 to June 1944 and then by an OTU operating Wellingtons, Hurricanes, Martinets, Oxfords, and Masters until flying ceased in June 1945. It reopened as a gliding site in 1965, and around 100 aircraft are based here, some of them powered. A single unlicensed grass runway is in use.

Husthwaite, Yorks
This unlicensed grass airfield at Baxby Manor opened before 1986, which is home to around twenty-five aircraft—mostly microlights that operate from three grass strips.

Hutton Cranswick, Humberside
This RAF fighter station opened in January 1942 and was home to mostly Spitfires until May 1946, although Typhoons, Hurricanes, and Mustangs were also based here. A target towing flight arrived in October 1943, equipped with Martinets, Henleys, Masters, and Lysanders, and stayed until February 1945. Flying ceased in May 1946, but crop sprayers used part of the runways from the 1960s to at least 1989.

Hutton-in-the-Forest, Cumbria
This SLG was used for storing Blenheims, Hurricanes, Bothas, Hudsons, Venturas, Wellingtons, and Mustangs between May 1941 and August 1945.

Huyton Hill, Merseyside
This AALG at Huyton Hill School opened in July 1932 and closed later in the 1930s.

Hyde Park, Gt. London

Two sites in Hyde Park—Marble Arch and Rotten Row—were designated as RNAS home defence night ELGs for use during 1914 and 1915.

Hylton

See Usworth.

Ibsley, Hants

This RAF station opened in February 1941 as a satellite for Middle Wallop. It was a fighter base for most of its life, Hurricanes and Spitfires being the main equipment. The USAAF arrived for a short stay of two months in August 1942 with P-38s and again in March 1944 with P-47s until the following July. After the departure of the fighters, a few miscellaneous units took over, including a glider training flight operating Dakotas and Hadrians; however, flying ceased in December 1945.

Ilfracombe, Devon

This AALG was in use in the 1930s.

Ince (Formby), Merseyside

This unlicensed microlight site opened before 1995 with three grass strips and around sixty residents. It is also open to light aircraft.

Inchinnan, Strathclyde

This RNAS airship station and associated LG opened in 1916 and closed around 1922. An AAP was set up in 1918, handling Cuckoos, DH9s, Fe2s, and V/1500s until closure in March 1918. William Beardmore and Company also test-flew aircraft constructed at Dalmuir here.

Ingham (Cammeringham), Lincs

This RAF bomber station opened in May 1942, but while incomplete, it was used briefly during October and November 1941 as a RLG for Shawbury. Wellingtons were operated until September 1943; it was then used again as a RLG, this time for Hucknall. This lasted until February 1944 when a couple of training flights arrived with Spitfires, Hurricanes, and Wellingtons and stayed until December 1944, when flying ceased.

Insch (Auchleven), Grampian

This unlicensed grass airfield opened in 1985 with one grass runway and is home to over twenty-five light aircraft.

Inskip, Lancs

This FAA station HMS *Nightjar* opened in March 1943 and was home to various units operating Swordfish, Barracudas, Fulmars, Avengers, Wildcats, and Fireflies. Flying ceased in September 1946.

Inverness (Longman), Highland

This civil airport opened on 5 May 1933 with scheduled services commencing a few days later, some of which continued during the Second World War. It became a RAF station in July 1940 and various units were based here, operating Lysanders, Rocs, Oxfords, Hornet Moths, Hurricanes, Blenheims, Masters, and Dominies until July 1945. It reverted to civil use in January 1946, and scheduled services recommenced, but these transferred to Dalcross (the new airport for Inverness) in 1947. Flying then ceased at Longman.

Inverness (Dalcross), Highland

This RAF station opened in July 1941 and was home initially to a gunnery school, which stayed until November 1945. It operated Defiants, Lysanders, Martinets, Ansons, and Wellingtons. An AFU equipped with Oxfords and Ansons was based from January 1942 to February 1944, and Spitfires were resident between January and April 1946. It became Inverness Airport in 1947 when scheduled services commenced and continue to this day. A FTS operated Oxfords and Chipmunks from May 1951 to December 1953 and a VGS was based here during 1968. A flight of S92s and AW189s is based here, providing SAR duties for the MCA.

Ipswich, Suffolk

Ipswich Airport was opened by the Prince of Wales on 26 June 1930 and became home to the Suffolk Aero Club. A modest scheduled service to Clacton was introduced in June 1936 by Southern Airways, but this was short-lived. In October 1938, the CAG commenced operations; this was followed by an elementary flying school flying Magisters and Harts until the outbreak of the Second World War. The aerodrome was then requisitioned by the RAF, and the first residents were Blenheims, which were followed by various aircraft of numerous units including Oxfords, Spitfires, Lysanders, Martinets, Austers, and Hurricanes. The RAF departed in December 1945, and civil flying resumed in 1946. Another attempt at scheduled services was by Suckling Airways, who introduced a service to Amsterdam in April 1986; however, this had to be moved to Cambridge two years later due to waterlogging of the grass runways (hard runways had never been provided).

Terminal building at Ipswich Airport on 16 May 1993 on the occasion of a Lions air show. The airport closed in 1996. (*Grant Peerless*)

Ipswich continued to be a busy GA airfield until 31 December 1996, when it closed as it was required for residential development.

Irby-on-Humber (Grimsby), Humberside

This private grass airfield was in use from the 1970s to 1990s.

Islay, Hebrides

Three aerodromes have been in use here, the first a short-lived one at Bridgend Sands, which was used for scheduled services from May 1933 to the spring of 1934. This was replaced by a new site at Duich Farm, which supported scheduled services until 1937 when it was again replaced by a larger site at Glenegedale. Scheduled services were operated until the outbreak of the Second World War when it was taken over by the RAF as Port Ellen. A few Beauforts and Ansons were the first occupants followed by a ferry training unit equipped with Beaufighters, Mosquitoes, and Bostons from December 1942 to December 1943. It received regular visits from naval aircraft, particularly Wildcats as well as being used as an ELG until flying ceased in November 1945. It reopened for civil use in 1947, and scheduled services soon recommenced, continuing to this day from two licensed hard runways.

Isle of Man

See Andreas, Jurby, Ramsey, and Ronaldsway.

Jersey, CI

Scheduled services were first operated from the beach at St Aubins in December 1933 and continued until March 1937, when they were transferred to the new States Airport. These continued until the outbreak of the Second World War when the FAA put in a brief appearance from March to June 1940 with Ospreys, Swordfishes, and Albacores. The RAF also based some Hurricanes for a few days in June 1940 until the Germans invaded in the following month. Civil flying and scheduled services resumed when peace was restored in 1945 and a hard runway was laid in 1952.

Joyce Green, Kent

This aerodrome was opened by Vickers in 1911 to test-fly their products. The first flights of various types took place here including No. 1 Monoplane (1911), Gunbus (1913) and Vimy (1917). It became an RFC first-class LG in December 1914 and was used initially for training and then for home defence duties. Types operated included FK8s, FB5s, DH2s, Fe8s, Be2s, Avro 504s, and Camels. It closed in December 1919 when Vickers moved their factory to Brooklands.

BEA Douglas DC3 (Pionair) G-ALXK *Rex Pierson* in front of the terminal building and control tower at Jersey Airport awaiting passengers in the 1960s. (*Richard Riding collection*)

Jura (Knockrome), Hebrides

This grass strip opened in 1964 and is used mainly by air ambulance flights.

Jurby, IoM

This RAF station opened in September 1939 and was home for most of its life to a variety of training units until military flying ceased in September 1963. Types operated over the years included Wallaces, Blenheims, Whitleys, Wellingtons, Ansons, Tiger Moths, and Chipmunks. A few Hurricanes and Spitfires were based from February to August 1941. Civil flying commenced after the RAF departed, and regular air shows were held, the last being in 2005. An airship production facility was in use in the late 1980s and early 1990s, and the Manx GC was resident in the early 1990s. The airfield is still largely intact, and while flying has officially ceased, a couple of microlights are based here. Gliding also takes place.

Keevil, Wilts

This RAF station opened in July 1942 and was used initially for the flight-testing of Spitfires built nearby. The first residents were the USAAF in November 1942, who operated L-4s, A-20s, C-47s, and C-53s until March 1944. A HGCU then took over with Stirlings, Horsas, Albermarles, and Hadrians; they departed in June 1945. Their place was taken by an OTU equipped with Spitfires, Harvards, Martinets, and Mustangs that stayed until October 1947. Flying then ceased but returned in January 1955 when it was used as a RLG for Hullavington by Harvards, Prentices, and Provosts until November 1957. It has been used since the early 1950s by the Bannerdown GC; this use continues today, with over twenty gliders being based here. It is also used for tactical training and military exercises by rotary and fixed-wing aircraft under the control of RAF Brize Norton.

Kelmscott, Oxon

This RAF station opened in July 1940 and was used mainly as a RLG for Watchfield until flying ceased in December 1946. Types using the field included Tiger Moths, Oxfords, and Ansons.

Kelstern (Louth), Lincs

This RFC first-class night LG was used for home defence between 1917 and June 1919. Types operated included Fe2s and F2bs. Just to the north-east, a RAF station opened in October 1943 as a satellite for Binbrook and was home to Lancasters until April 1945 when flying ceased.

Kemble, Glos

This RAF station opened in June 1938, its main user being a MU for the next forty-five years. It handled thousands of types including Hurricanes, Typhoons,

Albermarles, Beauforts, Lancasters, Wellingtons, Sabres, Meteors, and Hunters until closure in March 1983. A variety of other units used the airfield for short periods operating assorted types, among them a glider training flight equipped with Whitleys from January 1942 to April 1944. It was used as a RLG for Little Rissington between October 1955 and April 1976 and by the famous Red Arrows aerobatic team from August 1966 to November 1982. The RAF finally vacated Kemble in July 1992 when it was passed to the army. Civil flying took over in 1993, and today, it is Cotswold Airport with a thriving GA population of around 100 and home to an airliner salvage operation. A hard and a grass runway are in use, both licensed.

Kenley, Gt. London

This AAP opened in June 1917, handling DH9s, Dolphins, Camels, RE8s, SE5s, F2bs, and 0/400s. It also hosted other units until flying ceased in January 1920. It became a permanent RAF station in April 1920 and was home to F2bs, Snipes, Gamecocks, Siskins, Gauntlets, Bulldogs, Harts, Hectors, and Gladiators until the outbreak of the Second World War. From May 1940, it became a fighter station operating predominantly Spitfires but also Hurricanes and Mustangs until April 1944. A communications flight was based here from September 1946 to March 1958, and an AOP squadron operated Austers between February 1949 and March 1957. During 1946 and 1947, it was used for maintenance and charter operations by various civilian companies including Westminster Airways and British Air Transport. Scenes for the film *Reach for the Sky* were filmed on the airfield in 1955. It was used by various reserve flights between 1959 and 1964, and an ACGS was based here from 1948, later becoming a VGS until disbanding in June 1962. It was placed on C&M in February 1966 but a VGS equipped with Vikings is currently based here, together with about fifteen gliders of the Surrey Hills GC.

Kensington Gardens, Gt. London

This RNAS home defence night ELG was in use during 1914.

Kenyon Hall Farm, Lancs

This unlicensed airfield with a single grass runway is operated by the Lancashire Aero Club, who moved here from Barton in July 2009.

Kettleness, Yorks

This RNAS LG was in use during 1915 and 1916.

Kibworth, Leics

This private grass airfield at Paddocks Farm was in use from the 1980s and possibly later.

Grumman American AA-5 G-PURR in front of the control tower at Kemble on 13 May 2008. It is now known as Cotswold Airport. (*Grant Peerless*)

Kiddington (Glympton), Oxon
This RAF station was used mainly as a RLG for Kidlington by a wide variety of types including gliders, from 1940 until June 1945. They included Hectors, Hinds, Hotspurs, Tiger Moths, Oxfords, Masters, Mentors, and Lysanders.

Kidlington
See Oxford.

Kilburn, Gt. London
This LG was used by the Central Aircraft Company to test-fly their Centaur prototype during the 1920s. It was also used occasionally by light aircraft.

Kilconquhar, Fife
This RFC second-class night LG was used for home defence from February 1918 to May 1919.

Kilkeel (Aughrim), NI
This unlicensed airfield opened in the 1990s with a single grass runway at which around six aircraft are based.

Kilkerran, Strathclyde
This private grass airfield opened in the 1960s at which around a dozen aircraft are based.

Killingholme (East Halton), Lincs
This RNAS coastal air station opened in 1914, operating mostly Sopwith Scouts. It was taken over by a US Navy marine observers school in early 1918 that was equipped with Shorts seaplanes and Curtiss flying boats. This use ceased in January 1919 when it was returned to the RAF and the station closed in 1925.

Kimbolton, Cambs
This RAF station opened in November 1941 as a satellite for Molesworth and was used briefly by Wellingtons until January 1942. The USAAF arrived in the following September and operated B-17s until June 1945 when flying ceased. Part of the eastern side of the wartime airfield is used for private flying from a site known as Stow Longa and a couple of aircraft are based here.

Kincairn (Stirling/Gargunnock) Central Region
This RFC third-class night LG was used for home defence from August 1916 to March 1917.

Kincraig
See Feshiebridge.

Kineton, Warks
This AALG, operated by Lord Willoughby de Broke, was in use between September 1931 and 1939.

Kingsbury (Church Lane), Gt. London
This aerodrome opened in 1916 in connection with a factory operated by the Kingsbury Aviation Company used to build DH6s, Snipes, and Vimys until 1919. It was later used by Fraser's Flying School until closure in 1924. A site at Grove Park 1 mile to the north was another manufacturer's aerodrome used by Airco for test-flying from 1916 to 1919.

Kings Cliffe (Wansford/Apethorpe), Northants
This RFC second-class night LG was in use for home defence from December 1916 to July 1917. It was used as a RLG for RAF Avro 504s and Audaxes from 1933 to 1936. Following expansion, it reopened as a satellite for RAF Wittering in October 1941 and was home to Spitfires until January 1943. The USAAF then arrived with P-39s, which were followed by P-47s, P-38s, and P-51s. They stayed until October 1945 when it returned to the RAF. Some local flying and joy-riding then took place until the airfield closed in September 1947. A private grass airfield in the vicinity known as Spa Farm was in use from around 1974 to 1998.

Kings Heath (Billesley), W. Midlands
This civil aerodrome was used by the Birmingham Aero Club from 1911 and also by the Midland School of Flying. It was taken over by the RFC in April 1916 as a night LG and was used for home defence until mid-1918. It was used by light aircraft during 1920.

Kings Lynn, Norfolk
This manufacturer's aerodrome was used by Savage Ltd to test-fly mostly DH1s from about 1915. A private grass airfield at Tilney St Lawrence has been in use since the 1970s.

Kingsmuir (Sorbie), Fife
This unlicensed airfield opened in the 1990s with a single grass runway; it is home to around six light aircraft.

Kingsnorth, Kent
This ALG was used by RAF Spitfires from July to October 1943 and USAAF P-47s between April and July 1944.

Kingston Bagpuize, Oxon

This RLG for RAF Shellingford was in use between January 1942 and July 1943 by Tiger Moths, Masters, Hotspurs, and Oxfords. From January 1944, a USAAF air depot handled P-51s, P-38s, and F-5s until August 1944 when flying ceased. A MU then took over and the station closed in June 1954.

Kingston Deverill (The Park), Wilts

This gliding site opened in 1992 and is operated by the Bath, Wilts and North Dorset GC; it is home to about thirty gliders.

Kingstown

See Carlisle.

Kingswinford (Dudley/Wall Heath), W. Midlands

This RFC second-class night LG was used for home defence from April 1916 to June 1917.

Kinloss, Grampian

This RAF station opened in April 1939 and was home initially to a FTS equipped with Oxfords and Harvards until they departed in April 1940. Bomber Command arrived in November 1939 with Whitleys, Hampdens and Blenheims and continued with an OTU operating Whitleys, Ansons, and Wellingtons until June 1945. A MU was based from April 1940 and dealt with Oxfords, Halifaxes, Whitleys, Wellingtons, Spitfires, Bostons, and Warwicks. After the war, a Coastal Command OTU was set up with Wellingtons, Warwicks, and Beaufighters and became an OCU operating Lancasters, Neptunes, and Shackletons until October 1956. The Shackletons were replaced with Nimrods in 1971, which carried on flying until May 2011. A flight of FAA Sea Kings was based from February 1981 to October 1989. The airfield closed in July 2012, but a VGS operated Vigilants until 2016. The Fulmar GC is based here, and it is used as an ELG by the RAF.

Kinnell, Tayside

This RAF station opened as a satellite for Tealing in April 1943. It was home to an OTU operating Lysanders, Hurricanes, Spitfires, Typhoons, and Mustangs until July 1944. A flying instructor's school then took over and used Oxfords, Masters and Harvards until July 1945 when flying ceased. Some parachuting took place during the 1980s and 1990s.

Kirkandrews, Dumfries and Galloway

This RLG for RAF Kingstown was in use from June 1940 to December 1947 by Tiger Moths, Magisters, and Battles.

Kirkbride, Cumbria

This RAF station opened in June 1939, its main use being as a storage unit. Large numbers of aircraft were handled here, including Battles, Ansons, Spitfires, Hampdens, Bothas, Wellingtons, Hudsons, Halifaxes, Airacobras, Mitchells, Venturas, Fortresses, Vengeances, and Meteors. An ATA ferry pilot's pool was resident here from July 1941 to September 1945 to cope with the amount of aircraft having to be moved. The RAF departed in June 1960, but private aircraft returned before 1974 operating from two of the wartime runways, one hard and one grass, both unlicensed. Over twenty aircraft are based here.

Kirkby Mallory (Stapleton), Leics

This RLG for RAF Desford was in operation from September 1939 to May 1947, with Tiger Moths and Magisters being the main types operated.

Kirkbymoorside, Yorks

This civil aerodrome started life as an AALG known as Welburn Hall in 1932. An ACGS was based here from June 1942 to February 1948. It was home to Slingsby Sailplanes from 1934 and many gliders were built here including Cadets and Sedberghs as well as Nippers and Fireflies. The factory remains, but the airfield had closed by 2015. Wombleton airfield is about 1.5 miles to the north-east.

Kirkistown, NI

This RAF station opened in July 1941 as a satellite for Ballyhalbert and was used as such until March 1944. A flight of Spitfires was based here from January to November 1942. It was then used occasionally by the FAA with Swordfish, Fulmars, and Seafires; it became HMS *Corncrake 2* in July 1945. The navy's tenure was short-lived as the base was returned to the RAF in January 1946 and flying then ceased.

Kirknewton, Lothian

This RAF station opened in October 1941 and was home to an AACU that operated Blenheims, Lysanders, Hurricanes, Defiants, and Oxfords until May 1942. Mustangs were based here between December 1942 and May 1943 when flying ceased. A VGS arrived in

April 1967, and its Vikings are based here today along with six or so light aircraft that operate from a single unlicensed grass runway.

Kirkpatrick, Dumfries and Galloway

This RAF station opened in July 1940 and was used mainly as a RLG for Kingstown until July 1945 by Magisters, Tiger Moths, and Battles.

Kirkwall (Grimsetter), Orkney

This RAF station opened in October 1940, but it was June 1942 before Spitfires arrived, which stayed until April 1943. It was then transferred to the FAA as HMS *Robin* and was used by a variety of units operating Avengers, Fireflies, Seafires, and Wildcats until April 1945. It reopened as Kirkwall Airport in 1948 and is served by scheduled services. Two licensed hard runways are in use.

Kirkwall (Hatston), Orkney

This FAA station HMS *Sparrowhawk* opened in August 1939 and was home to numerous units, mostly those on 'shore leave' until closure in September 1945. Most naval types then in service were operated, including Gladiators, Martlets, Swordfish, Skuas, Dominies, Expeditors, Avengers, and even Hoverflies. After the war, it became Kirkwall Airport until 1948 when it was found to be too small to safely accommodate scheduled services. The Orkney Flying Club used part of the airfield from 1953 to 1957 and flying then ceased. Hatston was probably the first airfield in the British Isles to be provided with hard runways.

Kirkwall (Quanterness), Orkney

This civil aerodrome opened in January 1936 for Aberdeen Airways' services.

Kirkwall (Wideford), Orkney

This civil aerodrome opened in 1933 with scheduled services commencing in May of that year. These continued until January 1940 when the airfield closed.

Kirmington (Humberside Airport), Lincs

This RAF bomber station opened in October 1942, although it was used briefly from the previous March as a RLG for Leconfield. Wellingtons and Lancasters were based here until November 1945, when the airfield was placed on C&M. Some limited flying then took place for a few years, mainly diversions from Binbrook, but it closed in 1953. It reopened for civil use in the early 1960s and was opened officially as Humberside Airport on 26 March 1974, with scheduled services commencing in April 1975. A flight of S92s and AW189s is based here, providing SAR duties for the MCA.

Kirton-in-Lindsey, Humberside

This RFC home defence flight station, known as Kirton Lindsey or Manton, was in use from October 1916 to June 1919. Types based here included Fe2s, F2bs, and Avro 504s. A site about 3 miles to the south opened in May 1940 as a RAF fighter station and was home to Spitfires, Hurricanes, and Defiants until April 1943. Its role then changed to training and was used by various units operating Spitfires, Masters, Dominies, Harvards, Oxfords, Ansons, Tiger Moths, and Prentices. This use continued until July 1957 when the station was placed on C&M. The USAAF was resident briefly between June and August 1942 with P-38s. Gliding became the main user from August 1950 and carried on until October 1965. The RAF finally departed in the following December. The Lincoln Aero Club was based here from 1958 to 1967 and civilian gliding clubs continued to use the airfield, including the Trent Valley GC. Around thirty gliders are currently resident here.

Knettishall, Suffolk

This RAF station opened as a satellite to Honington in January 1943 but transferred to the USAAF in the following June. They operated B-17s, B-24s, and B-34s until August 1945 when the base closed. Civil flying returned from a grass strip on part of the wartime airfield in the 1970s, and a few light aircraft are based here.

Knockin (Oswestry), Salop

This unlicensed airfield opened before 1982 with one grass runway; it is home to a couple of light aircraft. It is also used by helicopters from RAF Shawbury for training, mostly on weekdays.

Knowle (Widney Manor), W. Midlands

This RFC night LG was used for home defence from April to October 1916. An ACGS was based here from July 1942 to January 1946.

Knowsley Park, Merseyside

This SLG was used to store Lysanders, Wellingtons, and Halifaxes from May 1942 to December 1944. It was used by Lord Derby, the landowner for his private aircraft in the 1950s.

Lacey Green, Bucks

This airstrip was used by Bomber Command communication flights from June 1944 to February 1946. Various types were operated here, including Austers and Stinsons.

Laddingford, Kent

This unlicensed airfield at Fowle Hall Farm with two grass runways opened in the early 1980s and is home to a dozen or so aircraft.

Laindon, Essex

This private airfield at Bensons Farm opened before 1982 with a single grass runway and is home to around ten aircraft. It may have been the same site used by an ACGS from January 1945 to January 1946.

Laira (Plymouth), Devon

This LG was used by the RAF from May to December 1918.

Lake Down, Wilts

This TDS opened in August 1917, equipped with Be2s, RE8s, Avro 504s, DH4s, DH6s, DH9s, FK8s, and Camels. It closed in September 1919.

Lakenheath, Suffolk

This RAF station was used originally as a decoy site for Feltwell before becoming a satellite for Mildenhall in November 1941. Stirlings, Wellingtons, and Lancasters were the main types operated here until May 1944. The airfield was then inactive until July 1947 when Lancasters of a signal school took up residence and stayed until February 1948. The USAF took over in August 1948 and remain to this day. Countless units operated numerous types over the years, including B-29s, B-50s, F-84s, KC-97s, B-47s, U-2s, F-100s, F-4s, F-111s, KC-135s, HH-43s, and SR-71s. F-15s and HH-60s are the main types currently operated. F-35s are due to be fully deployed here by 2021.

Lambert Arms, Oxon

Two separate AALGs on either side of the A40 road were in use between 1933 and 1939.

Lamb Holm, Orkney

This unlicensed airfield with two grass runways opened before 2000 and is home to around six aircraft.

Lambley, Notts

This unlicensed airfield at Jericho Farm with a single grass runway opened in 1992 and is home to about ten light aircraft.

Lanark, Strathclyde

Flying commenced from the racecourse here in 1910, and it was later used as a RLG by the Scottish Flying Club during 1935. It closed in the 1950s.

Lancaster (Morecombe), Lancs

This RFC day LG, known as Scale Hall, opened in July 1912. It later became an AALG and supported limited scheduled services during 1935 but closed in 1939.

Land's End (St Just), Cornwall

This civil aerodrome was first used for flying in 1935 and opened officially as Land's End Airport in September 1937. Scheduled services then commenced, and while suspended on the outbreak of the Second World War, they soon restarted to the Scilly Isles until November 1941 when flying ceased. It saw little military activity during the Second World War, although some Lysanders were based here briefly between late 1940 and early 1941. It reopened for civil use in May 1945, and scheduled services soon resumed, continuing to this day, along with a lively GA operation. Four licensed runways are provided, two being hardened in 2014.

Langar, Notts

This RAF station opened in May 1942 and was used initially as a RLG for Ossington until the following August. It was then designated as a satellite for Bottesford, and Lancasters arrived, only staying until October 1943. USAAF transport units then came on the scene with C-47s, C-53s, and CG-4s, but again, their stay was short, leaving in April 1944. During their occupation, the Americans assembled several hundred CG-4 gliders here. The RAF returned in August 1944 with a HCU equipped with Halifaxes and Lancasters, but these departed in March 1945. The base was then placed on C&M and closed in December 1946. It reopened in October 1952 for the Royal Canadian Air Force and was their only UK base. It operated as a supply and service depot and various types were based here, including Bristol Freighters, C-45s, C-47s, and DC-4Ms. The Canadians departed in August 1963. Avros set up a workshop on the airfield in September 1942 to repair Lancasters; this continued to be in use until September 1968. During this time, they serviced

Yorks, Shackletons, Avro 748s, and Meteors. Today, the airfield is used mainly for parachute training (from 1977) and is provided with two unlicensed hard runways. A couple of aircraft are based here.

Langford Lodge, NI

Originally selected as a SLG, this aerodrome was taken over instead by the USAAF in July 1942 who set up a base air depot to repair and service its aircraft. Over 14,000 were dealt with, including P-38s, P-39s, P-47s, B-17s, B-24s, A-20s, and C-47s. Although the depot closed in August 1944, many aircraft were stored until March 1946. It was later used by Martin-Baker for ejector seat production and by their company aircraft; it is still in use by the company who maintain a test track on the airfield.

Langham, Norfolk

This RAF station opened in October 1940 and was home initially to an AACU operating Henleys, Magisters, Lysanders, Hurricanes, and Defiants. Beaufighters arrived for a short stay of four months in April 1944, and a variety of types followed, including Wellingtons, Spitfires, Hurricanes, Warwicks, Mosquitoes, and Oxfords until May 1946 when the base was placed on C&M. It was reactivated in March 1953 for a CAACU operating Mosquitoes, Beaufighters, Spitfires, Meteors, and Vampires until November 1958 when this unit departed. It then became an ELG for Sculthorpe and finally closed in 1961. It had opened for civil use in 1958 from one hard and one grass runway, both unlicensed; a few aircraft are based here.

Langley, Bucks

A Hawker factory and associated aerodrome opened here in 1938. It produced Hurricanes, Typhoons, Tempests, and Sea Furies until the company moved to Dunsfold in 1950. Ansons and Austers of a RAF film production unit were based here from January 1944 to January 1946, and an ACGS operated here until September 1955, when flying ceased. It also saw use by several charter airlines from 1946 to 1949 as a maintenance base.

Larkhill, Wilts

This aerodrome opened in 1909 and was used for trials until 1914. It was used by an RFC unit between May 1912 and June 1913, but it closed in 1914. RAF Atlases were based here from September 1931 to 1933. In February 1940, an AOP flight arrived with Taylorcrafts, followed by Tiger Moths, Lysanders, and Austers until they departed in August 1944. The area, being part of Salisbury Plain, is still used for military exercises, mainly with helicopters.

Larks Barrow, Hants

Intended as an ALG, it was not used for this purpose; it was used instead as a RLG and FLG from 1942 to 1945.

Lasham, Hants

This RAF station opened in March 1943 and was home initially to Typhoons and Spitfires until the following June. Light bombers in the shape of Mitchells arrived in August and were followed by Mosquitoes and Bostons until they departed in October 1944. A group support unit then arrived, which operated Spitfires, Typhoons, Mosquitoes, Tempests, Martinets, and Masters until December 1945. From March 1945, General Aircraft Ltd overhauled Mosquitoes and test-flew its experimental gliders until 1948 when flying ceased. Gliding was established in 1951 and is still going strong today, Lasham being the major gliding centre in the UK with over 200 sailplanes being based here. Dan-Air set up a maintenance base in 1955 and airliners are still overhauled here today. One unlicensed hard runway is in use as well as grass areas for gliders.

Lashenden (Headcorn), Kent

Confusingly, there are two airfields known as Headcorn and Lashenden. An ALG near Egerton Forstal was used from July to October 1943 by RAF Spitfires and again from April to July 1944 by USAAF P-47s. A second site 2 miles to the south-west at Shenley Farm opened for private flying around 1927 and became another ALG for two weeks in August 1943 when RAF Spitfires were based here. It was used again from April to June 1944 by USAAF P-47s. It reopened for private flying in the late 1950s and is now a popular GA airfield with about eighty residents operating from a single licensed grass runway and one unlicensed one.

Lavendon, Bucks

This RFC first-class night and day LG, also known as Bedford, was used for home defence from October 1916 to mid-1918. It saw some civil activity after the First World War and closed in the 1920s.

Lavenham, Suffolk

This USAAF bomber station was in use from April 1944 to August 1945, initially with B-24s and then B-17s. Half a dozen light aircraft still fly from part of the old airfield.

Leadenham, Lincs
This RFC Home Defence Flight Station was in use from September 1916 to June 1919 with mostly Fe2s and Avro 504s.

Leagrave, Beds
Hewlett and Blondeau set up a factory here, known as the Omnia Works, in 1914 and built over 700 aircraft until the factory closed in 1920. Types constructed included Farmans, Caudrons, Hanriots, Be2s, FK3s, and Avro 504s. Some of these were flown out from an adjacent field.

Leamington Spa (Bishops Tachbrook), Warks
This AALG opened in July 1932 and was used by flying schools as well as the Leamington, Warwick and District Aero Club until closure on the outbreak of the Second World War. It was used as a RLG for Elmdon and Church Lawford from September 1939 to November 1942, mostly by Tiger Moths and Oxfords.

Leanach (Culloden), Highland
This ELG opened in September 1933 for Highland Airways. It became an SLG in September 1941 and was used to store Hurricanes, Defiants, Wellingtons, Beaufighters, and Spitfires until March 1945. It was also used as a RLG by Oxfords from RAF Dalcross from June to November 1943.

Leavesden, Herts
Construction of a factory and associated airfield for the MAP commenced here in 1940, which built over 700 Halifaxes and nearly 1,400 Mosquitoes. During the Second World War, a coastal command communications flight was based here from April 1944 to May 1946 and a USAAF communications flight from October 1944. Both units flew A-28s, C-64s, and C-47s. An ACGS also operated from April 1946 to September 1947. The DH Engine Company moved in during 1946 and went on to produce thousands of aero engines, latterly as Rolls Royce until the factory closed in June 1993. DH set up a repair facility in 1946, which dealt with many DH and other types until 1963. In 1959, DH developed Leavesden as a commercial airport, and it became home to many charter, air taxi, sales, and training companies over the years. It even hosted scheduled services to Hull and Chester by Humber Airways from March 1970 to September 1971. Airship operations took place during the 1970s and '80s, and Jetstreams were refurbished from 1971 to 1975. It closed to flying on 31 March 1994 and the site is now occupied by film studios.

Leckhampstead, Berks
This unlicensed airfield at Firs Farm opened in around 1998 with a single grass runway and has about six residents.

Leconfield, Humberside
This RAF bomber station opened in December 1936 with Heyfords and Whitleys. These departed in October 1939 and were replaced with fighters, mainly Spitfires, Hurricanes, and Blenheims. Bombers returned in December 1942 in the shape of Wellingtons and Halifaxes; these stayed until August 1945 when the station was placed on C&M. Fighters returned when it reopened in January 1955 and were to remain until 1976. Types operated included Vampires, Meteors, Sabres, Hunters, Javelins, and Lightnings. A helicopter SAR flight arrived in October 1957 with Sycamores and departed in April 2015, latterly with Sea Kings. A UAS operated between March 1969 and August 1975 with Chipmunks and Bulldogs. Leconfield was used as the Hull terminal for scheduled services in the late 1960s and early 1970s. Flying ceased in January 1977 when the base was transferred to the army.

Ledbury (Preston Cross), Herefs
This unlicensed airfield opened before 1974 and is home to a few light aircraft that operate from a single grass runway. It is also known as Preston Court, Much Marcle, Velcourt, and Dymock International.

Leeds/Bradford
See Yeadon.

Leeds (Roundhay Park), Yorks
This LG was first used in 1909 to test-fly aircraft built by Blackburns, mostly Be2s and Babies. It continued to be used by the company until 1930 when it transferred to Brough. It was used for scheduled services from 1919 to 1920 and was visited by flying circuses in the 1930s.

Leeming, Yorks
This AALG, known as Leeming Lane or Newton House, opened in July 1932 and was used for pleasure flying and training until requisitioned by the RAF in 1938. It opened as a bomber station in June 1940 and was home to all the 'heavies' at one time or another: Whitleys, Stirlings, Halifaxes, Wellingtons, and Lancasters. They departed in May 1946 and were replaced briefly with an OTU operating Mosquitoes,

Left: Westland Whirlwind XJ398 hovering in front of the control tower at Leavesden in 1958. This helicopter was powered by a Rolls-Royce Gnome engine built on the site. The airfield closed in 1994, and the site is now occupied by a Warner Bros film studio. (*Craig Woods*)

Below: A 1990 aerial view of No. 1 flight shed at Leavesden featuring a variety of aircraft on the apron and grass. This building is still in use by Warner Brothers having been re-clad and re-roofed. (*Craig Woods*)

Below: The farm strip at Firs Farm, Leckhampstead, on 15 May 2018. Grumman American AG-5 D-ENTO is parked on the grass in front of the hangar and control building in the afternoon sun. (*Grant Peerless*)

Robin DR400 G-GCUF and Grumman American AA-5 G-PURR in front of the two hangars at Ledbury on 22 June 2015. This airfield has various names including Preston Court, Much Marcle, and Dymock International. (*Grant Peerless*)

Wellingtons, Tempests, and Oxfords until May 1947. An OCU then arrived and operated Mosquitoes, Oxfords, Meteors, Brigands, Buckmasters, Javelins, Tempests, Valettas, and Canberras until September 1961. Trainers then returned in the shape of Vampires, Jet Provosts, Chipmunks, and Bulldogs, which stayed until April 1984. Some of these belonged to an AEF and UAS that is still operating today with Tutors. A flight of Jetstreams was present from May 1977 to April 1979 and Tornadoes from June 1988 to April 2008. Today, Hawks are the main type operated here, which arrived in September 1995.

Lee-on-Solent, Hants

This RNAS station opened in July 1917 but was used only by flying boats until an aerodrome was established in October 1934. It was used by a variety of units operating Queen Bees, Fairey3Fs, and Sharks until May 1939 when it transferred to the FAA as HMS *Daedulus*. They operated many types during the Second World War including Walruses, Swordfish, Fulmars, Seafoxes, Albacores, Barracudas, Seafires, Fireflies, Chesapeakes, and Wellingtons.

After the war, most types in naval service were operated until fixed-wing flying all but ceased in July 1963, Sea Hawks being the last to leave. Helicopters continued to fly until September 1991, and UAS Bulldogs were based here from July 1991 to April 1993. The station closed in September 1996, but civil flying continued, and today, Lee is a busy GA facility also known as Daedulus airfield or Solent Airport. It is home to over 125 aircraft that operate from a licensed hard runway and one unlicensed grass strip. Britten-Norman set up a maintenance and production facility in 2010 to support their Islander aircraft and the Portsmouth Naval GC is also present. A flight of S92s and AW189s is based here, providing SAR duties for the MCA.

Leicester (Aylestone Lane), Leics

One of six aerodromes serving Leicester, it was first used in June 1919 by the Berkshire Aviation Co. and later leased to the Leicester Aero Club. It probably closed in 1920.

Leicester (Braunstone), Leics

This municipal aerodrome officially opened in July 1935, but flying had been taking place since June 1934. Scheduled services commenced in March 1935 and continued until September 1939. During the Second World War, it was used as a RLG by Tiger Moths from Desford and briefly during 1944 by L-4s of the US Army. It closed at the end of the war and did not reopen for private flying.

Leicester (Desford), Leics

This RFC second-class day LG, known as Peckleton, was used for home defence from October 1916 to August 1918. It reopened for civil use in 1929 and became home to the Leicestershire Aero Club until they moved to Braunstone in March 1935. A reserve flying school arrived in November 1935 and training continued during and after the Second World War, finally coming to an end in June 1953 when flying ceased. Types based included Tiger Moths, Audaxes, Harts, Ansons, Magisters, Prentices, and Chipmunks. Reid and Sigrist, a CRO, repaired Mitchells and Defiants during the war. An AOP flight equipped with Austers was resident from

September 1949 to June 1953.

Leicester (Ratcliffe), Leics

This civil aerodrome opened in September 1930 and was used for private flying until the outbreak of the Second World War. It was used by an ATA ferry pool during the war. It reopened for civil use after the war and closed in 1950.

Leicester (Rearsby), Leics

This civil aerodrome opened in 1938 and was used initially by the County Flying Club. In the same year, the Taylorcraft Aeroplane Co. built a factory on the site and produced Taylorcrafts, Austers, and Beagle types until 1969. During the Second World War, the company repaired Tiger Moths and Hurricanes, and an ACGS was resident from October 1943 to December 1945. Following the demise of the Beagle Aircraft Company, the airfield closed in May 1971.

Leicester East, Leics

This RAF station opened in November 1943, the first residents being Stirlings and then Wellingtons until October 1944. An OTU arrived in May 1944 equipped with Dakotas, Oxfords, and Austers, staying until October 1945. It was then placed on C&M and closed in December 1947. It was reopened by the Leicester Aero Club in 1950 and became Leicester Airport in 1977. Today, it is a busy GA airfield with over 100 resident aircraft operating from three licensed hard runways and two grass strips.

Leigh (Tonbridge), Kent

This RFC night LG was used for home defence for only two months from October to December 1916.

Leigh Green (Tenterden), Kent

This RFC third-class night LG was used for home defence from October 1916 to June 1919.

Leighterton (Bowldown Farm), Glos

This RFC training squadron station opened in January 1918, which was home to Avro 504s, Pups, Camels, and Snipes until closure by early 1920. It reopened as an AALG in the summer of 1931 and was used sporadically by private aircraft and gliders of the Bristol GC. On the same site, an unlicensed airfield with two grass runways is still in use today. Babdown Farm, the Second World War airfield, was just to the south-west.

Leighton Buzzard (Scotts Field) Beds

This LG was used by Morgan and Co., car body manufacturers, to test-fly 1½ Strutters, DH6s, Avro 504s, and Vimys from 1917 to the end of 1919. It was probably the site of a Cobham's Flying Circus appearance in 1932.

Leiston, Suffolk

This USAAF fighter station opened in November 1943 with P-47s followed by P-51s until closure in July 1945.

Lenham, Kent

This civil aerodrome opened in 1930 and closed on the outbreak of the Second World War. It saw use by the Kent GC before the war and was used by AOP Austers during March and April 1943.

Lennoxlove (Haddington), Lothian

This private LG on the Haddington Estate was in use in the 1930s. A SLG opened here in April 1941 and was used to store Blenheims, Whirlwinds, Welkins, and Wellingtons until March 1946.

Lerwick (Tingwall), Shetland

There have been two airfields serving Lerwick. The first was grass-surfaced and was in use from 1971 to 1976. The second was opened in October 1976 with a licensed hard runway, with scheduled services currently being operated.

Leuchars, Fife

This military aerodrome was home to a torpedo training squadron and gunnery school operating various types from November 1918 to 1920. From March 1920, a succession of naval units were based here until August 1938, mainly on 'shore leave.' Types operated were numerous but included Nieuports, Panthers, Flycatchers, Fairey 3D/Fs, and Ospreys. RAF Coastal Command then arrived and used Ansons, Hudsons, Beauforts, Hampdens, Beaufighters, Mosquitoes, and Liberators until June 1945. A BAT flight of Ansons, Oxfords, and Wellingtons was resident here from January 1941 to August 1944 and a PRU equipped with Spitfires and Mosquitoes was based here from October 1941 to February 1944. BOAC operated flights to Sweden with Hudsons and Mosquitoes between 1941 and May 1945. After the war, Coastal Command continued operations with Halifaxes and Lancasters until December 1950. Fighter Command took over in May 1950 and operated Meteors, Vampires, Hunters, Venoms, Javelins, Lightnings, Phantoms,

Above: Grumman American AA-5 G-PURR parked on the grass in front of the Second World War control tower at Lee-on-Solent on 16 February 2012. It is now known as Daedulus airfield (after its naval name) or Solent Airport. (*Tony Yarnold*)

Right: Hangars, control tower, and various light aircraft at Leicester (Ratcliffe) on 1 June 1947. It closed in 1950. (*Eddie Riding*)

Below: Leicester (Rearsby) photographed from an Auster on 26 March 1946, the same month that Auster Aircraft Ltd was formed from Taylorcraft Aeroplanes (England) Ltd. Several of their products can be seen on the ground. The airfield closed in 1971. (*Eddie Riding*)

and Tornadoes. Typhoons replaced the Tornadoes in September 2010 but moved to Lossiemouth in 2014, leaving an AEF and UAS with Tutors the only unit still flying today. Scheduled services were briefly operated in the late 1960s when the airfield at Dundee was unserviceable. The site was handed over to the army in March 2015, but it continues to be used as an ELG by the RAF.

Leven, Fife

This LG was used by the RFC during 1913 and 1914.

Levington, Suffolk

This RNAS night LG was used as a shore base for ship-borne aircraft during 1916 and 1917.

Lewes, Sussex

This unlicensed airfield at Swanborough Farm opened before 1998 with a single grass runway and is home to dozen or so aircraft.

Leysdown (Shellbeach), Kent

Claimed to be the first aerodrome in Britain, Shorts flew a Wright biplane from here in March 1909. Flying continued until 1913, but before this, in 1911, the RNAS made use of the LG. In April 1918, the RAF arrived with a gunnery school equipped with Avro 504s, DH4s, DH9s, RE8s, and Pups. This closed in late 1918 when it was replaced with a coastal patrol flight that operated DH9s, RE8s, Pups, and 1½ Strutters until September 1919. Flying then ceased, but the aerodrome was used as an ELG until the end of the Second World War.

Lichfield (Fradley), Staffs

This RAF station opened in March 1940 and was occupied by a MU until March 1957. Types handled included Oxfords, Hurricanes, Ansons, Typhoons, Liberators, Fortresses, and Spitfires. Training also took place from April 1941 with Wellingtons and Ansons and continued after the war with Varsities and Valettas until December 1953. An ACGS was based from May 1947 to September 1955, and the airfield closed in April 1958. A microlight site at Roddige, about 1.5 miles east of the Second World War aerodrome, was opened before 1993 and is home to over forty aircraft. Another grass strip 2 miles south of the Second World War site at Streethay Farm was opened around 1988 at which six aircraft are based. Also, Sittles Farm strip is about half a mile south of Roddidge.

Lilbourne (Catthorpe), Northants

This RFC first-class night LG opened in June 1916 and was used mainly for training but also home defence. Various types were operated here, including Be2s, Avro 504s, SE5s, Camels, DH9s, F2bs, and Snipes until flying ceased in April 1919.

Limavady, NI

This RAF Coastal Command station opened in August 1940 and was home to Whitleys, Blenheims, Hudsons, Ansons, and Wellingtons until June 1945. An OTU equipped with Wellingtons and Ansons operated here from April 1942 to May 1944, and an ASR flight with Warwicks and Sea Otters from March to August 1945. The FAA was based here briefly from June to November 1944 with Wildcats, Swordfish, and Avengers. The airfield closed at the end of 1945.

Lincoln (Handley Page Field), Lincs

This field was used by Clayton and Shuttleworth to fly out aircraft constructed in their factory to West Common aerodrome for flight-testing. It was in use from about 1916 to the 1920s; types handled included 0/400s, Vimys, Camels, and Snipes.

Lincoln (West Common), Lincs

This manufacturer's aerodrome situated on the racecourse was used from 1915 to test-fly various types. An AAP opened in March 1917, handling Kangaroos, F2bs, 0/400s, Be2s, DH5s, DH6s, DH9s, Camels, and Cuckoos. It closed in 1919 but was later used by an ACGS from 1942 to 1945.

Lindholme (Hatfield Woodhouse), Yorks

This RAF bomber station opened in July 1940 and was home to Hampdens, Wellingtons, Manchesters, Lancasters, Halifaxes, and Lincolns until December 1949, although latterly, some of these were operated in the training role. A target towing flight was based here from November 1942 to May 1945 with Lysanders, Whitleys, and Martinets. An ANS arrived in March 1951 equipped with Wellingtons, Ansons, Varsities, and Valettas, staying until November 1952. This was replaced with a bombing school that operated Lincolns, Varsities, Oxfords, Hastings, and Canberras until September 1972. The station then closed, but an ACGS carried on flying until March 1982, and it was used as a RLG for Finningley until 1985.

Lingfield, Surrey

This RFC night LG was established on the racecourse, which was used for home defence for a short period between April and October 1916.

Linton-on-Ouse, Yorks

This RAF bomber station opened in April 1938 and was home to Whitleys, Halifaxes, and Lancasters until July 1946. Fighter Command then arrived and operated Mosquitoes, Hornets, Meteors, Sabres, and Hunters until March 1957. Training then took over with Provosts, Vampires, and Jet Provosts and continues to the present day with Tucanos. A VGS flew Vigilants until 2016 and Tutors of an AEF and UAS are currently based here, but the airfield is due to close by 2020.

Lisky (Strabane), NI

A civil aerodrome was in use here before the Second World War.

Lissett, Yorks

This RAF station opened in October 1942 and was used mainly as a RLG for Catfoss by Blenheims, Beaufighters, and Ansons until February 1943. It then became a bomber base that was home to Halifaxes and Stirlings until it closed in August 1945.

Litchborough, Northants

This RFC second-class night LG was used for home defence for a short period only from October 1916 to March 1917.

Little Downham (Ely), Cambs

This RFC second-class night LG was used for home defence from April 1916 to April 1919.

Little Gransden, Cambs

This unlicensed airfield at Fullers Hill Farm opened in 1966 and is home to around sixty aircraft that operate from two grass runways.

Little Horwood, Bucks

This RAF station opened in September 1942 as a satellite for Wing and was used as a RLG by an OTU operating Wellingtons, Warwicks, Ansons, Hurricanes, Oxfords, and Masters until November 1945. A communications flight was resident here from September 1942 to July 1945, using Oxfords, Ansons, Proctors, and Magisters. Flying ceased in November 1945.

Little Rissington, Glos

This RAF station opened in August 1938 and was used initially for training by Harts, Tutors, Ansons, Harvards, Tiger Moths, and Oxfords until December 1945. A BAT flight operated Oxfords from October 1941 to December 1945, and a communications flight used various types between February 1939 and July 1957. A MU handled thousands of aircraft during the Second World War including Spitfires, Wellingtons, Halifaxes, Battles, Hampdens, Typhoons, and Horsas. The CFS arrived in May 1946 and operated Tiger Moths, Chipmunks, Harvards, Prentices, Provosts, Meteors, Vampires, Jet Provosts, and Bulldogs for the next thirty years. The RAF departed in August 1976 and flying then ceased although a couple of VGSs that arrived in November 1977 still operate from the airfield, currently flying Vikings. Civil flying resumed from part of the wartime airfield in 2006 and a few aircraft are based here. Three hard licensed runways are available. Devonair moved in from Kemble at the end of 2006 and occupied some of the RAF hangars but departed in 2012.

Little Snoring, Norfolk

This RAF station opened in August 1943, with Lancasters being the first residents, followed by a variety of types including Wellingtons, Whitleys, Halifaxes, Mosquitoes, and Beaufighters until December 1946 when it was placed on C&M. Mosquitoes were stored from November 1945 to December 1946. It reopened in July 1951 for a CAACU operating Spitfires, Beaufighters, Mosquitoes, Vampires, and Meteors until closure in March 1953. Part of the airfield reopened again in 1957 for private flying, and around twenty light aircraft are currently based here, operating from an unlicensed hard/grass runway.

Little Staughton, Cambs

This RFC first-class night LG, also known as Bedford, was used for home defence from October 1916 to September 1917. An RAF station opened about 1 mile south-east in December 1942 but was used initially by a USAAF strategic air depot until March 1944. The RAF then arrived and operated Lancasters and Mosquitoes here until September 1945. A communications flight was based here from March 1946 equipped with Ansons, Messengers, Proctors, and Austers, staying until April 1948. It then saw use by Brooklands Aviation, which maintained Valettas, Varsities, and Mosquitoes. Today, it is still primarily a maintenance base, but twenty or so aircraft are based here, operating from a single unlicensed hard runway.

Grumman American AA-5 G-PURR in front of a type 'E' hangar at the Cotswolds airfield of Little Rissington on 13 May 2008. This type of hangar was normally used for storage purposes. (*Grant Peerless*)

Little Sutton, Cheshire

This RLG for RAF Sealand opened in November 1941 and was used mainly by Tiger Moths until December 1942. An ACGS was based here from July 1944 to July 1945, and the airfield closed in May 1946.

Little Walden (Hadstock), Essex

This USAAF station opened in March 1944 and was home initially to A-20s. These were followed by P-51s and P-47s until they departed in September 1945. The airfield closed in January 1946.

Littleworth, Worcs

This RLG for RAF Worcester was in use between 1941 and 1945.

Liverpool (Speke), Merseyside

This aerodrome was licensed in July 1930 when scheduled services commenced, but the official opening did not take place until 1 July 1933. Services were operated by several airlines up to the outbreak of the Second World War, some continuing during the war. In May 1936, the RAF based a squadron here that flew Harts, Hinds, and Spitfires. Rootes set up a factory on the aerodrome in September 1937, which produced nearly 2,500 Blenheims and over 1,000 Halifaxes. In February 1939, Lockheed set up a facility to assemble Hudsons and went on to handle T-6s, P-38s, P-47s, P-51s, and P-61s for the USAAF until well into 1946. The aerodrome was requisitioned by the RAF in September 1939 and was home to a wide variety of units operating Hampdens, Hurricanes, Spitfires, Chesapeakes, Rocs, Skuas, Sea Hurricanes, Swordfish, Lysanders, and Hornet Moths until June 1946. It returned to civil use in July 1944 and scheduled services recommenced the following November. After the war, hundreds of USAAF fighters were prepared for return to the USA, the majority being P-47s and P-51s, and in the 1950s, Airwork carried out maintenance work on Vampires and Sabres. In May 1966, a completely new runway was opened to the south-east of the old airfield together with a new terminal building and scheduled and charter services began to increase. Today, it is the busy Liverpool John Lennon Airport.

Llanbedr, Gwynedd

This RAF station opened in June 1941, the first residents being Ansons and Dominies. From the following October, it became a fighter base, operating mostly Spitfires until the end of the war. A CAACU was based here from September 1951 to January 1958 with Beaufighters, Mosquitoes, Spitfires, Vampires, Oxfords, and Ansons. In 1954, its role changed to the evaluation of pilotless aircraft and this continued until closure in December 2004. Types used included Fireflies, Meteors, Canberras, Sea Vixens, Jindiviks, Hawks, and Navajos. It reopened for civil use in 2014 and is known as the Snowdonia Aerospace Centre. It is open to visiting aircraft for which three unlicensed hard runways are available.

BEA DH Dragon Rapide G-AGUG in front of the iconic control tower and terminal building at Liverpool (Speke) Airport on 21 February 1947. The terminal is now a luxury hotel. (*Eddie Riding*)

Llandow, Glamorgan

This RAF station opened in 1937 with Hinds and Hectors that moved out in September 1939. An aircraft storage unit arrived in April 1940 and handled Spitfires, Whitleys, Albermarles, Bostons, Mustangs, and Lancasters. A similar use continued from July 1943 when an overseas aircraft preparation unit moved in, which prepared and ferried Beaufighters, Wellingtons, Warwicks, Venturas, Halifaxes, Dakotas, and Lancasters until August 1945. An OTU was based here from July 1941 to May 1943, equipped with Spitfires and Masters. A RAuxAF squadron arrived in May 1946 that operated Spitfires and Vampires and stayed until March 1957. An AOP flight with Austers was resident here between July 1949 and March 1957. A long taxi track linked the airfield to nearby RAF St Athan. While flying all but ceased in 1957, the airfield was used to support St Athan until 1960.

Llandrindod Wells, Powys

This civil aerodrome opened in 1931 on the site of an old racecourse and was used mainly for pleasure flying and training until closure in 1935.

Llandudno, Gwynedd

This civil aerodrome opened around 1930 and was possibly home to an Air Pageant in July 1936.

Llanishen, Gwent

This field was used by an ACGS from October 1943 to August 1947.

Llantysilio, Clwyd

This gliding site is operated by the North Wales GC and is home to around a dozen gliders.

Lleweni Parc, Clwyd

This private grass airfield opened before 1993 and is home to about a dozen aircraft, mostly microlights as well as gliders of the Denbigh GC.

Loch Doon, Strathclyde

Ths RNAS aerodrome was home to a gunnery school equipped with Be2s and DH2s from January 1917 to January 1918.

London Air Park

See Hanworth.

London City Airport, Gt. London

This airport situated in the London Docklands was opened by HM the Queen on 5 November 1987, although scheduled services had commenced a month earlier. It is used for mostly short-haul flights to European destinations from a single short runway.

London Colney, Herts

This RFC second-class night LG opened in April 1916 and was used for training and home defence with Be2s, Spads, Pups, SE5s, Scouts, and Avro 504s. A TDS was formed in July 1918, equipped with Avro 504s, Snipes, and SE5s; it stayed until flying ceased in November

Above: View of London City Airport from across the Royal Albert Dock on 27 March 2015. On the apron, a couple of British Airways' City Flyers Embraer ERJ190s are awaiting passengers. (*Grant Peerless*)

Below: Spad S.VII A8817 in front of flight sheds at RFC London Colney in 1917. The aerodrome closed in 1919. (*Alan Curtis*)

1919. Less than 1 mile to the east is a microlight site known as The Dell, which opened in 1992 and is operated by the Hertfordshire Microlight Club with around a dozen residents.

Londonderry (Eglinton), NI

This RAF station opened in August 1941 for Coastal Command but was used instead as a fighter base by Hurricanes and Spitfires. It was taken over by the FAA as HMS *Gannet* in May 1943 and remained in naval hands until February 1963, latterly as HMS *Sea Eagle* (from May 1960). During this time, it was used by most types then in-service, including Swordfish, Corsairs, Fireflies, Wildcats, Hellcats, Sea Furies, Avengers, Gannets, Whirlwinds, and Wessexes. In September 1965, it became a civil airport under the control of Londonderry City Council and is now Derry Airport.

Londonderry (Gransha Asylum), NI

This civil aerodrome opened in around 1925 and was used for short-lived airmail services by Northern Airlines.

Long Crendon, Bucks

This private grass strip at Baileys Farm opened before 2009; it is home to about ten light aircraft.

Long Kesh, NI

This RAF station opened in September 1941 and was initially home to Lysanders and Tomahawks of an AACU, later a target towing flight until April 1942. A Coastal Command OTU was based here from December 1942 to February 1944 and operated Beauforts, Hampdens, Hudsons, and Venturas. The FAA was in occupation from March 1944 to February

1945 and used Swordfish, Wildcats, Hellcats, and Seafires. Shorts set up an assembly line for Stirlings during the war; these were test-flown from the airfield. It closed in 1946, but a VGS operated here until 1958 and Shorts GC until 1968. The base was taken over by the army in January 1972, who flew Scouts, Sioux, and Gazelles until flying ceased in December 1977.

Long Marston, Warks

This RAF station opened in late 1941 as a satellite for Honeybourne and was used briefly by a ferry training unit. In May 1942, it became a RLG for an OTU operating Whitleys, Wellingtons, and Ansons; this use continued until July 1945. A MU arrived in the following November, which stored mainly Wellingtons and Hamilcars until September 1947. It became a RLG again in January 1952 when it was used by Oxfords, Harvards, and Chipmunks until March 1954, when flying ceased. Part of the wartime airfield reopened for civil use in the early 1980s but closed in November 2017 to make way for 3,500 homes to be known as Long Marston Village.

Long Mynd, Salop

This gliding site was opened in 1934 by the Midland GC, which is still in operation today. Around forty sailplanes are based here. It was home to an ACGS from 1942.

Long Newnton, Glos

This RAF station opened in September 1940 as a satellite for Babdown Farm and was used mainly as a RLG for nearby aerodromes. Types operated included Harts, Masters, and Oxfords. Flying ceased in May 1945, after which it was used by a MU until closure around 1950. The Cotswolds GC was based here from 1964 to 1967.

Longbridge (Northfield), W. Midlands

This LG, known as Cofton Hackett, was opened in the First World War by the Austin Motor Company to test-fly aircraft built at their factory at Longbridge. Types included RE7s, RE8s, SE5s, and F2bs. It was used by civil aircraft between the wars, but activity was light until the Second World War, when aircraft production and flight-testing returned with Battles and Hurricanes. The last flight from Cofton Hackett was probably in around October 1942.

Longbridge Deverill, Wilts

This unlicensed airfield at Wing Farm with one grass runway was opened before 1972 and is home to around twenty-five aircraft, mostly microlights.

Longhorsley, Northumberland

This RFC second-class night and third-class day LG was used for home defence from January 1917 to June 1919.

Longtown, Cumbria

This RAF training station opened in July 1941 as a satellite for Crosby-on-Eden and was used later by a HCU. Together, they operated Hurricanes, Beauforts, Beaufighters, Halifaxes, Stirlings, Liberators, and Oxfords. It closed in April 1946.

Lopcombe Corner, Hants

This RFC aerodrome opened in September 1917 and was later used as a TDS until June 1919. Types operated included Avro 504s, Be2s, Pups, Camels, DH5s, and DH6s. SE5s were based here from February to October 1919, when flying ceased. It was used by AOP Austers from Old Sarum between April and August 1943 and by US Army L-4s in 1944.

Lords Bridge, Cambs

This RLG was used between 1942 and 1944 by Tiger Moths, Magisters, and Masters based mainly at Teversham.

Lossiemouth, Grampian

An AALG was in use here between 1934 and 1938. It was requisitioned by the RAF and opened in May 1939, its first occupants being Harvards and Oxfords of a training school until April 1940. Its main use during the Second World War was maintenance and bomber training. A bomber OTU arrived in May 1940 and stayed until July 1945, operating mainly Wellingtons, Ansons, Defiants, and Oxfords. A MU was set up in April 1940 that handled Hurricanes, Tiger Moths, Wellingtons, Defiants, Masters, Beaufighters, Lancasters, Yorks, Lincolns, and Warwicks until disbanding in February 1947. An ATA ferry pilot's pool was based here between October 1941 and July 1945 and was used mostly Ansons and Arguses while Blenheims, Halifaxes, and Lancasters carried out operations from April 1940 to November 1944. Coastal Command took over in July 1945 with an OTU equipped with Liberators and Wellingtons but only stayed until May 1946. It transferred to the FAA in July 1946 as HMS

Fulmar and went on to operate nearly every naval type then in service, many on 'shore leave' from carriers. These included Fireflies, Seafires, Attackers, Sea Furies, Seahawks, Gannets, Buccanneers, and Scimitars. The base reverted to RAF control in September 1972 but continued to be used by the Navy until May 1993 with Gannets, Sea Harriers, and Sea Kings. From July 1973, the RAF operated Shackletons, Jaguars, Hunters, Hawks, and latterly Tornadoes. Typhoons arrived in summer 2014, and with the closure of Leuchars, Lossiemouth is the only front line station in Scotland. Poseidons are due to be based from 2020.

Loughborough, Leics

An aerodrome at Loughborough Meadows was used by the Brush Electrical Works to test-fly aircraft constructed by them between October 1915 and April 1919. These included Longhorns, Avro 504s, Short 827s, and 184s. It fell into disuse after the First World War and saw no further activity. Another aerodrome to the north-west of the First World War site on a former racecourse was again used by the Brush Company during the Second World War and built over 300 Dominies between March 1943 and March 1946. It also repaired Hampdens as a CRO. An ACGS operated from October 1943 to January 1946. The airfield finally closed around 1960.

Loughton, Bucks

This AALG was in use between 1932 and 1939.

Low Eldrig, Dumfries and Galloway

This SLG was used for the storage of Battles and Blenheims from June 1941 to September 1942.

Lower Beeding (Horsham), Sussex

This RFC second-class night and first-class day LG was used for home defence from January 1917 to August 1919. Be2s and Be12s were the main types operated.

Lower Kingswood (Rookery Farm/ Kingswood Knoll), Surrey

This civil aerodrome opened in around 1928 and was used mainly for aircraft restoration. It was visited regularly by various flying circuses until falling into disuse by the start of the Second World War. It was used as a FLG for Redhill during the war.

Lower Upham, Hants

There are two airfields here very close to each other. Phoenix Farm opened before 1989 with a single unlicensed grass runway and is home to Solent Flight and six light aircraft while Roughay Farm, opened before 1992, also has one grass strip and around ten residents.

Lowthorpe, Yorks

This was predominantly an airship station, but it was used by RNAS DH6s during the latter part of the First World War.

Loxwood, Sussex

This RLG for Gatwick was used mainly by an elementary flying school from February 1938.

Luce Bay

See West Freugh.

Ludford Magna, Lincs

This RAF bomber station opened in July 1942 with a detachment of Wellingtons until the following September. Lancasters arrived in June 1943 and remained here until October 1945 when flying ceased. It was reactivated in July 1959 for the deployment of Thor missiles, which departed in May 1963.

Ludham, Norfolk

This RAF fighter station opened in December 1941 as a satellite for Coltishall operating mainly Spitfires and some Typhoons until closure in July 1945. It was transferred briefly to the FAA from August 1944 to February 1945 as HMS *Flycatcher* and was used as a mobile naval airfield organisation depot to repair and service aircraft for use on carriers. It reopened for private flying before 1974 from a section of the wartime east–west hard runway and around a dozen aircraft are currently based here.

Lullington (Burton-on-Trent), Derbys

This RFC second-class night LG was used for home defence for a short period only from October 1916 to March 1917.

Lulsgate Bottom

See Bristol.

Lundy Island, Devon

This landing strip was licensed in June 1934, which supported scheduled services to Barnstaple and Torbay until the outbreak of the Second World War. It saw no action during the war, and scheduled services resumed in 1950, continuing until 1956 when fixed-wing services were stopped on safety grounds. They were replaced by helicopters in 1981 and continue to operate today from November to March from a heliport at Hartland Point. It is open to visiting aircraft, but pilots have to take great care when using the short grass strip.

Luton, Beds

Flying commenced here in March 1937, but Luton Municipal Airport was not opened officially until 16 July 1938. Luton Flying Club was formed in March 1938, and Percival Aircraft set up a factory in 1937. Before and during the Second World War, they built Vega Gulls, Q6s, Proctors, Oxfords, and Mosquitoes. An elementary flying school was formed in August 1938, which operated Magisters, Harts, and Ansons until February 1942. Napiers opened a factory in March 1940 and used the airfield to fly its test-bed aircraft. The ATA arrived in April 1942 and trained pilots as well as operating a ferry pool until May 1943. After the war, Percivals produced Prentices, Princes, Provosts, and Jet Provosts, latterly as Hunting Percival and then BAC until production ceased in 1966. Civil flying resumed after the war, mainly with charter flights followed by scheduled services in 1958 and inclusive tour charters in 1962. During the 1960s, several airlines used Luton as a diversion airport when Heathrow was fogbound. Today, it is the busy London Luton Airport with numerous scheduled and charter flights to mainly European destinations, predominantly by 'low cost' airlines.

Lydd, Kent

A temporary LG at Dering Farm was in use by the RFC during 1913 and 1914. Nearby, an RFC third-class night LG was used for gunnery and home defence purposes from January 1917 to October 1919. Various types were operated here, including RE8s, Be2s, FK8s, Pups, and F2bs. In June 1943, an ALG was established 2 miles north-west of the First World War aerodrome; this was used by RAF Typhoons until October 1943. The third airfield in the area was 4 miles east of the ALG and opened as Ferryfield on 13 July 1954 for Silver City Airways and their car ferry operations. Around fifty aircraft are based here today, operating from a single licensed hard runway. A flight of S92s and AW189s is also based here, providing SAR duties for the MCA.

Lymington, Hants

This AALG was in use from 1933 to 1938. A site near here was used as an ALG by USAAF P-47s from April to June 1944.

Lympne (Hythe), Kent

The first of two aerodromes was opened in November 1915 and was used by a gunnery school until March 1916. A second site just to the west opened as a RFC first-class LG in September 1916 and was used for home defence and as a gunnery school. An AAP was set up in October 1918 and handled a variety of types until closure in November 1921. Civil flying commenced in 1920 with freight services, and the aerodrome became an ELG for airliners. Short Bros used the airfield to test-fly their aircraft between 1924 and 1929, and the Cinque Ports Flying Club was formed in 1928. It was requisitioned by the RAF in November 1936 as a temporary bomber station but only Hinds arrived. It was transferred to the FAA as HMS *Buzzard* in July 1939 but only for a couple of months. It was renamed HMS *Daedulus 2* in January 1940 but returned to the RAF in May 1940 when Lysanders arrived and stayed until November 1941. It became a fighter station in June 1942, and Spitfires, Hurricanes, and Typhoons were operated until May 1945 when it was placed on C&M. Civil flying resumed in January 1946 and scheduled services commenced in July 1948, which continued until October 1974. A concrete runway was built in 1967–1968, after which it was renamed Ashford Airport. Flying ceased in 1989.

Lyneham, Wilts

This RAF station opened in May 1940, its first resident being a MU communications flight that stayed until December 1966. It was next used for training by Oxfords, Harvards, and Ansons until February 1942 when a ferry unit arrived. This stayed until March 1944 and operated Beauforts, Hudsons, Marylands, Liberators, Wellingtons, and Oxfords. It was taken over by Transport Command in February 1944, and this remained its primary role for the next sixty-eight years. Types operated over the years included Warwicks, Dakotas, Liberators, Stirlings, Yorks, Hastings, Comets, Britannias, and Hercules. The base closed in December 2012.

Lyveden, Northants

This gliding site opened in 1990 and is home to the Welland GC, which operates over a dozen gliders.

Machrihanish

See Campbeltown.

Macmerry (Tranent), Lothian

This RFC second-class night LG, known as Hoprig Mains, was used for home defence from August 1916

Left: The old control tower at Luton, which opened in September 1952 but was replaced by a new 'Eurotower' in January 1995. This view was taken in April 1959 just before the long-awaited concrete runway was brought into use and features an Auster, Miles Hawk Trainer, and Aeronca. (*Grant Peerless*)

Above: EasyJet Boeing 737 taxiing past the new 'Eurotower' at Luton Airport on 11 May 2003. (*Grant Peerless*)

Below: Bristol Freighter and Douglas DC3s of Silver City Airways and a Bristol Freighter of Cie. Air Transport (a subsidiary of Silver City) on the apron at the then new airport at Lydd, also known as Ferryfield, in the early 1960s. The airfield opened in July 1954 and was famous for its car ferry operations to the continent. (*Aerofilms*)

to July 1917. It reopened for civil use in 1929 by the Edinburgh Flying Club and was used by some scheduled services up to the outbreak of the Second World War. It was taken over by RAF in August 1940 and was used by various units operating Whirlwinds, Hurricanes, Blenheims, Lysanders, Mustangs, and Spitfires until late 1943. It was transferred to the FAA in June 1945 as HMS *Nighthawk 2* but saw little use. It was returned to the RAF in December 1945 and was used by an ACGS until April 1946. Cunliffe-Owen had a facility on the airfield during the Second World War, which overhauled Hudsons. The airfield reopened for civil use in August 1946 but closed in 1953.

Madley, Herefs

This RAF station opened in August 1941 and was used by a signals school equipped with Proctors, Dominies, Magisters, and Oxfords, which stayed until flying ceased in January 1947. An ACGS was based here for the last year.

Maghaberry, NI

This RAF station opened as a satellite for Long Kesh in November 1941. Its first residents were Lysanders and Tomahawks of an AACU that stayed until December 1942. A Coastal Command OTU then arrived and operated Beauforts, Hampdens, and Venturas until February 1944. The USAAF came on the scene in November 1943 and set up a ferry/training squadron that delivered aircraft to England. Types handled included P-38s, P-47s, P-51s, B-17s, B-24s, and C-47s until the facility closed in May 1944. It was then returned to the RAF and placed on C&M. A MU arrived in January 1945, storing and scrapping Stirlings until the airfield closed in October 1947. Ironically, Shorts had a Stirling assembly line here during the war.

Malmesbury (Charlton Park), Wilts

Two unlicensed grass strips on the Earl of Suffolk and Berkshire's estate opened before 1998. A couple of aircraft are based here.

Malton (Heslerton), Yorks

This private grass airfield was in use from the 1970s to 1980s.

Manby, Lincs

This RAF station opened in August 1938, its first resident being an air armament school equipped with Battles, Wallaces, Hinds, Wellingtons, Martinets, Hurricanes, Mosquitoes, Lancasters, and Harvards. This stayed until July 1949 when the RAF Flying College took over and operated Valettas, Varsities, Meteors, Canberras, Provosts, Hastings, and Lincolns until July 1962. This unit became the College of Air Warfare and used many of the foregoing types as well as Hunters, Dominies and Jet Provosts. The College departed in March 1974 and the airfield then closed. There is a private grass strip at Eastfield Farm just to the east of the wartime airfield that opened before 1993, which is home to about six light aircraft.

Manchester

See Barton.

Manchester (Alexandra Park/ Didsbury), Gt. Manchester

This AAP, known as Hough End Fields, was in use from 1917 to 1919, which handled Avro types built locally. Scheduled services commenced in May 1919 but ceased a year later. Avros continued using the site for test-flying until it closed in August 1924.

Manchester, Gt. Manchester

An aerodrome at Burnage was used occasionally during the First World War, and another at Miles Platting was used by Avro for test-flying during the war. Yet another aerodrome at Trafford Park was opened by the Manchester Aero Club in 1911 and saw occasional use during the First World War.

Manchester (Ringway), Gt. Manchester

This was officially opened as Manchester's airport on 25 June 1938 as a replacement for Barton, although Fairey had set up a factory here in June the previous year to assemble Battles. Scheduled services were operated until the outbreak of the Second World War. The RAF arrived in March 1939, and the airfield became home to a wide variety of units operating Lysanders, Hurricanes, Spitfires, Ansons, Tiger Moths, Hectors, and Hotspurs. Its major use during the war was parachute training with mostly Whitleys and Dakotas. The RAF departed in March 1957, and the last aircraft they operated were Vampires, Austers, and Chipmunks. Avro had a factory here during the war, which produced and test-flew Manchesters and Lancasters. Commercial operations resumed in June 1946. During the 1950s, Faireys serviced B-26s and F-86s for the USAF and

Camouflaged hangar at the earl of Suffolk and Berkshire's Charlton Park Estate airstrip near Malmesbury with Grumman American AA-5 G-PURR visiting on 14 August 2016. (*Grant Peerless*)

test-flew Fireflies, the last leaving in April 1956. Today, Manchester International Airport is the second largest in the country after Heathrow.

Manchester (Wythenshawe) Gt. Manchester

This temporary municipal airport for Manchester was in use from April 1929 to January 1930, when Barton became Manchester's airport. It was however used as a RLG and for limited private flying after this but for how long is not known.

Manningford (Bohune Common) Wilts

This RAF station opened in September 1939 and was used as a RLG for various local airfields. Types using the field included Tutors, Tiger Moths, Magisters, Masters, and Oxfords. It closed in April 1947.

Manorbier, Pembrokeshire

This RAF station opened in June 1938 for target towing with mainly Queen Bees and closed in 1946.

Manston, Kent

This RNAS night LG, also known as Manstone opened in 1915 and was used mostly for training until April 1918 when a TDS was formed. This was equipped with Be2s, RE8s, DH4s, DH6s, DH9s, Avro 504s, Camels, and SE5s until it closed in December 1919. A coastal patrol flight arrived in May 1918 and operated Camels and DH9s until December 1919. A FTS came on the scene in May 1921 and operated Avro 504s, F2bs, and Snipes until April 1922. From March 1924, a variety of units used the station with an assortment of types until the outbreak of the Second World War, including F2bs, Snipes, Vimys, Atlases, Virginias, Fairey 3Fs, Clouds, and Ansons. It became a fighter station in September 1939, and numerous types were based here, including Hurricanes, Blenheims, Spitfires, Defiants, Havocs, Mosquitoes, Mustangs, Typhoons, Whirlwinds, Swordfish, Avengers, Tempests, and Meteors until June 1946. During the latter part of the war, an extra-long runway was laid to enable it to be used as an emergency diversion airfield and many aircraft in difficulties made successful landings. This was one of three airfields designated for this purpose, the others being Carnaby and Woodbridge. In April 1946, it was designated a civil customs aerodrome. RAF Transport Command arrived in September 1946 with Dakotas, Yorks, and Lancastrians and stayed until December 1947. An overseas ferry unit was based here from May 1948 to July 1950. The USAF then took over and operated F-84s, SA-16s, B-29s, F-86s, B-54s, and T-33s until May 1958 when it was placed on C&M. The RAF disposed of the airfield in 1999. Civil operations recommenced in April 1959 and various charter companies and airlines came and went until, as Kent International Airport, it closed in May 2014.

British Airways DHC Dash 8 G-BRYY parked on the apron in front of the control tower and terminal building at Manchester Airport in August 1999. (*Barry Abraham*)

Manywells Height (Cullingworth), Yorks

This RFC day and third-class night LG was used for home defence from April 1916 to June 1919. Types operated included Be2s and RE8s.

Mapperley, Derbys

This unlicensed microlight site at Park Hall Farm opened in around 2001 with around twenty residents that fly from a single grass strip.

Marchington, Staffs

This gliding site was operated by the Marchington GC from 1980 until it moved to Tatenhill in 1999.

Marden (Staplehurst), Kent

This RFC second-class night LG was used for home defence from October 1916 to October 1919. Types operated included Be2s, Be12s, SE5s, and Camels. It saw limited use as a diversion airfield for airliners in the early 1930s but closed in June 1935. The Second World War ALG at Staplehurst was about 3 miles to the east.

Margam, Glamorgan

This unlicensed grass airfield at Old Park Farm opened in around 2005 with two runways and is home to over twenty aircraft, mostly microlights.

Margate (Chapel Hill), Kent

This civil aerodrome was operated by the Cornwall Aviation Company, which was used for joy-riding between July and August from 1926 to 1931.

Marham, Norfolk

This RFC home defence flight station opened in September 1916 and was home to Fe2s, Be2s, Be12s, DH6s, and Camels until flying ceased in May 1919. Following expansion, it became a RAF heavy bomber station in May 1937 with Hendons, followed by Wellingtons, Stirlings, Halifaxes, Mosquitoes, and Blenheims. These stayed until April 1944 when the airfield closed for runway improvements. The first unit to return in September 1945 was the Central Bomber Establishment, which operated Lancasters, Lincolns, Mosquitoes and Meteors until April 1949. Before this, in June 1947, the USAF arrived with B-29s followed by B-50s and stayed until February 1951. The RAF then took over and operated a variety of aircraft belonging to numerous units based here, including Washingtons, Canberras, Lincolns, Valiants, Victors, Lightnings, and Tornados. Bloodhound missiles were deployed between 1959 and 1964. F-35 Lightnings started to arrive in June 2018 to replace Tornados, which were retired in March 2019. It is also used by the Fenland GC. Marham remains one of the RAF's main bases in the UK.

Market Deeping, Lincs

This RFC second-class night LG was used for home defence from March 1917 to June 1919. Types based here included Fe2s and Avro 504s.

Market Harborough, Leics

This RAF training station opened in August 1943 and was home to Wellingtons, Defiants, Lysanders, Hurricanes, and Tomahawks until June 1945. Flying then ceased, but in February 1946, it reopened as a sub storage depot that dismantled Horsas and stored Monitors and Queen Martinets until October 1949.

Market Lavington, Wilts

This RAF LG opened in 1918 and closed in June 1919.

Market Rasen, Lincs

This landing strip inside the racecourse was in use from before 1974 to 1990.

Marlborough (High Trees), Wilts

This AALG opened in 1935 and was in use until the outbreak of the Second World War. The CFS made use of the airfield as a FLG from January 1936 to 1942. It may have been open until 1950.

Marsham, Norfolk

This RFC RLG was used for home defence between 1915 and October 1916. Types operated included Be2s and FB5s.

Marshfield, Wilts

This unlicensed airfield at Garston Farm with a single grass runway opened in 1984 and is home to about twenty aircraft.

Marshland (Wisbech), Cambs

This unlicensed airfield with a single grass runway opened before 1982.

Marske, Yorks

This aerodrome was first used by a flying school in July 1910. The RFC arrived in November 1917 and used it for training until October 1919. A variety of types were based here, including DH4s, DH9s, F2bs, Dolphins and Camels.

Marston Moor (Tockwith), Yorks

This RAF bomber training station opened in December 1941 with Halifaxes, which were later joined by Stirlings. Some Hurricanes, Spitfires, and Oxfords were also operated here. Flying ceased in November 1945, but private flying returned in 1991 from part of the wartime runways.

Martlesham Heath, Suffolk

This RFC third-class night LG (later a second-class and first-class night LG) opened for home defence in April 1916 and was in use as such until 1919. In January 1917, it also became an experimental station that operated numerous types of aircraft. This evolved into the A&AEE in March 1924 and stayed until the outbreak of the Second World War. The first operational RAF unit arrived in August 1936 with Demons and was followed by many more operating Blenheims, Hurricanes, Defiants, Spitfires, Typhoons, and Mustangs. The USAAF arrived in October 1943 with P-47s and P-51s that stayed until November 1945. After the war, various RAF units were based here, including a SAR flight and the Battle of Britain Memorial Flight, using a wide variety of weird and wonderful aircraft. Flying eventually ceased in May 1966.

Marwell Hall, Hants

This aerodrome was opened in September 1941 by Cunliffe-Owen Aircraft Ltd to test-fly aircraft constructed or modified at their factory at Eastleigh. Types handled included Spitfires, Blenheims, Bostons, Hudsons, Airacobras, Halifaxes, Venturas, Liberators, and Seafires until flying ceased in 1944.

Matching, Essex

This USAAF station opened in January 1944 with B-26s that were resident here until October 1944. The RAF then took over, and the operational refresher training unit moved in with Stirlings, Halifaxes, Horsas, Spitfires, and Oxfords until October 1945 when flying ceased. Around the same time, Martinets of a target towing flight were based for a short period.

Matlaske, Norfolk

This RAF station opened as a satellite for Coltishall in October 1940. Various units were based here, operating Spitfires, Whirlwinds, Walruses, Lysanders, and Typhoons until flying ceased in September 1945.

Mattishall, Norfolk

This RFC home defence flight station was in use from April 1916 to May 1919 with mostly Be2s, Fe2s, and Be12s.

Visiting Piper PA28 G-BCGI and Grumman American AA-5 G-PURR at Marshland on 21 August 2012. The airfield has a good 800-m grass runway but is probably home to only one aircraft. (*Grant Peerless*)

Maxstoke, Warks

This RLG for RAF Castle Bromwich and RAF Elmdon operated from September 1939 to February 1946. Types operated included Tiger Moths, Magisters, Ansons, and Oxfords. It may also have been used as a decoy site from late 1940 to late 1944.

Maydown, NI

This RAF station was intended as a SLG but opened instead as a satellite for Eglinton in August 1942. However, its first residents were Spitfires and P-38s of the USAAF that stayed only until the following December. It was taken over by the FAA in May 1943 as HMS *Shrike*, later HMS *Gannet 2* until the Navy departed in February 1947. Various types were based here, including Swordfish, Barracudas, Avengers, Wildcats, and Seafires. The airfield closed in January 1949.

Maylands

See Romford.

Maypole (Chislet), Kent

This unlicensed airfield opened in the mid-1970s with a single grass runway and is home to around twenty aircraft.

Meir

See Stoke-on-Trent.

Melbourne, Humberside

This RAF station opened in late 1940 as a RLG for Leeming and was used mainly by Whitleys. Halifaxes arrived in August 1942 but only stayed until the following January. They were replaced from January 1945 with several Oxford and Dakota training flights until flying ceased in July 1946. Part of the wartime airfield reopened for private flying before 1982 and is now used mainly by microlights from a site known as Melrose Farm. About a dozen aircraft are based here, using a single hard runway.

Melksham, Wilts

This AALG was in use in the 1930s. An unlicensed airfield with a single grass runway opened in the 1980s at nearby Craysmarsh Farm and is home to around a dozen light aircraft.

Melton Mowbray, Leics

This RAF station opened in September 1943, which was home to an overseas aircraft preparation unit, ferry training unit, and an OTU. Between them they operated Spitfires, Mosquitoes, Corsairs, Hellcats, Beauforts, Beaufighters, Bostons, Oxfords, Dakotas, Halifaxes, Horsas, Hadrians, and Stirlings. Flying ceased in October 1945, and the base was then placed on C&M. It was reactivated in December 1959 for a deployment of Thor missiles that stayed until August 1963 when it finally closed.

Membury, Berks
This aerodrome was originally intended as a RAF bomber OTU but was occupied instead by the USAAF. They arrived in September 1942 and operated B-17s, P-38s, Spitfires, P-51s, C-47s, CG-4s, and P-47s until February 1945. RAF Transport Command Dakotas were based here from July 1945 to October 1946 when flying ceased. Part of the wartime airfield reopened for civil flying by Campbell Aircraft Ltd in the mid-1960s, and today, twenty-five or so aircraft are based here, some belonging to Membury Flying School. Two hard and three grass runways are in use, all unlicensed.

Mendlesham, Suffolk
This RAF station opened at the end of 1943, with the first aircraft to arrive being Spitfires in February 1944. They only stayed for a couple of months when their place was taken by B-24s of the USAAF, which were followed by B-17s. They remained until flying ceased in July 1945. A few light aircraft operate from part of the wartime runways.

Menthorpe Gate (North Duffield) Yorks
This RFC second-class day and third-class night LG was used for home defence between January 1917 and May 1919, mainly by Avro 504s. Breighton airfield is about 1.5 miles to the east.

Mepal, Cambs
This RAF bomber station opened in April 1943 and was home to Stirlings and Lancasters until July 1946 when flying ceased. Thor missiles were deployed here between July 1959 and July 1963.

Meppershall, Beds
This private airfield at Standalone Farm with a single grass runway opened in 1984. It is normally only open to aircraft requiring maintenance, but a few are based here.

Meriden, W. Midlands
This RFC day and second-class night LG was used for home defence from April 1916 to August 1918.

Merrow (Burwood Farm), Surrey
This RLG for Fairoaks was in use from September 1939 to May 1947. Tiger Moths and Ansons were the main types operated here.

Merryfield (Isle Abbots), Somerset
This RAF station opened in February 1944 as a satellite for Westonzoyland, but its first residents were C-47s, C-53s, and CG-4s of the USAAF. They stayed until September 1944, and their place was taken by RAF Transport Command with Dakotas, Halifaxes, and Yorks. These departed in May 1946 when it was placed on C&M. In 1949, Westlands began using the airfield for flight-testing Wyverns; this activity continued throughout the 1950s with other types, particularly Sabres and Meteors rebuilt at Yeovilton. In November 1951, Vampires and Meteors arrived for various training units. These were replaced in April 1955 by Canberras of Bomber Command, but their stay was short, leaving in October 1956. The station then transferred to the FAA and Sea Venoms were based here, mostly on 'shore leave' from aircraft carriers until October 1960. It then reverted to C&M until 1972 when it became a RLG for Yeovilton known as HMS *Heron 2*. No units are based here, but it is currently used mainly by helicopters on exercises and also gliders.

Merston, Sussex
This RAF station opened in May 1941 as a satellite for Tangmere and was home to mainly Spitfires and Typhoons until flying ceased in August 1944.

Metfield, Suffolk
This USAAF station opened in August 1943 with P-47s followed by B-24s until August 1944. After this, various transport aircraft (including C-47s and C-54s) occupied the airfield until closure in late 1945.

Metheringham, Lincs
This RAF bomber station was home to Lancasters between November 1943 and February 1946.

Methven, Tayside
This SLG opened in April 1941 and was used to store Ansons, Wellingtons, Stirlings, Beauforts, Defiants, Hurricanes, and Hudsons (Cunliffe-Owen had a facility on site to maintain these) until September 1944. It was also used by an AOP flight of Austers from March to July 1943.

Methwold, Suffolk
This RFC night LG was used for home defence for a short period from April to October 1916. Following expansion, it reopened for the RAF as a satellite to Feltwell in September 1939 and became home to Wellingtons, Venturas, Stirlings, and Lancasters until April 1946. The station was then placed on C&M until

the following December when it was used as a RLG for Feltwell by Harvards, Prentices, and Tiger Moths until February 1954 when flying ceased.

Michaelchurch, Herefs

This civil aerodrome was in use between 1930 and 1939.

Middle Farm (Mixbury), Oxon

This SLG opened in February 1941 and was used to store Hampdens, Halifaxes, Spitfires, Gladiators, Tomahawks, and Wellingtons until closure in January 1946. It was also used during 1942 as a RLG for RAF Kidlington and Croughton by Masters, Hotspurs, and Hectors.

Middle Wallop, Hants

This RAF fighter station opened in April 1940, but the first resident was a training unit operating Harvards and Oxfords until the following June. Hurricanes, Spitfires, Blenheims, Beaufighters, Mustangs, and Mosquitoes then started to arrive. For a brief period between December 1943 and July 1944, the USAAF were present with Spitfires, P-51s, and F-6s. In November 1945, the station was transferred to the navy as HMS *Flycatcher* and many naval types were based here. This phase only lasted until April 1946 when Spitfires returned. A Fighter Command control and reporting school was set up in December 1945 with Spitfires, Oxfords, and Balliols, and they stayed until September 1957. Another change of role occurred in January 1948 when the army set up an AOP school equipped mainly with Austers. This led to Middle Wallop becoming the army air corps centre in September 1957, and this establishment continues to this day but mainly with helicopters. Types operated by the army over the years include Hoverflies, Chipmunks, Sycamores, Whirlwinds, Skeeters, Sioux, Beavers, Scouts, Tutors, and Islanders. Gazelles, Bell 212s, Wildcats, and Apaches are the current residents. For the whole of its seventy-eight-year life, the airfield has remained grass-surfaced and is reputed to have one of the largest areas of mown grass in Europe. Today, Middle Wallop is also home to the Museum of Army Flying, which opened in July 1984.

Middleton, Northants

This gliding site was used by the Welland GC from 1981 to 1989.

Middleton, Yorks

This RFC second- and third-class night LG was used for home defence from April 1916 to the summer of 1918.

Middleton Sands, Lancs

The beach here was used for pleasure flying by Kendal and Westmoreland Aero Club and Loxhams Flying Services from about 1935 to 1961. Microlights started flying from the beach in 2002.

Middleton St George (Teesside Airport), Cleveland

This RAF bomber station opened in April 1941 with Whitleys, which were followed by Halifaxes, Wellingtons, and Lancasters until June 1945. They were replaced by an OTU that operated Mosquitoes, Spitfires, Ansons, and Dominies until April 1947. An ANS then arrived equipped with Wellingtons, Ansons, and Oxfords, which departed in May 1950. Training then took over with Meteors, Vampires, and Oxfords until June 1956. In February 1957, the base transferred to Fighter Command and Javelins, Hunters, Meteors, and Lightnings were operated until the RAF departed in April 1964, although an AEF and UAS flew Chipmunks and Bulldogs from December 1985 to January 1988. After major redevelopment, Teesside Airport was opened officially on 1 November 1966, although scheduled services had commenced in October 1964. It was known as Durham Tees Valley Airport from 2004 but reverted to Teesside International Airport in 2019.

Midhurst (Cowdray Park), Sussex

This AALG situated on a polo field was in use during the 1930s. It was commissioned by the Admiralty in June 1941 and used for storing naval aircraft until closure in September 1945.

Midhurst (Wispers), Sussex

This AALG was owned by the Duchess of Bedford and was also used as an ELG during the 1930s.

Mildenhall (Beck Row), Suffolk

This RAF station opened in October 1934 and was home to many types of aircraft from various units, including Heyfords, Wellingtons, Harts, Gauntlets, Gladiators, Stirlings, Battles, Oxfords, Lancasters, and Lincolns until March 1950. In the following July, the USAF took over and they remain to this day. They have operated a variety of aircraft over the years, including B-29s, B-50s, KC-97s, C-47s, C-119s, C-117s, C-131s, and SR-71s. The main residents today are C-130s, KC-135s, and CV-22s, but the airfield is due to close by 2027.

Control tower at the Army Air Corps base at Middle Wallop on 6 July 2013 on the occasion of a model aircraft rally. (*Grant Peerless*)

Middleton St George after the RAF vacated the airfield in 1964 and before it became Teesside Airport in 1966. It was later renamed Durham Tees Valley Airport. (*Aerofilms*)

Milfield (Wooler), Northumberland

A RFC first-class night LG, known as Woodbridge, opened in February 1917 and was used for home defence with Be2s and RE8s. A site just to the west opened as a RAF station in August 1942 and was home to two OTUs operating Hurricanes, Masters, Typhoons, and Tempests until February 1946. A fighter leaders school arrived in January 1944, equipped with Spitfires, Hurricanes, Typhoons, Masters, and Oxfords and stayed until December 1944. Flying ceased in 1946, but it reopened for gliding in 1969 by the Borders GC and is now known as Galewood Farm.

Millom, Cumbria

This RAF station opened in January 1941 and was home to several training units operating Bothas, Ansons, Battles, Oxfords, Henleys, Defiants, Hurricanes, and Mosquitoes until flying ceased in January 1945.

Milltown, Grampian

This decoy site for Lossiemouth was converted into a RAF station and opened in June 1943. It was occupied by an OTU equipped with Wellingtons and Ansons until June 1945 and by Coastal Command Liberators, Wellingtons and Halifaxes from September 1944 to May 1946. It was then transferred to the FAA as HMS *Fulmar 2*, but no units appear to have been based here. It was eventually returned to the RAF in September 1972 and saw use by Harriers and Hercules on tactical exercises. An ACGS was based here from June 1973 to March 1977 when flying ceased.

Milson (Cleobury Mortimer/ Kidderminster), Salop

This unlicensed airfield opened before 1974 with a single grass runway and is home to around ten aircraft.

Minchinhampton

See Aston Down.

Molesworth, Cambs

This RAF bomber station opened in November 1941 with the arrival of Wellingtons, but their stay was brief, departing in January 1942. The USAAF took over in the following June and operated A-20s, P-38s, and B-17s until June 1945. The RAF then resumed control and various fighters were based here until October 1946, including Spitfires, Mustangs, Tempests, and Meteors. It was then placed on C&M until February 1954 when the USAF returned, this time with B-29s, C-119s, C-54s, and SA-16s. The Americans departed in December 1957 and flying then ceased. It was reactivated in December 1986 for the deployment of Tomahawk cruise missiles, which were airlifted in to nearby Alconbury and stayed until January 1989.

Mona, Gwynedd

This RAF station opened in April 1942 and was home to various training units operating Bothas, Battles, Ansons, Martinets, and Magisters until 1944. It was placed on C&M after the war and in July 1951 became a RLG for Valley. It was used by Vampires, Meteors, Gnats, and Hawks; this use continues today by the latter type. The airfield is also used by light aircraft and over twenty are based here.

Monewden (Ipswich), Suffolk

This unlicensed airfield at Cherry Tree Farm opened in 1971 with one grass runway and has about a dozen resident aircraft.

Montford Bridge, Salop

This RAF station opened in April 1942 as a satellite for Rednal and was home to various training units operating Spitfires, Mustangs, Masters, Hurricanes, and Oxfords. Flying ceased in June 1945, but a MU broke up Masters and Hotspurs until the following December. Some civil flying took place in the 1980s, possibly into the 1990s.

Montrose (Broomfield), Grampian

This RFC aerodrome opened in February 1913 and was used initially for reconnaissance and then for training, becoming a TDS in July 1918. Types operated included Be2s, Shorthorns, Longhorns, Avro 504s, RE8s, SE5s, DH4s, and Camels until closure in May 1919. Following expansion, it reopened for the RAF in January 1936 and was home to an FTS operating Harts, Audaxes, Oxfords, and Masters until March 1942. Coastal Command arrived in August 1938 and used Ansons and Hudsons for a year before Spitfires came on the scene in January 1940. These were followed by Blenheims and Hurricanes, which stayed until March 1942. A flying instructors school was then set up, operating Oxfords, Magisters, Harvards, and Tiger Moths until July 1945, while a flight of AAC Lysanders and Martinets was based here between May 1943 and August 1944. Flying ceased in July 1945, but it saw some use by light aircraft post-war to at least 1993 as well as being used by RAF Hercules for tactical exercises during 1978.

Visiting Yak 52 G-BVVW parked on the grass by the control hut and windsock at the grass airfield at Monewden on 28 August 2018. (*Grant Peerless*)

Moorby (Horncastle), Lincs

This RFC first-class night LG was used for home defence from October 1916 to June 1919.

Moor Side (Kirkby Moor), Cumbria

This gliding site was used by the Furness GC from October 1930 to 1939.

Moreton-in-Marsh, Glos

This RAF station opened in November 1940 as a satellite for Edge Hill and was home to a couple of OTUs operating Hurricanes, Wellingtons, Ansons, Lysanders, Martinets, and Defiants until November 1946. A ferry training unit used Wellingtons, Ansons, and Oxfords from May 1942 to May 1944, and an AFU flew Oxfords and Harvards between December 1946 and January 1948. It was then placed on C&M but was reactivated for training in October 1949 with Harvards and Prentices until April 1955 when flying ceased.

Moreton Valence, Glos

This RAF station opened in September 1939 as a satellite for Staverton and was used mainly as a RLG by various training units operating Ansons, Dominies, and Oxfords. This continued until December 1945 when the RAF departed, although an ACGS carried on to October 1946. In October 1943, the MAP set up a factory on the site for Glosters, where they built and test-flew Meteors and Javelins. The factory closed in July 1962 and flying then ceased.

Morpeth (Stannington) Northumberland

This RAF station opened in March 1942 and was home initially to a gunnery school equipped mainly with Bothas, but also Lysanders, Ansons, and Martinets until December 1944. An AACU with Henleys and Martinets was based here briefly from April to June 1943, and an OTU arrived in April 1945 with Spitfires, Masters, Martinets, and Dominies. This unit departed in July 1945 and flying then ceased, although a MU took over until the airfield closed in July 1948.

Morridge (Leek) Staffs

This gliding site was used by the Staffordshire GC from 1972 to 1992.

Moulton (Northampton), Northants

This RFC second-class night and day LG was used for home defence from December 1916 to February 1918.

Mount Farm, Oxon

This RAF station opened in August 1940 as a satellite for Benson and was used by Battles, Wellingtons, and Ansons of an OTU until February 1942. From December 1940 to May 1943, it was used as a dispersal site for PRU Spitfires, Blenheims, and Venturas from Benson. The USAAF arrived in February 1943 with a PRU operating L-4s, F-5s, P-38s, Spitfires, and P-51s until departing in March 1945. The RAF then returned with an OTU that operated Mosquitoes and Spitfires until flying ceased in October 1946.

Mountnessing, Essex

This RFC third-class night LG was used for home defence from April to December 1916.

Movenis, NI

This unlicensed airfield at McMasters Farm opened before 2000 with one hard runway and is used mainly for parachuting. Visiting light aircraft are welcome and a few are based here.

Mullaghmore, NI

This RAF station opened in October 1942 as a satellite for Limavady and was used initially by an OTU operating Wellingtons and Ansons until January 1944. The USAAF then arrived and it became a reserve airfield as well as a storage facility. B-26s were among the types handled until the Americans departed in May 1944. The FAA took up residence for a brief period from November 1944 to March 1945 and operated Swordfish, Barracudas, Avengers, Wildcats, and Fireflies. The airfield closed in May 1945.

Mullion, Cornwall

This RNAS airship station opened in June 1916 with an associated LG used by a coastal patrol flight operating DH6s, DH9s, and 1½ Strutters from April 1917 to May 1919.

Murlough (Dundrum), NI

This SLG opened in March 1941, storing mostly Blenheims and Wellingtons until closure in February 1945.

Murton, Yorks

This RFC second-class LG was used for home defence from October 1917 to June 1919, mainly by Avro 504s.

Myreside (Edinburgh), Lothian

This RFC LG was in use for home defence during the First World War.

Nantwich (Worleston), Cheshire

This grass airfield at Dairyhouse Farm opened in the 1970s. The Cheshire Microlight Centre moved here in 2019 when their base at Arclid closed.

Narborough (Great Government Aerodrome), Norfolk

This RNAS night LG opened in August 1915 but was taken over by the RFC as a home defence first-class night LG from April 1916. It was also used for training and became a TDS in September 1918. Types based here included Fe2s, Camels, RE8s, FK8s, Avro 504s, Be2s, SE5s, and DH6s until flying ceased in November 1919. Marham airfield is just over half a mile to the west.

Nayland, Suffolk

This unlicensed airfield at Hill Farm opened in 1962 with two grass runways and has around a dozen resident aircraft.

Neatishead, Norfolk

A landing strip at the radar station here was used by Austers from Horsham St Faith during the 1950s and later by helicopters from Coltishall.

Needs Ore Point, Hants

This ALG was used by RAF Typhoons from April to July 1944.

Netheravon, Wilts

This RFC aerodrome opened in June 1913 and was used for training with FB5s, RE7s, Be12s, Pups, SE5s, Camels, Avro 504s, Fe2s, F2bs, and 0/400s. Training continued after the war with Tutors, Harts, Hectors, Hotspurs, Whitleys, Tiger Moths, and Masters. Flycatchers, Fairey 3Fs, and Nimrods were also used for naval training. During the Second World War, gliding and parachute training took place as well as army co-operation duties. Transport Command took over in January 1944 with Halifaxes, Stirlings, Yorks, Buckinghams, and Mosquitoes until only Dakotas were left in 1950. Austers and Ansons arrived in January 1952 and stayed until November 1958 when flying ceased. The station was taken over by the army in March 1965 and they operated mostly helicopters including Scouts, Sioux, Gazelles, and Lynxes as well as fixed-wing Beavers. The army still makes use of the airfield, and it is also open to private pilots who can use two unlicensed grass runways.

Netherthorpe, Yorks

This civil aerodrome was licensed in April 1935 and was home to the Sheffield Aero Club until the outbreak of the Second World War. It was used briefly by RAF Lysanders between June and September 1940 and an ACGS from September 1943 to May 1946. It reopened for civil use in 1951 and is now a thriving GA airfield with around fifty resident aircraft operating from two licensed short grass runways. It is still operated by the Sheffield Aero Club.

New Haggerston (Berwick), Northumberland

This RFC home defence station opened in October 1916, later becoming a first- and second-class night LG. Be2s and Be12s were the main types operated here until April 1917. A coastal patrol flight was based here from May 1918, which operated DH6s until flying ceased in June 1919.

New Holland, Humberside

This RFC second-class night LG was used for home defence from October 1916 to August 1919. It may have still been in use during the 1930s.

New Romney (Littlestone), Kent

This RFC aerodrome opened in August 1917 and was home to a gunnery school equipped with DH4s, DH9s, F2bs, RE8s, Avro 504s, Pups, and 0/400s until November 1919. From 1927, it was used as an ELG for airliners using Croydon until the mid-1930s and then as a private LG up to the outbreak of the Second World War. An ALG known as Honeychild opened some 2 miles to the west in July 1943 and was used by RAF Typhoons until October 1943. After this, it became a reserve ALG until closure in November 1944.

New York, Lincs

This unlicensed airfield at Whaley Farm opened in around 1994 with two grass runways and has around six residents.

New Zealand Farm (Lavington) Wilts

This RAF station opened in October 1940 and was used as a RLG for Upavon by Oxfords and Masters until December 1943. The USAAF arrived in March 1944 with L-4s and L-5s and stayed until the following September. After the war, it was used as an outstation for Boscombe Down for weapons trials and also by the army as a LG.

Newbridge, Cornwall

This unlicensed airfield with two grass strips at Lower Botrea Farm has been in use from the 1990s.

Newbury, Berks

This landing strip inside the racecourse was in use from around 1950 to 2005.

Newcastle (Cramlington), Tyne and Wear

This RFC home defence station opened in December 1915 and was home to Be2s and Be12s. Its role changed to training in October 1916 and it became a TDS in July 1918 until flying ceased in October 1919. Types based here included DH4s, DH6s, DH9s, Avro 504s, FK3s, and RE8s. It reopened for civil use in 1924 and limited scheduled services operated from here during

A busy scene at Netherthorpe on a sunny Sunday in October 2001. It features Vans RV6 G-RVIN and Jodel DR1050 G-BXYJ. (*Grant Peerless*)

1934. The Newcastle Aero Club was based here from 1925 to 1935, and the aerodrome closed in April 1936.

Newcastle (Dukes Moor), Tyne and Wear

This LG was used by Armstrong Whitworth to test-fly aircraft built on the site, mostly Be2s, from 1913 to June 1916 when they moved to Town Moor. The RNAS moved in during November 1914 and used a few TB8s for home defence until departing in March 1915.

Newcastle (Gosforth/Town Moor), Tyne and Wear

This aerodrome was used by Armstrong Whitworth from June 1916 to build and test-fly FK8s and F2bs. In August 1917, an AAP was formed that handled FK8s, F2bs, and Cuckoos built by AW as well as other types until July 1919. It reopened for civil use in late 1919 but was only used sporadically during the 1920s.

Newcastle (Woolsington), Tyne and Wear

Officially opened as Newcastle's municipal airport on 26 July 1935, scheduled services commenced soon afterwards and continued until the outbreak of the Second World War. An elementary flying school arrived in June 1939 with Hinds, Audaxes, Tiger Moths, and Magisters and stayed until September 1939. It then became a RAF station and was used by various units during the war. A MU arrived in July 1940 and salvaged crashed aircraft while an ASR flight was based here from June to December 1943 with Ansons and Walruses. It was used as a RLG for an OTU based at Ouston from November 1943 to June 1945, Hurricanes, Oxfords, Ansons, and Wellingtons being the main types operated here. A UAS equipped with Tiger Moths operated here from January 1941 to September 1946 and an ACGS was based here until June 1948. It returned to civil use after the war, and scheduled services recommenced in 1948. Today, Newcastle is a busy international airport.

Newchapel (East Grinstead), Surrey

This RFC second-class night LG was used for home defence from October 1916 to August 1919.

Newchurch, Kent

This ALG was used by RAF Spitfires, Hurricanes, Typhoons, and Tempests from July 1943 to September 1944.

Newmarket Heath, Suffolk

A RFC first-class night LG opened on the racecourse in April 1916 and was used initially for home defence. From November 1917, it was used for training with Fe2s, DH6s, Avro 504s, Pups, and Be2s until flying ceased in May 1919. It reopened for civil use in October 1934 by the Jockey Club and was available for use between April and November. It was also an AALG. A number of licenses were issued for scheduled services, but it is not clear if any were actually flown. All civil flying ceased on the outbreak of the Second World War when the airfield was taken over by the RAF. They used it for various activities with many types of aircraft including Wellingtons, Lysanders, Whitleys, Stirlings, Defiants, Martinets, Spitfires, Lancasters, Halifaxes, Mosquitoes, and Blenheims. The RAF departed in February 1945, and it reopened to civil flying in 1946 from an unlicensed grass strip on the racecourse known as Rowley Mile. It is still in use today but on race days only, together with another strip just to the south-west known as the July Strip.

Newquay

See St Mawgan.

Newton, Notts

This RAF station opened in 1936 but it did not become operational until July 1940, initially as a bomber base with Battles and Wellingtons. Its role changed to training in July 1941; this continued until flying ceased in November 2000. Types operated over the years included Oxfords, Masters, Tiger Moths, Magisters, Ansons, Harvards, Chipmunks, and Bulldogs. It became an important gliding centre in 1947 and continued as such until closure. It remained grass-surfaced throughout its life.

Newton Mearns (Windhill), Strathclyde

This civil aerodrome was used by a flying club between 1934 and 1936.

Newton Peveril (Sturminster Marshall), Dorset

This unlicensed airfield opened in the 1960s and is home to fifteen or so light aircraft operating from a single grass runway.

Newtownards (Ards), NI

Ards Airport opened on 31 August 1934, although scheduled services had commenced a few days earlier.

These lasted until March 1938 when they transferred to the new airport at Sydenham. Club and private flying continued until the outbreak of the Second World War. It was taken over by the RAF in November 1939 and was used by a variety of units, including army co-operation, target towing, and communications. An assortment of types was operated including Tiger Moths, Lysanders, Henleys, Masters, Defiants, and Oxfords. The RAF departed in March 1944, but an ACGS continued flying until 1953. Civil flying resumed after the war, and Silver City Airways operated a car ferry service to Stranraer from 1955 to 1957. F. G. Miles set up a factory on the site after the war, producing Geminis and Messengers until closure in 1948. A VGS arrived in November 1995 but departed with its Vigilants in 2016. Today, Newtownards is a busy GA airfield with three licensed hard runways and over eighty residents.

North Benfleet (Sadlers Farm), Essex

This RFC second-class night LG was used for home defence from April 1916 to March 1919.

North Coates, Lincs

A RFC third-class night LG, known as North Coates Fitties, was used for home defence from 1916. A coastal patrol flight was based here from September 1918 to March 1919, employing mostly DH6s. A site about half a mile to the west opened in January 1932 for armament training; this use continued until 1939. Types operated included Harts, Fairey 3Fs, Gordons, Wallaces, Audaxes, and Battles. It then became an operational station mostly in the coastal patrol role equipped with Blenheims, Hurricanes, Beaufighters, Swordfish, and Hudsons until flying ceased in June 1945. A flight of SAR Sycamore helicopters was based here between February 1954 and October 1957. Bloodhound missiles were deployed at various times from December 1958 to June 1990. Part of the wartime airfield reopened for civil use in 1995 and is now home to around twenty light aircraft that use a single unlicensed grass runway.

North Creake, Norfolk

This RAF bomber station opened in November 1943 and was home to Stirlings and Halifaxes until July 1945. It was then placed on C&M until October 1945 when it was used for storing Mosquitoes. This use ceased in September 1947 and the airfield then closed.

North Duffield, Yorks

This private grass airfield at Birchwood Lodge is home to around ten light aircraft.

North Elham (Dereham), Norfolk

This RFC third-class night LG was used for home defence in February and March 1917.

North Hill (Honiton), Devon

This gliding site opened in 1966 and is home to the Devon and Somerset GC. Over fifty gliders are based here.

North Killingholme, Lincs

This RAF bomber station opened in November 1943 and was home to mostly Lancasters until October 1945 when flying ceased. Killingholme First World War aerodrome was about 2 miles to the north-east.

North Luffenham, Leics

This RAF station opened in December 1940, its first residents being an FTS equipped with Tiger Moths, Magisters, and Ansons. It transferred to Bomber Command in July 1941 and received Hampdens, Manchesters, and Lancasters that stayed until April 1942. An OTU then took over with Wellingtons, Ansons, Lysanders, and Defiants until March 1944. Next on the scene was an HGCU with Whitleys, Albermarles, Horsas, Dakotas, and Halifaxes that were resident until December 1947. Stirlings, Lancasters, and Mosquitoes of a HCU were based here from November 1944 to October 1946. In December 1947, a transport OCU was formed with Ansons, Dakotas, Valettas, and Devons; this was resident here until March 1951. The Royal Canadian Air Force arrived in November 1951 with Sabres; these stayed until April 1955. The station was then handed back to the RAF who used it for all-weather training with Meteors, Brigands, Balliols, and Mosquitoes until March 1958. Hunters were briefly based between February and June 1958 and the base was then placed on C&M. It was reactivated in December 1959 for a deployment of Thor missiles that stayed until August 1963 when flying ceased, although Chipmunks of an AEF used the airfield in the early 1970s.

North Moor (Messingham), Lincs

This unlicensed airfield at Low Hill Farm opened before 2002 with a single grass runway and is home to over twenty aircraft, mostly microlights. Another private strip in the vicinity at Sandcroft Farm has around six residents.

North Ockendon, Essex

This RFC home defence night LG was in use from April to October 1916.

North Pickenham, Norfolk

This USAAF station opened in January 1944 and was home to mainly B-24s, C-47s, and Mosquitoes. The Americans departed in July 1945 and the station was placed on C&M until 1958. Thor missiles were deployed in July 1959, which were resident here until July 1963. Between October 1964 and February 1965, the airfield was used as a RLG by Kestrels from West Raynham. Flying then ceased.

North Ronaldsay, Orkney

This civil aerodrome was opened in August 1934 by Highland Airways who operated scheduled services until the outbreak of the Second World War. It was used as an ELG by the RAF from 1939 to 1945. It then returned to civil use, and today, it has two hard and one grass runways, all licensed. It is currently served by scheduled services.

North Shotwick

See Sealand.

North Thoresby (Grimsby), Humberside

This private grass airfield at Eastfield House was in use from the 1970s to 1990s.

North Uist (Sollas), Hebrides

This civil aerodrome opened in February 1936 with scheduled services that continued until the outbreak of the Second World War. Some essential civilian operations continued during the war, including use as an ELG. Currently, an unlicensed runway is situated on the beach and is available to visiting aircraft as well as air ambulance flights.

North Weald, Essex

This RFC home defence flight station known as North Weald Bassett opened in April 1916 and was used by several units operating Be2s, Be12s, Camels, and F2bs until December 1919 when flying ceased. It became a RAF fighter station in September 1927 and was used by Siskins, Bulldogs, Demons, Gauntlets, Gladiators, and Hurricanes up to the outbreak of the Second World War. It remained a fighter base during the war when Hurricanes and Spitfires were the main types operated, along with Blenheims and Mustangs. It transferred briefly to Transport Command in July 1945, who used a few Warwicks but returned to fighters in March 1949 in the shape of Spitfires, Vampires, Meteors, and latterly Hunters until February 1958. Communication and reserve flights were based in the post-war years until the RAF departed in September 1964, although a VGS continued flying until February 1965. It was used by light aircraft and gliders during the 1960s, and in 1968, scenes for the *Battle of Britain* film were shot on the airfield. In August 1979, Epping Forest District Council purchased the airfield, and civil flying then gained momentum. Today, North Weald is a busy GA airfield with over 150 residents including warbirds and jets, which operate from one grass and two hard runways, all unlicensed.

North Witham, Lincs

This USAAF air depot opened in December 1943 and was home to C-47s and C-53s until April 1945. It was then placed on C&M and used by a MU until it closed in April 1956.

Northampton

See Sywell.

Northleach, Glos

This RLG for RAF Stoke Orchard was used mainly by Tiger Moths from September 1941 to November 1942 and then Masters, Hotspurs, and Horsas of a GTS until January 1945, when flying ceased.

Northolt, Gt. London

This RFC first-class LG opened in March 1915 and was used for home defence and training, latterly as a TDS, until April 1920. Types operated included Be2s, FB5s, Scouts, RE7s, Avro 504s, Shorthorns, Camels, SE5s, Spads, and Dolphins. After the First World War, it was jointly used by the RAF, who operated a communications flight, and civil companies, who used it for flying training and charter work. The RAF returned in force in April 1923 and used DH9s, Snipes, Siskins, Bulldogs, Fairey 3Fs, Tutors, and Harts until July 1934. It then became a fighter station and Demons, Bulldogs, Gauntlets, Harts, and Hurricanes were based here up to September 1939. This use continued throughout most of the war, Blenheims, Spitfires, Hurricanes, and Mosquitoes being the main occupants. In February 1946, it was designated the main airport for London and scheduled services commenced soon after, but they relocated to Heathrow by October 1954. In the post-war years, it was used by a variety of RAF units but mostly by communications flights using Ansons, Oxfords, Pembrokes, Bassetts, and Devons, as well as currently BAe125s and 146s. The USAF was present from May 1951 to 1975 with C-47s, C-54s, C-131s, and T-29s. Today, Northolt is still a joint RAF and civil airport and is well used by the Royal Squadron and many corporate jets.

Above left: Inside the control tower at North Weald on 26 October 2014, showing a view over the airfield. (*Tony Yarnold*)

Above right: Northolt in the 1950s. It was the main airport for London from 1946 until 1954 when Heathrow took over. It is still used jointly by the RAF and civilian traffic. (*Aerofilms*)

External view of the substantial control tower at North Weald on 25 September 2015. (*Grant Peerless*)

Northwick Park (Harrow) Gt. London
This small field was used by an ACGS from October 1942 to April 1946.

Norwich (Aylsham Road), Norfolk
This LG was used by Mann Egerton Ltd to test-fly Shorts 184s, 1½ Strutters, DH9s, and DH10s built by them on site from 1916 to 1919.

Norwich (Mousehold Heath), Norfolk
This RFC first-class LG opened in July 1915 and closed in July 1919. It was home to training and home defence units and from March 1917 by an AAP. Numerous types were based including Fe2s, Avro 504s, Be2s, DH9s, Camels, and SE5s. It was used by Boulton Paul from 1917 for test-flying its products and by the Norfolk and Norwich Aero Club from February 1927 until September 1939. It became Norwich Airport on 21 June 1933 and soon attracted scheduled services. The RAF returned in March 1937 with a storage unit and an elementary flying school in August 1939 equipped with Magisters, Audaxes, and Hinds. This was disbanded on the outbreak of the Second World War, and civil flying then ceased. A communications flight was based here between April 1939 and April 1940 and the aerodrome served as a dispersal site for Horsham St Faith for a short while before becoming disused.

Nottingham
See Tollerton.

Novar
See Evanton.

Nuneaton, Warks
This RAF station opened in February 1943 as a bomber training airfield and was used as a RLG for Bramcote until November 1945 when flying ceased. Types operated included Wellingtons, Ansons, Dakotas, Lancastrians, and Oxfords. It closed in September 1946.

Nuneaton (Attleborough Fields) Warks
This civil aerodrome was first used for flying in July 1912, but the official opening was not until August 1913. Its use during the First World War is doubtful. Limited scheduled services and pleasure flights were operated from 1919 until it closed in March 1921.

Nuthampstead, Herts
This RAF station opened in May 1943 but was used instead by the USAAF. They arrived in the following September and operated P-38s, followed by B-17s until June 1945. Flying then ceased, but it resumed before 1974 from an unlicensed grass strip alongside one of the wartime runways. A few light aircraft are based here.

Nutts Corner
See Belfast.

Nympsfield, Glos
This gliding site opened in 1956 and is operated by the Bristol and Gloucestershire GC. About seventy gliders are based here, and visiting powered aircraft are accepted.

Oakington, Cambs
This RAF bomber station opened in July 1940 and was home initially to Blenheims. These were followed by Stirlings, Lancasters, Wellingtons, and Mosquitoes until July 1945 when Transport Command took over. They operated Yorks, Dakotas, and Liberators until December 1950 when training became the main role and was to continue for nearly twenty-five years. Harvards were the first trainers to be used followed by Meteors, Vampires, Varsities, and Jetstreams until fixed-wing flying ceased in December 1974. The station was reactivated in January 1979 when the army arrived with Scouts and Siouxes, and later Gazelles and Lynxes, until final closure in January 1992.

Oakley, Bucks
This RLG for RAF Westcott was used mainly by Wellingtons and Martinets of an OTU from September 1942 to September 1945, when flying ceased. It was also used as a diversion airfield for bombers during the Second World War. Private flying takes place on the western part of the wartime airfield on Field Farm, and around a dozen aircraft are resident here, mostly microlights of the Bucks Microlight Club who have been based here since before 1986.

Oaksey Park, Wilts
This unlicensed airfield opened before 1992 with two grass runways and has over fifty resident aircraft.

Oatlands Hill, Wilts
This RAF station opened in June 1941 as a satellite for Old Sarum and was used by Tomahawks, Harvards, Mustangs, and Austers until flying ceased in April 1945.

Oban (Connel/North Connel), Strathclyde

This RAF station opened in 1943 and was home to Mustangs and Lysanders until February 1944. It was used as an ELG from August 1944 to December 1945 when flying ceased. It reopened for civil use in 1967, and scheduled services were operated until 1976. Around twenty-five light aircraft are based here, using a single licensed hard runway. It is also used by air ambulance flights and again supports scheduled services.

Odiham, Hants

This RAF station was used briefly during the summer of 1933 by Audaxes before opening officially in February 1937. It was home to AACUs until June 1945, operating Lysanders, Hectors, Blenheims, Tomahawks, Mustangs, Spitfires, Hurricanes, Mosquitoes, and Typhoons. A forward repair unit arrived in November 1943 and handled Halifaxes, Stirlings, Albermarles, Wellingtons, Mosquitoes, Spitfires, and Typhoons before departing in November 1944. A BAT flight of Oxfords was based briefly from September 1944 to September 1945. Transport Command came on the scene for a year from June 1945 with Dakotas and then the station passed to Fighter Command. They operated Tempests, Spitfires, Vampires, Meteors, Hunters, and Javelins until July 1959 when it was placed on C&M. It reopened in May 1960, again for Transport Command, but this time with helicopters including Sycamores, Whirlwinds, Belvederes, Wessexes, Pumas, and Lynxes. Pioneers and Twin Pioneers were also operated from here, and a communications flight equipped with Ansons, Devons, Pembrokes, Austers, and Chipmunks was based here from May 1960 to May 1972. Chinooks continue to operate today along with the Kestrel GC and a VGS equipped with Vikings was based here until 2016.

Okehampton (Folly Gate), Devon

This LG was first used in June 1929 in connection with artillery practice camps on Dartmoor. Types operated here included F2bs, Atlases, and Audaxes until they departed in September 1937. The RAF arrived in August 1940 with Lysanders and stayed there until 1942 when the airfield was taken over by a MU. This moved out in July 1945 and it then closed. AOP Austers made occasional use of the airfield after the war as did FAA helicopters.

Old Buckenham, Norfolk

This USAAF bomber station opened in December 1943 and was home to B-24s until flying ceased in May 1945. It reopened around 1990 for civil use and is now home to some thirty aircraft, operating from one hard runway and two grass strips, all licensed.

Old Heton (Cornhill), Northumberland

This RFC third-class night LG was used for home defence from January to August 1917.

Old Leake, Lincs

This private grass airfield at Tofthouse Farm was in use from the 1970s to 1990s.

Old Sarum, Wilts

This RFC training aerodrome, known as Ford Farm, opened in August 1917 and was home to Be2s, DH4s, DH6s, DH9s, Pups, RE8s, and Avro 504s until March 1920. Training continued by the army, who used Hectors, Atlases, Ansons, Blenheims, Lysanders, Harvards, Magisters, Tiger Moths, and Austers until December 1944. The School of Land/Air Warfare arrived in May 1947 and operated various aircraft until March 1963 while the helicopter development unit used Whirlwinds between June 1961 and April 1963. Flying ceased in September 1970, but a VGS continued until November 1978; it finally closed as a military base in 1979. It reopened for civil flying from a single licensed grass runway in 1982 but closed to private flying in October 2019. However, commercial operations such as skydiving and parachuting are due to continue.

Old Warden, Beds

This civil aerodrome was opened in 1932 by Richard Shuttleworth as a base for his collection of vintage aircraft. During the Second World War, a CRO was set up, specialising in Proctors, Harvards, and Magisters. The Shuttleworth Collection, opened to the public in 1963, is still going strong, and regular air displays are held here. The airfield is also open to visiting aircraft for which a licensed grass runway is available.

Old Weston (Thrapston), Cambs

This RFC home defence aerodrome was in use from October 1916 to September 1917. Types operated included Be2s and Be12s. Molesworth airfield is about 1 mile to the west.

Omagh (Gortin), NI

This LG was used by RAF F2bs from May 1918 to January 1919.

Orfordness, Suffolk
This RFC home defence night LG opened in April 1916 but was used mainly for experimental flying with various types until September 1939.

Oronsay, Hebrides
This private airfield opened in around 1950 and is used mainly by air ambulance flights.

Orsett (Thurrock), Essex
This RFC first-class night LG was used for home defence from July 1916 to May 1919.

Orston, Notts
This RAF station opened in July 1941 and was used mainly as a RLG for Newton. It was utilised by Battles, Oxfords, Masters, Harvards, and Ansons until November 1945 when flying ceased.

Orton (Peterborough), Cambs
This RFC second-class LG was used for home defence from December 1916 to November 1918.

Ossington, Notts
This RAF station opened in January 1942 and was home to various training units for most of its life. Oxfords, Harvards, Ansons, Wellingtons, Tomahawks, and Martinets were the first types to be operated here, followed by Lancasters and Yorks. These were operated jointly with BOAC from January 1945 to train aircrews for civil operations, which lasted until April 1946. Flying then ceased, and the airfield closed in August 1946.

Oswestry
See Knockin.

Otterburn Hall, Northumberland
This AALG was associated with the Otterburn Hall Hotel and in use between the end of 1932 and 1939. It continued to be used after the war but had closed by 2016.

Oulton, Norfolk
This RAF bomber station opened in August 1940 as a satellite for Horsham St Faith and was home initially to Blenheims. These were followed by Bostons, Hudsons, Beaufighters, Fortresses, and Liberators until June 1945, when flying ceased. The airfield became a MU in October 1945 and was used to store Mosquitoes until closure in October 1947.

Ouston, Northumberland
This RAF station opened in July 1940 and was home initially to a MU equipped with a few Blenheims and Hornet Moths until May 1941. Fighter Command then arrived and operated Hurricanes, Spitfires, Defiants, and Mustangs until October 1943. Two OTUs were next on the scene with Ansons, Wellingtons, Hurricanes, Spitfires, and Masters, which were resident here until March 1946. A FTS equipped with Harvards, Ansons, and Tiger Moths was then based until February 1948. Fighters returned in October 1951 in the shape of Vampires of a RAuxAF squadron; these stayed until March 1957. Communications flights operated here from January 1955 to September 1961 and a UAS/AEF from September 1946 to September 1974, firstly with Tiger Moths but graduating to Chipmunks, Balliols, Provosts, and Bulldogs. It was used as a RLG by Jet Provosts from Acklington from 1961 to 1968 and by a VGS until December 1974, when flying ceased.

Out Skerries (Bruray), Shetland
This unlicensed airfield opened in 1974 with a single grass runway. It is used by air ambulance flights and some scheduled services.

Overbury (Tewkesbury), Glos
This AALG on two adjacent fields was in use in the 1930s

Overley, Glos
This SLG was used to store Mustangs, Hampdens, and Stirlings from May 1941 to September 1944. It was also used as a RLG by Oxfords and Harvards from RAF South Cerney between June and October 1942.

Overton Heath, Wilts
This RLG for RAF Upavon opened in September 1940 and was used by mainly Oxfords until flying ceased in August 1945. Just to the east of the Second World War airfield is an unlicensed microlight site known as Clench Common, which opened before 1993 with around twenty-five residents. Two grass strips are in use.

Owthorne (Withernsea), Humberside
This RFC third-class night LG was used for home defence from December 1916. A coastal patrol flight was based here from June 1918 and flew mainly DH6s and DH9s until flying ceased in June 1919.

Oxenhope, Yorks

This unlicensed airfield at Hawksbridge Farm opened in the 1970s with two grass runways and has around eight resident aircraft.

Oxford (Kidlington), Oxon

This civil aerodrome opened in June 1938 for the Oxford Flying Club but closed on the outbreak of the Second World War. An elementary flying school arrived in June 1938 and used Hinds, Magisters, and Tiger Moths until September 1939. This was replaced by an FTS that operated mainly Harvards, Ansons, and Oxfords until February 1942, when a GTS took over with Hotspurs and various tugs. An AFU was based here with mostly Oxfords from March 1943 to June 1945, and a UAS flew Harvards, Oxfords, and Chipmunks between April 1949 and January 1959. It reopened for civil flying by the Oxford Flying Club in July 1946 and scheduled services were later operated. A hard runway was laid in 1970. Today, Kidlington is the busy Oxford Airport with over eighty residents including business jets that operate from two licensed hard runways.

Oxford (Stanton St John), Oxon

This AALG was in use from 1933 to 1939, but it saw little activity.

Paddock Wood (Old Hay), Kent

This unlicensed airfield opened in 1989 with two grass runways and has around six resident aircraft.

Padstow (Trevose Head), Cornwall

This LG was used by a RAF coastal patrol flight equipped with DH6s and DH9s from May 1918 to May 1919.

Page Bank, Co. Durham

This civil airfield was in use from after the Second World War to around 1978.

Palmers Farm (Shenfield), Essex

This RFC third-class night LG was used for home defence from September 1916 to June 1919. It was later used by an ACGS from May 1944.

Panshanger (Holwell Hyde), Herts

A decoy factory opened on land at Holwell Hyde in November 1940 to divert attention from the DH factory at Hatfield and was in use until September 1942. From the autumn of 1940, it began to be used as a RLG for Tiger Moths from an elementary flying school at Hatfield, and in June 1941, it moved in completely. It became a RFS in May 1947 and operated Tiger Moths and later Chipmunks and Ansons until March 1953.

Piper PA28s G-AVLT, ATPN, and AVFZ of the Oxford Air Training School in front of the company's premises at Oxford (Kidlington) in the late 1960s. (*Barry Abraham*)

An ACGS was based here from June 1943 to May 1948, and the aerodrome was renamed RAF Panshanger in September 1943.

It reopened for civil use in March 1946 by the London Aeroplane Club and was also used by a variety of other clubs, private owners, and crop-spraying companies. From 1960 to 1963, Airwork assembled and test-flew Cessna aircraft imported from the USA and also set up a sales organisation. T. D. Keegan was based here in the early 1960s and operated large types including DC4s and Vikings. The aerodrome closed temporarily in April 1992, reopened in June 1993, and closed finally in September 2014.

Papa Stour, Shetland
This unlicensed airfield opened in 1969 with one hard runway. It is used mainly by air ambulance flights.

Papa Westray, Orkney
This licensed airfield opened in 1967 with one hard runway and two grass strips. It is served by scheduled services, including the world's shortest commercial flight—to nearby Westray, which takes approximately two minutes.

Papplewick Moor (Nottingham), Notts
This RFC LG opened in April 1916 and was used for home defence with Be2s, Be12s, and Fe2s until May 1917. In April 1918, it became a RLG for Hucknall until closure in 1919, although some civil flying is reported to have taken place in the late 1920s. It reopened for the RAF in July 1941, again as a RLG for Hucknall and was used mainly by Tiger Moths and Ansons. It closed in November 1945.

Parham Park (Pulborough), Sussex
This private civil aerodrome was in use in the 1930s. It was used as an ELG for RAF Tangmere during July 1940 and by AOP Austers in 1944. It was reopened for the Southdown GC in 1974 and is now an active gliding site with over fifty aircraft being based here, including gliders and powered aircraft.

Park Royal, Gt. London
This rough field was used for limited flying by Claud Grahame-White between April 1910 and about 1912.

Peckleton
See Leicester.

Pembrey, Pembrokeshire
This RAF station opened in September 1939 and was home to an assortment of training and fighter units operating Wallaces, Harts, Ospreys, Spitfires, Hurricanes, Blenheims, Lysanders, Ansons, Wellingtons, and latterly jets such as Vampires, Meteors, and Hunters. It closed in September 1957 but reopened as a GA airfield in August 1997; it now has around six resident aircraft operating from a single licensed hard runway.

Pembroke
See Carew Cheriton.

Pengam Moors
See Cardiff.

Penkridge (Pillaton), Staffs
This RLG for Wolverhampton was used mainly by Tiger Moths between May 1942 and July 1945. It reopened for civil flying by the Staffordshire Aeroplane club in the 1980s known as Otherton, and three unlicensed grass strips are in use here, with around fifty resident aircraft, mostly microlights.

Penrhos, Gwynedd
This RAF station opened in February 1937 and was home to numerous training units operating Wallaces, Harrows, Henleys, Battles, Blenheims, Spitfires, Hurricanes, Ansons, and Oxfords. Flying ceased in June 1945, and the station closed in March 1946. Part of the site reopened for civil use before 1977 from a new hard runway.

Penshurst, (Chiddingstone Causeway), Kent
This RFC first-class night LG was used as a home defence flight station from December 1916 to November 1918. It then became a wireless school equipped with DH6s, Be2s, Avro 504s, Camels, and Snipes until March 1919. It transferred to civil use in 1920 when it became a diversion airfield for Croydon, but it was closed for various periods until March 1940, when it was designated a RLG for Redhill. It was used by mainly Tiger Moths and Magisters but only until June 1940. An AOP flight of Austers arrived in September 1942 and stayed until March 1945 when flying ceased.

Penston, Lothian
This RFC first-class night LG opened in December 1916 and was used for home defence until a new flight

Vickers Supermarine Spitfire OO-ARE in front of the London Aeroplane Club's hangar at Panshanger in May 1961. The nose of another Spit, G-AIDN, can be seen behind. (*Richard Riding*)

Various light aircraft parked on the grass at Panshanger on 13 August 2014. The airfield closed less than a month later. (*Grant Peerless*)

station opened on the other side of the road in August 1917. Avro 504s were the main type operated here until flying ceased in June 1919.

Pentney, Norfolk

This RLG for RAF Marham was in use from 1939 to 1941, mainly by Wellingtons.

Pentridge, Dorset

This LG was used by the RFC/RAF during the First World War.

Pen-Y-Parc, Clwyd

This gliding site was operated by the North Wales GC in the 1980s.

Peplow (Childs Ercall), Salop

This RAF station opened in September 1940 as a RLG for Tern Hill and was used by Masters and Hurricanes. It then became mainly a training station used by various units that operated Wellingtons, Albermarles, Horsas, Hadrians, Oxfords, Harvards, Fireflies, and Lancasters. It closed at the end of 1949, but parts of the eastern wartime perimeter tracks are used by light aircraft with a couple being based here.

Perranporth (Trevellas), Cornwall

This RAF station opened in April 1941 as a satellite for Portreath, initially as a fighter base, operating mostly Spitfires until April 1944. It then passed to the FAA for a few months with Avengers and Swordfish until placed on C&M in September 1944. It was then used briefly as a Transport Command staging post and by an ACGS until closure in April 1946. Civil flying commenced in May 1951 with short-lived scheduled services, but these had ceased by the following year. Flying restarted in 1957 when the Cornish GC took up residence and light aircraft also returned. Today, Perranporth is home to over thirty aircraft that operate from two unlicensed hard runways.

Pershore (Throckmorton), Worcs

The Worcestershire Flying Club began flying from a site near Tilesford in June 1934 with Moths and continued until the outbreak of the Second World War. The RAF arrived in February 1941, and the first residents were Wellingtons belonging to an OTU. They stayed until March 1944 and were followed by other training units that operated Tomahawks, Oxfords, Hurricanes, and Chipmunks, until April 1954. During the war, a ferry unit was set up that dispatched aircraft abroad. Types handled included Mosquitoes, Beaufighters, Halifaxes, Venturas, Wellingtons, and Warwicks, which lasted until the spring of 1948. The Radar Research Establishment moved in from Defford in September 1957 and operated Hastings, Meteors, Venoms, Valettas, Hunters, Canberras, and Devons until flying ceased in 1978.

Perth (Scone), Tayside

Opened as Perth Municipal Airport on 27 January 1936, scheduled services commenced the following December and continued until April 1940. An elementary flying school was formed in January 1936 and operated Tiger Moths, Harts, Battles, and Magisters. Training continued until June 1954, latterly as a RFS with Ansons, Harvards, Prentices, and Chipmunks. A flight of AOP Austers was based here from May 1949 to March 1957, and a UAS commenced operations in December 1950. Equipped with Tiger Moths, Magisters, Harvards, Chipmunks, and Bulldogs, it moved out in January 1993. Scheduled services were operated for a brief period in the early 1960s. Air Service Training continued with training in 1954, and today, Perth is a busy GA airfield with over 100 resident aircraft. Two hard and one grass runways are available, all licensed.

Perton (Wolverhampton), Staffs

This RFC night and day LG, originally known as Fern Fields, opened in April 1916 with Fe2bs. It closed in August 1918, but some civil use took place during the 1920s. It was reopened by the RAF in August 1941 as a RLG for Shawbury and later Wheaton Aston and was used by Oxfords, Harvards, and Hurricanes until placed on C&M in August 1946. During the Second World War, it was used for the flight-testing of Bostons and Havocs. It saw spasmodic use by light aircraft during the 1960s, and there were hopes that it could replace Wolverhampton Airport, which had closed in 1971.

Peterborough

See Horsey Toll.

Peterborough (Westwood), Cambs

This RAF station opened in August 1932 and was used initially by an air storage unit until February 1935. After this, Hillson Pragas were assembled and test-flown. RAF training commenced in December 1935 and continued with various units until April 1946. Types operated included Harts, Tutors, Audaxes, Battles, Oxfords, Tiger Moths, Masters, Harvards, and Ansons. Civil flying resumed after the war, mostly by

Spalding Airways and continued until closure in 1965. Between June 1948 and 1950, BEA based its S51 and Bell 47 helicopters here. The Perkins Engines GC was based from 1959 to 1963.

Peterhead (Longside), Grampian

This RNAS airship station, also known as Lenabo, was established in March 1916, but an LG on the site was used by a coastal patrol flight for a brief period in November and December 1918. About 4 miles to the north-east, a RAF station opened in July 1941 and was home to mostly fighters, numerous units being based until August 1945. Types operated here included Spitfires, Hurricanes, Fulmars, Typhoons, Beaufighters, and Mustangs. Flying ceased in around August 1945, but it reopened for civil helicopter operations in 1975 and for fixed-wing flying in 1977. Over twenty light aircraft are currently based here, operating from part of one of the wartime hard runways, which is unlicensed.

Peterlee, Co. Durham

This unlicensed airfield opened in 1987 is situated on reclaimed land from Shotton Colliery and is used primarily for parachuting. One hard runway is available and around six aircraft are based here.

Pett, (Hastings), Sussex

This RFC third-class night LG was used for home defence from December 1916 to August 1918.

Pickering, Yorks

This private grass airfield was in use from the 1970s to around 1984.

Pilling, Lancs

This unlicensed microlight site at Brook Farm has two grass strips and over twenty residents.

Plainville, Yorks

This dispersal site was used by Whitleys from RAF Linton-on-Ouse from early in the Second World War to October 1941.

Plaistowes (St Albans), Herts

This unlicensed microlight site opened in 1984 and has over fifty residents; it is also available to STOL light aircraft. It has two short grass strips.

Plockton, Highland

This unlicensed airfield opened in 1966 with a single hard runway and is home to a few light aircraft. It was used by FAA Sea Kings between September 1985 and March 1994.

Plough Corner (Little Clacton), Essex

This RFC second-class night and day LG was used for home defence from October 1916 to July 1919.

Pluckley, Kent

Ths RFC second-class night LG was used for home defence from January 1917 to May 1919. Types operated included Be2s and Camels.

Plumpton, Cumbria

This civil airfield was in use from about 1952 to 1978.

Plumstead Marshes, Gt. London

This RFC third-class night LG was used for home defence from April 1916 to May 1917. It continued to be used by the RAF into the 1930s.

Plungar, Leics

This RFC first-class night LG was used for home defence from October 1916 to June 1919.

Plymouth (Chelson Meadow), Devon

The racecourse here was used for flying before and during the First World War. Civil flying continued after the war until activities transferred to the new aerodrome at Roborough in 1931.

Plymouth (Roborough), Devon

A polo field was first used for flying in 1923 when short-lived scheduled services were operated from here. It was later developed as Plymouth's airport and opened officially on 15 July 1931, with scheduled services being operated from April 1933 up to the outbreak of the Second World War. The RAF began using the airport for communications flights from 1935, and their presence intensified in 1939 when fighters arrived in the shape of Gladiators. These were joined by a variety of units operating Magisters, Swordfish, Defiants, Battles, Hurricanes, and Oxfords, some of which belonged to FAA squadrons. Military flying ceased in February 1945, apart from an ACGS, which operated until 1948. It reopened as a civil airport in 1946, and scheduled services recommenced in 1952. A FAA AEF was formed in June 1960 equipped initially with Tiger Moths, but these were replaced with Chipmunks and eventually Tutors. A commando unit operated a few Sioux helicopters between April 1967 and July 1971. A hard runway was laid in 1975 and a second one in

1980. The airport closed in December 2011 but there are plans to reopen it.

Pocklington, Humberside

This RFC first-class night LG, known as Barmby Moor, opened in April 1916 and was used sporadically for home defence until June 1919. Just to the east, a RAF bomber station opened in June 1941 and was home initially to Wellingtons, which were followed by Halifaxes and Liberators until September 1945 when flying ceased. Part of the wartime airfield reopened for gliding in 1971, and today, over thirty aircraft are based here, mainly gliders of the Wolds GC. Two hard and two grass runways are available, all unlicensed.

Podington, Beds

This USAAF station opened in July 1942 as a satellite for Chelveston and was home to C-47s, B-17s, P-38s, and A-20s until June 1945. Flying then ceased and the airfield is now the site of Santa Pod Raceway, which opened in 1966. Before this, gliders of the Northamptonshire GC used the airfield from 1959 to 1965. Some private flying still takes place from part of the old airfield, and a couple of light aircraft are based here.

Polebrook, Northants

This RAF station opened in January 1941 and was home initially to an OTU operating Wellingtons. These stayed until June 1941 when Fortresses arrived, followed by Liberators until April 1942. The USAAF then took over and operated B-17s until June 1945. A MU then moved in and handled mostly Stirlings and Mosquitoes until departing in September 1947 when military flying ceased. The Perkins Engines GC was based here from 1956 to 1959, and the station was reactivated in December 1959 for the deployment of Thor missiles, which departed in August 1963.

Pontefract, Yorks

This RFC second- and third-class night LG situated on the racecourse was used for home defence between April 1916 and June 1919. Be2s were among the types based.

Ponteland (High West House), Northumberland

This RFC second-class night LG was used for home defence from April 1916 to August 1919.

Popham, Hants

This unlicensed airfield opened in 1977 alongside the A303 with two grass runways. It is a popular GA facility and is home to over 100 aircraft.

Port Ellen

See Islay.

Port Meadow, Oxon

This civil aerodrome was opened in 1911 by the Imperial Aero Club but was only used by them for a year or so, although it is possible that some flying took place after this. It was taken over by the RFC in August 1916, but it may have been used by them before the

Air Southwest DHC Dash 8 G-WOWA taxies past the control tower at Plymouth on a cloudy day in July 2011. The airport closed five months later but there are plans to re-open it. (*Grant Peerless*)

war. It was used mainly for training until June 1919. Types based included Camels, Dolphins, Avro 504s, Pups, Be2s, and F2bs. It was used for barnstorming and joy-riding during the 1930s.

Porthcawl (Locks Common), Glamorgan

This civil aerodrome was used by light aircraft and for limited scheduled services from 1919 to September 1939.

Portholme Meadow, Cambs

This aerodrome was opened in 1911 for the Portholme Aircraft Co., which built several types of aircraft before securing a contract to build Camels and Snipes. The RFC arrived in August 1916 and it was used from April 1918 by a TDS equipped with DH6s, DH9s, Be2s, and F2bs until flying ceased in October 1918.

Portmoak, Tayside

Primarily a gliding site, it opened in 1957 and is home to the Scottish Gliding Centre. Over sixty gliders are based here, and visiting light aircraft are accepted. Three unlicensed grass strips are available.

Porton Down, Wilts

This LG was in use from 1920 to 1949 by light aircraft associated with the Chemical Defence Establishment. It was used by the RAF for experimental flying with Battles from September 1937 and as a RLG for Odiham-based Hectors during 1938.

Portreath, Cornwall

This RAF fighter station opened in March 1941 and was home to Whirlwinds, Spitfires, Blenheims, Mustangs, Beaufighters, and Mosquitoes until September 1944. An overseas aircraft despatch unit arrived in December 1941 and ferried hundreds of aircraft abroad, including B-17s, B-24s, C-47s, P-38s, P-39s, Halifaxes, and Horsas; they stayed until October 1945. An ASR unit was based here from April 1944 to February 1945, operating Warwicks, Walruses, and Lysanders. Flying ceased in October 1945.

Portrush, NI

This civil aerodrome was first used for joy-riding in 1919 but its further use is uncertain.

Portsmouth, Hants

Portsmouth Airport opened on 2 July 1932 and soon attracted scheduled services, predominantly to the Isle of Wight. It was well-used by airlines and flying clubs until the outbreak of the Second World War when it became a satellite for RAF Thorney Island. In April 1933, Airspeed set up a factory on the site, which built Couriers, Envoys, Oxfords, Mosquitoes, and Horsas. Portsmouth Aviation (a CRO) repaired and overhauled RAF aircraft during the war. Civil flying resumed in April 1946 with scheduled services commencing soon afterwards. Airspeed converted Oxfords to Consuls and produced components for Ambassadors, Comets, and Vampires until the mid-1960s. An ACGS was based from October 1944 to September 1946. The airport, which had remained grass-surfaced, closed in December 1973.

Portstewart Strand, NI

This LG was used for pleasure flying during the 1930s.

Postling, Kent

This unlicensed airfield at Pent Farm opened in 1992 with one grass runway. It is home to around twenty aircraft.

Poulton, Cheshire

This RAF station opened in March 1943 as a RLG for Hawarden and was also home to various training units. Types operated included Mustangs, Hurricanes, Harvards, Masters, Spitfires, Oxfords, Blenheims, and Typhoons. It closed in June 1945, but some private flying took place after this until the early 2000s when it ceased.

Prawle Point, Devon

This LG was used by a RAF coastal patrol flight equipped with DH6s and DH9s from May 1918 to February 1919.

Predannack, Cornwall

This RAF station opened in May 1941 as a satellite for Portreath. It was mainly a fighter base and was home to Hurricanes, Havocs, Spitfires, Beaufighters, Mosquitoes, Typhoons, and Tempests until June 1946. Wellingtons and Liberators were also based here from December 1943 to August 1944. It was placed on C&M in June 1946 but reopened briefly as a RLG for Culdrose in 1953 when it was used by mainly Sea Furies. It closed again in October 1954 but was reopened in December 1958 by the FAA as a facility for helicopter training away from the main base of Culdrose and this continues to this day. An ACGS was formed in 1969 and this is now a VGS operating Vikings.

Preston Candover, Hants

This private grass airfield was used as a base by Air Pegasus from about 1974. It was still in use in 1977.

Prestwick, Strathclyde

A civil aerodrome, known as Monkton, opened in 1933 but closed in September 1934. It was absorbed into a new Prestwick Airport, which opened on 17 February 1936; an elementary flying school was formed on the same day. Training continued until July 1941 and types operated included Tiger Moths, Harts, Ansons, and Battles. Spitfires arrived in December 1939 followed by Hurricanes; these stayed until April 1941. An ATA ferry pilot's pool was set up in September 1940 and was resident until October 1945 with Ansons, Arguses, and Puss Moths. A radio school was based here from December 1940 to December 1942 and used mainly Bothas while a BAT Flight with Hudsons and Oxfords was resident here from October 1941 to February 1946.

Prestwick is most famous as a transatlantic ferry terminal, and over 37,000 American- and Canadian-built aircraft were delivered from November 1940 to September 1945. Types flown in included Hudsons, Liberators, Fortresses, Dakotas, Mitchells, Mosquitoes, and Lancasters. Transatlantic and other scheduled flights commenced in October 1945 and continue to this day. The USAF arrived in November 1953 and operated KC-97s, HC-130s, SC-54s, and SA-16s until they departed in September 1966. Scottish Aviation maintained various types during the Second World War and even built some Queen Bees. After the war, they overhauled C-47s, C-54s CF-100s, and T-33s as well as building new Pioneers, Twin Pioneers, Bulldogs, and Jetstreams. The FAA returned in October 1971 (as HMS *Gannet*) with a flight of Sea Kings that were based here until 2016, when they were replaced in the SAR role with privately operated S92s and AW189s.

Pulham St Mary, Norfolk

This was predominantly an airship station in use from 1916 to 1918, but it included a LG that was used by communication flights and possibly a coastal patrol flight during the First World War.

Pwllheli (Broom Hall), Gwynedd

This civil aerodrome opened before 1937 and was home to the Pwllheli and District GC. It was acquired by Billy Butlin in 1946, and pleasure flights were offered to holidaymakers at his nearby camp. Scheduled services, mainly for Butlin's residents, were operated during the summer months by Dragon Airways in the 1950s. The aerodrome had two grass runways and closed at the end of the 1960s.

Queniborough, Leics

This RFC day and third-class night LG was used for home defence from early 1916 to August 1918.

Rackheath, Norfolk

This short-lived USAAF bomber station opened in March 1944 with B-24s and closed in June 1945.

Radcliffe-on-Trent (Shelford), Notts

This RFC second-class night LG was used for home defence from April to November 1916.

Radlett (Park Street), Herts

This aerodrome and factory for Handley Page was opened in July 1930, but they had been test-flying their products here since June 1929. Their new factory on the site produced Heyfords, HP42s, Harrows, and Hampdens before the outbreak of the Second World War. During the war, Halifaxes were the main product, with over 1,500 being built. After the war, Hastings, Hermes, Victors, Heralds, and Jetstreams were produced. The annual SBAC show took place at Radlett in 1946 and 1947. The airfield closed in June 1970 on the demise of Handley Page.

Raeburnfoot, Dumfries and Galloway

This RLG for RAF Kingstown was used by Magisters, Tiger Moths, and Battles during the Second World War.

Ramsbury, Wilts

This RAF station opened as a satellite for Membury and was proposed initially as a bomber OTU. Instead, it was handed over to the USAAF in August 1942, and they operated C-47s, C-53s, and CG-4s until February 1945. RAF Oxfords used the airfield as a RLG during 1943, and it was used for glider training from June to December 1945, the main types operated being Dakotas and Hadrians. It was then used as a RLG for Little Rissington by Oxfords and Harvards until flying ceased in May 1946. A private landing strip at nearby Baydon Manor was in use from around 1974 to 1989.

Ramsey

See Upwood.

Ramsey (Hall Caine), IoM

The island's first airport opened in April 1935 with scheduled services, which continued until September

1937. Limited flying then took place until the outbreak of the Second World War, when it was used as a RLG until January 1943.

Ramsgate (Nethercourt), Kent
This civil aerodrome opened in 1932 and closed when the new Ramsgate Airport opened in 1935.

Ramsgate, Kent
This civil airport opened officially in July 1937, although flying had started by June 1935. Limited scheduled services operated before the war but ceased for the duration. In 1940, it was used as a dispersal site for Manston but no other use was made by the armed forces during the Second World War. It reopened for civil flying in June 1953 with scheduled services and joy-riding but closed in 1968.

Ramster (Ramsnest), Surrey
This AALG was used mostly as an ELG during the 1930s.

Randalstown, NI
This civil aerodrome was in use before the Second World War.

Rattlesden, Suffolk
This USAAF bomber station opened in December 1942, initially with B-26s but later B-17s. Flying ceased in August 1945, but Bloodhound missiles were deployed from December 1959 to January 1964. Part of the site is now used by the Rattlesden GC, who arrived in 1987 and operate over twenty-five gliders.

Rattray (Crimond), Tayside
This FAA station HMS *Merganser* opened in October 1944 and was home to various units operating mostly Barracudas until August 1946. Some Ansons, Harvards, Fireflies, and Oxfords were also based just before the station closed in September 1946.

Raydon, Essex
This USAAF station opened in November 1943 and was home to P-51s and P-47s until closure in October 1945. Part of the north-east corner of the wartime airfield reopened for private flying in 1997 and is known as Raydon Wings. A single unlicensed grass strip is available.

Rayne Hall Farm (Braintree), Essex
This unlicensed airfield opened before 1982 with a single grass runway and has around twenty-five resident light aircraft.

Reading
See Woodley.

The futuristic terminal building incorporating a control tower at Ramsgate in July 1937. BAC Drone G-AEEN and BA Swallow G-AERK are parked in front. The airfield closed in 1968. (*Aerofilms*)

Hangar and workshop at the grass airfield at Rayne Hall Farm in Essex on 30 September 2010. (*Grant Peerless*)

Reading (Coley Park), Berks

This RFC aerodrome opened in December 1915 and was used for training with Martynside S1s, Shorthorns, Longhorns, and Avro 504s until flying ceased in January 1919.

Redcar, Cleveland

The racecourse here was used by the RNAS/RAF from July 1915 for training with Avro 504s, Longhorns, Pups, Camels, Dolphins, SE5s, and F2bs until September 1919. A coastal patrol flight was based here briefly with DH6s between May and July 1918.

Redhill, Surrey

This civil aerodrome opened in May 1934 and was used mainly for training and private flying. An elementary flying school was set up in July 1937 equipped with Harts, Magisters, Battles, and Ansons; it stayed until June 1940. RAF fighters then arrived, Spitfires being the main type but also Blenheims, Beaufighters, Hurricanes, and Mustangs. These departed in February 1944 and were replaced with various units operating Ansons, Tiger Moths, Oxfords, and Tempests until May 1945. Training returned in April 1948 when an RFS was formed; it operated Tiger Moths, Ansons, Oxfords, and Chipmunks until June 1954. Civil flying resumed in May 1947 by the Redhill Flying Club, and today, it is a busy GA airfield with over 100 residents operating from three licensed grass runways.

Redmires (Sheffield), Yorks

This RFC third-class night LG was used for home defence from April 1916 to September 1917.

Rednal, Salop

This RAF station opened in April 1942 and was home to only one main unit, an OTU that operated Spitfires, Masters, Battles, Martinets, Lysanders, Mustangs, and Harvards until closure in June 1945. Private flying returned in 1990 from part of the wartime north-east and south-west hard runway and a few aircraft are resident here.

Regents Park, Gt. London

This RNAS home defence night ELG for Hendon was in use during 1914.

Rendcomb, Glos

This RFC training squadron station opened in June 1916, becoming a TDS in August 1918. Types operated here included Be12s, F2bs, RE8s, DH6s, and Avro 504s. It closed in December 1919, but part of the site reopened for private flying in 1990 and today over a dozen aircraft are based, many of them vintage types.

Renfrew

See Glasgow.

Modern control tower at Redhill on 17 July 2018. (*Grant Peerless*)

Bucker Jungmeister G-AXIH in front of the control tower and hangar at Redhill, *c.* 1970. (*Richard Riding*)

Rennington (Stamford/Alnwick), Northumberland

This RFC second- and third-class night and second- and third-class day LG was used for home defence from December 1916. A coastal patrol flight was based here from June 1918, operating a few DH6s until flying ceased in June 1919.

Retford

See Gamston.

Rhigos, Glamorgan

This gliding site opened in the early 1980s and is home to the Vale of Neath GC with about six sailplanes. Powered aircraft are also accepted.

Rhoose

See Cardiff.

Riccall, Yorks

This RAF bomber station opened in September 1942 and was used mainly for training with Halifaxes, Whitleys, Liberators, Dakotas, and Yorks until flying ceased in November 1945.

Ridgewell, Essex

This RAF bomber station opened as a satellite for Stradishall in December 1942. It was home to Stirlings but only for a short time as the USAAF arrived in the following May with B-17s, staying until June 1945 when flying ceased. Gliding now takes place from part of the site by the Essex GC, who operate around twenty sailplanes.

Ringmer, Sussex

This RLG for RNAS Eastbourne was in use during 1915 and 1916. A gliding site at Kitson Field opened before 1978 and is operated by the East Sussex GC; it is home to around twenty-five gliders.

Ringway

See Manchester.

Ripe, Sussex

This unlicensed airfield at Kittyhawk Farm has two grass strips at which nearly a dozen aircraft are based.

Ripon, Yorks

This RFC second-class night LG was situated on the racecourse and was used for home defence from October 1916 to March 1919 with Be2s, Be12s, and Avro 504s. Training also took place from December 1917 with Avro 504s, Pups, RE8s, F2bs, DH6s, and Camels. Flying ceased in early 1920.

Riseley, Beds

This unlicensed airfield at Sackville Farm opened before 1989 with a single grass runway; it is home to around fifty aircraft, mainly microlights and gliders of the Sackville Vintage GC.

Rivar Hill, Wilts

This gliding site opened before 1982 and is operated by the Shalbourne GC; it is home to about twenty gliders.

Rivenhall, Essex

This USAAF station opened in January 1944. P-51s and B-26s were operated here until the following August when the RAF took over with Stirlings; they stayed until flying ceased in January 1946.

Roborough

See Plymouth.

Roche, Cornwall

This unlicensed airfield at Woodlands Barton Farm has two grass strips and has been in use since the 1970s; it is home to around ten aircraft, mostly microlights.

Rochester, Kent

This aerodrome and associated factory were built by Shorts in 1933. It was also used as a civil airport, with scheduled services commencing in June 1934. Shorts built several types, but their main output was 500 Stirlings during the Second World War before moving to Belfast in 1946. An elementary flying school was set up in April 1938 with Avro 504s, Tutors, Tiger Moths, Harts, and Magisters; training continued, latterly by an RFS. This operated Tiger Moths, Ansons, Prentices, and Oxfords until disbanding in March 1953. An FAA flight arrived in November 1949 with Oxfords, Harvards, and Fireflies; it stayed until May 1955 while Shorts operated a ferry flight between November 1950 and June 1960 equipped with Dominies, Sea Devons, and Sea Princes. Shorts also opened a maintenance facility in 1954 that handled Beaufighters, Brigands, Mosquitoes, and Sturgeons until departing in 1959. Scheduled services were operated from 1960 to 1967, and today, Rochester is a busy GA airfield, which is home to over 100 aircraft. Three licensed grass runways are available.

Rochford

See Southend.

Rollestone Camp (Larkhill), Wilts

This LG was used for balloon training from 1916 and later as a RLG during the Second World War. It closed in July 1946.

Romford (Maylands), Gt. London

This civil aerodrome opened in 1928 and was used by Hillman's Airways for its scheduled services from November 1931 to June 1934, when it moved its operations to Stapleford Tawney. The aerodrome then fell into decline, and while its licence was withdrawn in January 1936, flying continued (mostly by the Romford Flying Club) until the outbreak of the Second World War.

Ronaldsway, IoM

Flying started from a field on the shore of Derby Haven in 1929, and it became an AALG in 1932. Scheduled services then commenced, which continued until September 1939. The RAF arrived in July 1940 with a gunnery school, which operated Gauntlets, Wallaces, Harts, and Lysanders until February 1943. It was commissioned for the FAA as HMS *Urley* in July 1944 and was used mainly for training with Barracudas, Swordfish, and Ansons until the navy departed in December 1945. Civil flying returned in 1946, and scheduled services resumed in 1947, which continue to this day.

Roston (Snelston), Derbys

This RFC second-class day and night LG was used for home defence from October 1916 to September 1918. It was then used occasionally by light aircraft, including a visit by Cobham's Flying Circus in 1929. It saw use during the Second World War as a RLG for Burnaston, and in September 1947, twenty-five Jersey cows arrived in three DC3s. There were no more recorded movements after this.

Rothesay, Strathclyde

This civil aerodrome on the Isle of Bute was in use from about 1919 to the 1930s and was served occasionally by scheduled services. A nearby beach airstrip at Ettrick Bay saw similar use. There is an unlicensed grass airfield at Mount Stuart on the south-west of the island.

Rougham (Bury St Edmunds), Suffolk

This USAAF bomber station opened in December 1942 and was home to B-26s and B-17s until December 1945. Part of the wartime airfield has been used for private flying since before 1974 from a single unlicensed grass strip; regular air displays are held here. About ten aircraft are based.

Rousay, Orkney

This civil aerodrome was used by Highland Airways between 1934 and 1939.

Rudbaxton, Pembrokeshire

This SLG was in use between April 1941 and September 1942, but it is not known what types were stored.

Ruddington (Nottingham), Notts

This RFC second-class night LG was used for home defence from October 1916 to November 1917.

Rufforth (York), Yorks

This RAF bomber station opened in September 1942 and was home to mainly Halifaxes in the training role until May 1945. A few Oxfords, Spitfires, and Hurricanes were also operated. A communications flight arrived in May 1946 and used various types until April 1947; another one operated here from August 1950 to February 1958. This one employed Ansons, Proctors, Oxfords, Austers, Chipmunks, Tiger Moths, Provosts, and Meteors. From April 1951 to April 1958, Valettas and Hastings from Dishforth used the airfield as a RLG. Between February 1953 and June 1954, a flight of Austers was present; it was used again as a RLG from July 1959 to November 1966, this time by Provosts, Vampires, and Jet Provosts from Linton-on-Ouse. Flying then ceased, but private flying returned to parts of the wartime runways in 1982, mostly gliders of the York GC; today, over 100 aircraft are based here. Three unlicensed hard runways are available.

Rugby (Lawford Heath), Warks

This AALG was in use from about 1932 to 1939.

Runwell (Wickford), Essex

This RFC second-class night LG was used for home defence from October 1917 to October 1918.

Rush Green, Herts

This unlicensed airfield opened in the late 1950s with two grass runways and has around six residents.

Rustington, Sussex

This day LG was used from 1917 for aircraft based at Gosport. It was then developed as a TDS for the

USAAS but never completed and work was abandoned in October 1919.

Ryde (Westridge), IoW

It opened as Isle of Wight Airport in June 1932 with scheduled services, initially to Portsmouth, followed by further destinations. These continued until the outbreak of the Second World War when the airport closed for the duration, although it was used as an ELG by RAF and FAA aircraft up to 1940. It reopened for civil flying after the war but closed in 1953.

Rye, Sussex

This RFC third-class LG was used for home defence from March 1917 to November 1918.

Sadberge, Yorks

This RNAS and later a RFC LG was in use from 1917 to 1919.

Salcombe

See Bolt Head.

Saltby, Leics

This RAF station opened in August 1941 as a satellite for Cottesmore and was home to Hampdens and Ansons until September 1943. The USAAF arrived in February 1944 with C-46s, C-47s, C-53s, CG-4s, and Horsas; they stayed for a year. The RAF then returned with a HCU that operated Stirlings, Halifaxes, Spitfires, and Oxfords until flying ceased in August 1945. A couple of MUs took over until October 1948 when the base closed. Part of the wartime airfield has been used by the Buckminster GC since 1971, and light aircraft are also welcome. Two hard runways and a grass strip are in use, all unlicensed. Around forty gliders and powered aircraft are based here.

Samlesbury, Lancs

This aerodrome was associated with an English Electric factory that opened in December 1939, which assembled and test-flew 770 Hampdens and 2,145 Halifaxes during the Second World War. They continued after the war with Vampires, Canberras, and Lightnings. As BAC/BAe, they worked on Tornadoes, Jaguars, Hawks, and Harriers, then latterly components for Airbus wings, Typhoons, and Goshawks. An RAF communications flight was based here from October 1940 to September 1944 and operated Hurricanes, Masters, and Oxfords. An ACGS was based after the war and a VGS was formed in June 1984, which continued until October 2008, although the majority of flying ceased in July 1988.

Sanday, Orkney

This civil aerodrome was used by limited scheduled services between 1934 and 1946. It was used as a RLG by Spitfires from RAF Skeabrae during 1944. A licensed airfield at Bea Ness opened in 1967 with one hard and two grass runways; it is served by scheduled services.

Sandbach (Arclid), Cheshire

This microlight site opened in around 1991 but closed in 2019.

Sandown, IoW

There have been three airfields serving the Sandown and Shanklin area. The first was at Apse, which opened in 1929 and was operated by the Island Aviation Co. as well as being home to the Isle of Wight Flying Club. Scheduled services commenced in October 1932, but all activities were transferred to a new site 1 mile away near Languard in 1934. This was short-lived, and operations were moved to the present site at Lea, where flying commenced at Easter 1935. Scheduled services started soon afterwards and continued until the outbreak of the Second World War. The IoW Flying Club became part of the CAG scheme in 1938, and training carried on until the aerodrome closed on the outbreak of the Second World War. It reopened in August 1948 and scheduled services were resumed by a variety of airlines that continued into the 1960s. Today, Sandown is known as the Isle of Wight Airport and is home to around thirty aircraft that operate from a single unlicensed grass runway.

Sandridge (Hill End Farm), Herts

This RLG for RAF Holwell Hyde/Panshanger was in use from 1940 to at least July 1945, mostly by Tiger Moths.

Sandtoft (Belton), Humberside

This RAF bomber station opened in February 1944 and was home to a HCU equipped mostly with Lancasters and Halifaxes until flying ceased in November 1945. It reopened for civil flying from part of the south-eastern perimeter track in 1982; today, it is a busy GA airfield with around thirty residents. One licensed hard runway is in use.

Sandy, Beds

This unlicensed microlight site at Longacre Farm opened before 1993 with two grass strips and over forty residents. It is also available to STOL aircraft.

Panoramic view across Sandown airfield on the Isle of Wight taken from the control tower on 21 August 2014. (*Tony Yarnold*)

Grumman American AA-5 parked in front of the control tower at Sandown on 21 August 2014. (*Grant Peerless*)

Sawbridgeworth, Herts

This RFC second-class night LG was used for home defence from April 1916 to June 1919. A LG at Matham's Wood was in use for exercises from 1937; this became RAF Sawbridgeworth in August 1940. It was home to a variety of units operating Lysanders, Mustangs, Tomahawks and Typhoons. Flying ceased in May 1944.

Saxthorpe (Aylsham), Norfolk

This RFC second-class night LG was used for home defence from August 1917 to November 1918.

Scalby Mills (Scarborough), Yorks

This LG on the beach was used by the RNAS from August 1914 to 1915.

Scale Hall

See Lancaster.

Scalford (Melton Mowbray), Leics

This RFC second-class night LG was used for home defence from October 1916 to November 1918.

Scampton, Lincs

This RFC home defence flight station, known as Brattleby, opened in October 1916. Training also took place, and a TDS was formed in July 1918. Types operated included Be2s, FK3s, RE8s, Avro 504s, Camels, DH4s, Pups, and Dolphins until closure in June 1919. Following expansion, it reopened as a RAF bomber station in August 1936 and was home initially to Heyfords, Virginias, Harrows, Wellesleys, and Hinds, then later Hampdens, Manchesters, and Lancasters. After the Second World War, Lincolns arrived, followed in October 1953 by Canberras. The USAF put in a brief appearance from July 1948 to January 1949 with B-29s. Vulcans came on the scene in May 1958 and stayed until February 1982. A bombing school was formed in September 1972 and operated Hastings and Varsities until July 1974. The Red Arrows arrived in November 1982 with their Hawks until they departed in February 1996; they returned in 2001 and are still based here. Between July 1990 and May 1996, Andovers of the joint arms control implementation group were based. Today, Scampton is still an active RAF base, but the 'Reds' are the only flying unit based here and it is due to close by 2022.

Scarborough, Yorks

A RAF second-class night LG, also known as East Heslerton or Ganton, was used for home defence from April 1918 to June 1919. It reopened in August 1932 for the Scarborough Aero Club but closed in 1936. Scarborough Racecourse was used by the RNAS as a home defence station by Be2s and Avro 504s between August 1915 and February 1917. It was the temporary home of the Scarborough Aero Club from May 1931 until August 1932. A site 3 miles to the south-west at West Ayton was the base of a coastal patrol flight from August 1918 to March 1919, equipped with DH6s. It was used by civil light aircraft for some time after the First World War.

Scatsta, Shetland

This RAF station opened in April 1940, but no operational units were based here during the Second World War. It was, however, used extensively by communication flights, for refuelling and diversions, with many types making use of the facility, from Hornet Moths to Lancasters. It was placed on C&M in 1946 but was reactivated in 1952 for a tactical exercise. It reopened for civil use in 1978 in connection with the Sullom Voe oil terminal and scheduled services were then operated. A flight of FAA Sea Kings was based from April 1983 to July 1985. Half a dozen civil helicopters are currently based here, and a single licensed hard runway is available.

Scilly Isles

See St Marys.

Scone

See Perth.

Scopwick

See Digby.

Scorton, Yorks

This RAF station opened in October 1939 as a satellite for Catterick, but it saw little action until October 1941 when fighters arrived in the shape of Blenheims, followed by Beaufighters, Spitfires, and Typhoons. The USAAF arrived in May 1944 for a short stay with predominantly P-61s but also a few A-20s and P-47s. They departed in August 1944 and flying then ceased.

Scoulton, Norfolk

This RFC third-class night LG was used for home defence from January to October 1917.

Sculthorpe, Norfolk

This RAF station opened in May 1943 and was home to Bostons, Venturas, Mosquitoes, and Fortresses until

October 1944. It was then inactive until February 1949, when the USAF arrived and operated B-29s, B-50s, B-45s, B-66s, F-84s, C-119s, C-47s, L-20s, and T-33s. The last units departed in June 1962, but some flying continued until June 1989. The airfield is still largely intact.

Scunthorpe, Lincs

This civil airfield was in use from around 1959 to 1978.

Seacroft (Winn Moor), Yorks

This RFC night LG was used for home defence for a short period only from March to October 1916.

Seaford (Stud Farm), Sussex

This civil aerodrome was used mainly for pleasure flying between about 1933 and 1935.

Seahouses (Elford), Northumberland

This RFC day LG opened in October 1916 and was used for home defence until June 1918. It then became home to a coastal patrol flight that operated DH6s and Kangaroos until flying ceased in January 1919.

Sealand (Chester/Queensferry), Clwyd

This RFC training station, known as North Shotwick, opened in October 1917, becoming a TDS in July 1918. Types operated included Pups, Camels, Dolphins, and Avro 504s until closure in April 1920. An AAP known as South Shotwick was under construction nearby in April 1918 but was never completed. The site became RAF Sealand in 1924, still in the training role, and went on to operate Avro 504s, Atlases, Siskins, Tutors, Harts, Audaxes, and Furies, then later Oxfords, Masters, Hurricanes, and Tiger Moths. A packing unit arrived in May 1929, which was responsible for crating aircraft to be sent overseas. An aircraft storage unit was formed in December 1935, which joined the packing unit and was to become a major user of the airfield. It dealt initially with Battles and went on to repair Mosquitoes, Wellingtons, and Lancasters. This use continued after the war, when the USAF took over some of the hangars to augment their facility at Burtonwood. They departed in August 1957. Regular flying ceased in March 1945, but there were occasional movements until about 1957. An ACGS operated here between March 1946 and September 1950; a VGS arrived in March 1963, which stayed until March 2006.

Seaton Carew, Cleveland

This RFC home defence station opened in May 1916 and was used by Be2s, Fe2s, Kangaroos, F2bs, and DH6s until closure in June 1919. It reopened as an AALG known as West Hartlepool and was in use during the 1930s. The later aerodrome at Greatham was just to the west.

Sedgeford, Norfolk

This RNAS home defence LG opened in August 1915 but was taken over by the RFC in May 1916. It was home to various units, some American, until flying ceased in December 1919. Types operated included Avro 504s, Be2s, RE8s, 1½ Strutters, Camels, Dolphins, SE5s, F2bs, DH6s, DH4s, and DH9s.

Sedlescombe, Sussex

This private grass airfield at Spilsted Farm opened in around 1992; it is home to around twenty aircraft, including some gliders.

Seething, Norfolk

This USAAF bomber station opened in December 1943 and was home to B-24s until flying ceased in July 1945. The Waveney Flying Group reopened part of the airfield in 1960, and it is still in use by the group and other light aircraft with around twenty-five being based here. A single unlicensed hard runway is in use.

Seighford, Staffs

This RAF station opened in September 1942 as a satellite for Hixon. It was home initially to an OTU operating Wellingtons; then a HGCU with Albermarles, Horsas, and Hadrians; then finally, an AFU equipped with Oxfords and Harvards. Flying ceased in July 1946 but recommenced in 1956 when Boulton Paul set up a facility to overhaul Canberras and Lightnings. They departed in January 1966, but private flying still takes place, mostly in the form of gliding by the Staffordshire GC, which moved in during 1992. About forty gliders are based here.

Selsey (Church Norton), Sussex

This AALG was in use in the 1930s. It was taken over as an ALG in May 1943 and used by RAF Spitfires and Typhoons until July 1943. It was used again from April to August 1944 by RAF Spitfires. An Auster is based on a private strip near here, which may be part of the old airfield.

Sennybridge, Powys

This airstrip was used by RAF Austers and US Army units during the Second World War. It later saw use by FAA helicopters from June 1973 to September 1992.

Cessna 177 N442BJ in front of the control tower and hangar at Seething on 27 July 2007. (*Grant Peerless*)

Shacklewell (Empingham), Leics
This unlicensed airfield opened before 1996 with a single grass runway and has over a dozen resident light aircraft.

Shaftesbury, Dorset
This AALG at Cannfield Farm was in use in the 1930s.

Shapinsay, Orkney
This private airfield opened in 1969 and is used mainly by air ambulance flights.

Shawbury, Salop
This RFC training aerodrome opened in June 1917 and was home to Camels, Pups, Avro 504s, DH4s, DH6s, DH9s, and RE8s until closure in April 1919. Following expansion, it reopened as a RAF station in February 1938, mainly for training with various units operating Harts, Audaxes, Blenheims, Hurricanes, Whitleys, Battles, Oxfords, Wellingtons, Stirlings, and Halifaxes. These were joined later by Ansons, Lincolns, Provosts, Vampires, Varsities, Jet Provosts, Chipmunks, and Bulldogs. A MU had been formed in February 1938 and was in place throughout the war. It handled a large number of types and scrapped Mosquitoes, Wellingtons, Lancasters, Spitfires, Javelins, Vampires, and Provosts after the war. Fixed-wing flying all but ceased in 1978, but earlier, in 1976, the station's role changed to helicopter training; this continues to this day. Types operated here included Whirlwinds, Wessex, Gazelles, Squirrels, and Griffins. Junos and Jupiters are the main types currently operated here. The airfield is still open to visiting private pilots who have the choice of two licensed hard runways.

Sheerness (Isle of Sheppey), Kent
This was predominantly an airship and balloon base, but it was also a day LG for RFC home defence units, which was in use from May 1917 to 1919.

Sheffield, Yorks
Officially opened as Sheffield Airport on 10 June 1997, the first landing took place in the previous December. Scheduled services commenced in February 1998 but ceased in 2002 due to lack of support. It was used by GA aircraft and flying schools until closure in April 2008.

Shellingford, Oxon
This RAF training station opened in September 1941 and was used by Tiger Moths until flying ceased in March 1948.

Shendish, Herts
This private grass strip was operated by Robert Pooley during the 1980s and '90s.

Shenington
See Edge Hill.

Shenstone, Staffs
This private grass airfield opened in around 1984; it is home to about twenty aircraft, mostly microlights.

Shepherds Grove, Suffolk
This RAF station opened in May 1944 as a satellite for Stradishall. Its first residents were Stirlings followed by Lancasters and various other types until October 1948 when it was placed on C&M. It reopened in August 1951 when the USAF arrived with F-86s and later F-84s, which departed in December 1958. Thor missiles were deployed between July 1959 and July 1963, and the base then closed.

Sherburn-in-Elmet, Yorks
This RFC second-class LG opened in 1917 and was used initially for home defence, albeit sporadically. From 1918, it became an AAP, and Blackburn built and test-flew Cuckoos until the facilities closed in 1920. It was reopened by the Yorkshire Aeroplane Club in January 1926 and flying continued until the outbreak of the Second World War. Airspeed test-flew some of its products here, including the Ferry in 1932, before moving to Portsmouth. Scheduled services were operated here from 1934. RAF Hurricanes were based for a short while between March and May 1941, and the AFEE was resident from July 1942 to January 1945 with Dakotas and Hadrians. An ATA ferry pilot's pool was based here for most of the war with their communications aircraft; a UAS was active here from January 1941 to December 1945 with Tiger Moths. The Blackburn Aircraft Company reopened the First World War factory on the airfield in 1940 and built some 1,700 Swordfish. They went on to repair many types of aircraft as a CRO, including naval and American types.

Civil flying resumed in 1946, but it was low-key until 1964 when Sherburn Aero Club was formed. Grumman light aircraft were assembled and test-flown here during the 1960s and 1970s. Today, it is a thriving GA airfield with over eighty resident aircraft operating from one hard and three grass runways, all of which are licensed.

Sherston, Wilts
This civil aerodrome was in use during the 1930s.

Shifnal, Salop
This unlicensed microlight site has been operated by the Wrekin Microlight Club since before 2011. It has two grass strips and over twenty residents.

Shipdham, Norfolk
This USAAF bomber station opened in June 1942. B-26s were the first residents, but they stayed for under a month and were replaced by B-24s until they departed in June 1945 and the airfield closed. It reopened for private flying in September 1969 from one of the wartime hard runways, now unlicensed and is currently home to around a dozen aircraft.

Shipton, Yorks
This RFC second-class night LG was used for home defence from October 1916 to November 1918, mainly with Be2s. It was used as a MU by the RAF during the Second World War.

Shobdon (Pembridge), Herefs
This RAF station opened in September 1940. It was home to an AACU operating Battles, Lysanders, Martinets, and Oxfords, as well as a GTS with Masters and Hotspurs. It closed in November 1945 but reopened for private flying in 1961. It is now a popular GA airfield with one licensed hard runway and two unlicensed grass strips. Over 100 aircraft are based here, including gliders of the Herefordshire GC.

Shopwhyke
See Goodwood.

Shoreham, Sussex
This is one of the oldest airfields in the UK. Flying began here in February 1911 and it soon attracted several flying schools. It was requisitioned by the RFC in August 1914 and used mainly for training with Farmans, Avro 504s, FK8s, Pups, and Camels during the First World War. The Canadian Air Force also made use of the aerodrome from March 1919 to February 1920 with SE5s. Civil flying resumed in 1923 when F. G. Miles offered joy-rides and scheduled services commenced in September 1932, initially to the Isle of Wight. Brighton, Hove, and Worthing Municipal Airport was opened officially on 13 June 1936 with a smart new terminal building. Scheduled services continued up to and just after the outbreak of the Second World War, but the airport closed to civil traffic in June 1940. A reserve flying school arrived in July 1937 with Tiger Moths, Harts, Hinds, and Ansons; it was resident until September 1939.

During the war, it was used mainly for ASR and target-towing duties, mostly with Lysanders but also Walruses, Defiants, Sea Otters, and Spitfires. It reopened for civil flying in June 1946 and F. G. Miles

The apron, control building, and hangars at Sherburn-in-Elmet on 13 September 2007. The ubiquitous Grumman American AA-5 G-PURR is present together with Cessna 152 G-BMSU and a Jodel. (*Grant Peerless*)

arrived in 1951 to overhaul and repair various types of aircraft. This company was absorbed into Beagle Aircraft Ltd in 1960 and produced 206s and Pups until going into liquidation in February 1970. Scheduled services resumed and taxi and training flights were operated, with a hard runway being constructed in 1982. Today, Shoreham is an extremely busy airport, now known as Brighton City, and is home to nearly 150 aircraft ranging from microlights to corporate jets. One hard and three grass runways are in use, all licensed.

Shotteswell, Oxon

This unlicensed airfield at Church Farm with two grass runways opened before 1974 and is home to around six light aircraft.

Shrewsbury (Monkmoor), Salop

This RAF aerodrome was home to an observer's school from October 1918 to May 1919 equipped with Be2s, RE8s, 0/400s, and DH9s. It reopened for civil use in 1923 but little use was made of it. It was used by a RAF MU during the Second World War and closed in 1947.

Shrewton, Wilts

This RAF station opened in July 1940 as a RLG for Netheravon and was used by Harts, Hinds, and Audaxes. From January 1942, it was used for glider training with Hectors, Masters, Hotspurs, and Horsas until the following December. Training then resumed with Tiger Moths and Austers until they departed in November 1944 when flying all but ceased. It was then placed on C&M and virtually abandoned in April 1946 but was retained for a number of years as an ELG and for occasional use by trials aircraft from Boscombe Down.

Shrivenham, Oxon

This gliding site at Sandhill Farm opened in the 1980s and is home to around twenty gliders that are operated mainly by the Vale of White Horse GC.

Sible Hedingham, Essex

This RFC second-class night LG was used for home defence from April 1916 to October 1918. The Second World War RAF airfield at Gosfield is just to the west. About 3 miles to the north-west at Blooms Farm is an unlicensed airfield with one grass runway.

Sibson (Peterborough), Cambs

This RLG for RAF Westwood opened in June 1940 and was used mainly for training by Battles, Harts, Harvards, Oxfords, Tiger Moths, Masters, and Ansons until flying ceased in April 1946. It reopened for private flying in 1969, and around twenty aircraft are based here, operating from two unlicensed grass runways. It specialises in parachute training.

Silloth, Cumbria

This RAF station opened in June 1939, its first resident being a MU that handled Hurricanes, Sea Hurricanes, and Hudsons. Later in the war, and afterwards, Yorks,

Miles Messenger G-AKVZ parked in the sunshine in front of the art deco terminal building at Shoreham Airport in June 1966. The visual control room above the pre-war terminal was a later addition. (*Richard Riding*)

Dakotas, Lancasters, Ansons, and Balliols were scrapped. In November 1939, Coastal Command arrived with Ansons, Bothas, Hudsons, and Beauforts. When they departed, OTUs took over, operating Wellingtons and Ansons. The final unit in residence flew Vengeances, Martinets, and Spitfires until July 1947. The RAF departed in December 1960. Limited scheduled services were operated from May 1959 to the late 1960s when they transferred to Crosby-on-Eden. Civil flying continued into the 1980s.

Silverstone, Northants

This RAF station opened in April 1943 and was home to an OTU operating Wellingtons and Martinets until November 1946 when flying ceased. Motor racing started from the perimeter tracks in 1948, the first Grand Prix being held in October of that year. Private civil aircraft used a wartime runway inside the racing circuit until 2010, but today, only helicopters are permitted.

Skateraw (Innerwick), Lothian

This RFC third-class night LG was used for home defence between February 1917 and November 1918.

Skeabrae, Orkney

This joint RAF and FAA station opened in October 1940 and was home to a number of mostly fighter units until June 1945. Types operated included Sea Gladiators, Hurricanes, Spitfires, and Seafires. A gunnery flight equipped with Lysanders and Masters was based here briefly from November 1942 to August 1943. Flying ceased in around September 1945, but a few microlights fly from part of the old airfield.

Skegness (Winthorpe), Lincs

This civil aerodrome opened in 1931 with scheduled services commencing soon afterwards. It closed in 1936, but some occasional flying may have taken place up to the start of the Second World War.

Skegness (Ingoldmells), Lincs

This civil airfield opened in June 1948 to provide pleasure flights for holidaymakers at the adjacent Butlin's camp. These continued, together with charter and training flights, until closure in 1993.

Skegness (Water Leisure Park), Lincs

This unlicensed airfield opened in 1992 to replace Ingoldmells, with two grass runways. It is situated within a leisure park and is home to around ten aircraft.

Skellingthorpe, Lincs

This RAF bomber station opened as a satellite for Waddington in August 1941 and was home to Wellingtons, Whitleys, Hampdens, and Manchesters. Following the laying of hard runways, Lancasters arrived in 1942 and stayed until flying ceased in

Grumman American AA-5 G-PURR basking in the sun at Skegness Water Leisure Park on 18 July 2016. This airfield replaced an earlier one at Ingoldmells in 1992. (*Grant Peerless*)

September 1945. The airfield remained open as a RLG for Swinderby until 1952 when it closed.

Skipton-on-Swale, Yorks

This RAF bomber station opened in August 1942 as a satellite for Leeming and was home to Wellingtons, Halifaxes, and Lancasters until flying ceased in October 1945.

Skirwith, Cumbria

This gliding site at Skelling Farm has been operated by the Eden Soaring GC since 2008 with around a dozen sailplanes being based.

Skitten, Highland

This RAF station opened in October 1940 as a satellite for Wick and was home to various units, some for only short periods, as well as being used as a diversion airfield. Hurricanes were the first residents and Hampdens operated shipping strikes here from August 1942 to October 1943. An anti-submarine unit operated Beaufighters and Mosquitoes between April 1943 and July 1944. The last unit based here flew Spitfires, Hudsons, Venturas, and Fortresses until flying ceased in November 1944. It closed soon after the end of the Second World War.

Skye, Hebrides

A civil aerodrome, known as Glen Brittle, opened in December 1935 with local scheduled services that continued until early 1938, but after this, the airfield fell into disuse. A strip at Skeabost was used by Strathallan Air Charter between 1947 and 1964. A new airfield at Broadford opened in 1972 with one unlicensed hard runway, and scheduled services were operated until 1988. It is hoped that they can resume in the future, but in the meantime, some flights are operated by Loch Lomond Seaplanes.

Slade Farm, Oxon

This SLG opened in December 1940 and was used to store mainly Blenheims and Wellingtons until closure in September 1945. It was also used during the Second World War as a RLG for glider towing operations by Hectors, Hinds, and Hotspurs.

Sleap, Salop

This RAF station opened in January 1943 as a satellite for Tilstock and was used mainly by training units. Various types were operated from here, including Whitleys, Wellingtons, Stirlings, Halifaxes, Ansons, and Horsas until July 1949 when flying ceased. It reopened in August 1956 as a satellite for Shawbury and was used by Chipmunks, Vampires, Provosts, and Varsities. The RAF finally departed in 1964, and civil flying then took over. Today, Sleap is a busy GA airfield equipped with two licensed hard runways and with over 100 resident aircraft, including those of the Shropshire Soaring Group.

Cessna 310 G-BTFF photographed in front of the control tower at Sleap in August 1994. (*Barry Abraham*)

Slindon, Sussex
This LG was in use by the RAF from April to December 1918.

Slinfold, Sussex
This unlicensed airfield at Wellcross Farm opened before 1975, and possibly in the 1950s with a single grass runway and is home to about a dozen light aircraft.

Smethwick, W. Midlands
This LG was used during the First World War by the Birmingham and Midland Carriage Company to test-fly aircraft built on the site, mostly DH10s and 0/400s.

Smiths Lawn, Berks
This private LG, known as Windsor Landing Ground, opened in 1929 for the Prince of Wales, which he used until the Royal Flight moved to Benson in 1937. Vickers set up a shadow factory in 1940 that assembled and test-flew Wellingtons and Warwicks. It became a RLG for Tiger Moths from Fairoaks from July 1941 to February 1945. The USAAF arrived in October 1943 with C-47s, C-53s, UC-61s, L-4s, and L-5s that were resident here until early 1945. The airfield closed the following July.

Smoogro, Orkney
This RNAS LG was used by naval aircraft as a shore base from 1917 to 1921.

Snailwell, Cambs
This RAF station opened as a satellite for Duxford in April 1941 and was home to Lysanders, Tomahawks, Typhoons, Whirlwinds, and Mustangs. Flying ceased temporarily in April 1944 but recommenced six months later when a Belgian Air Force training squadron arrived with Tiger Moths and Masters. They stayed until March 1946 when the airfield closed.

Snaith, Yorks
This RAF bomber station opened in July 1941 and was home to Wellingtons and Halifaxes until October 1945. A BAT flight of Oxfords was resident from September 1945 to July 1946 when flying ceased.

Snelston
See Roston.

Snetterton Heath, Norfolk
This USAAF station opened in June 1943 and was home initially to B-26s. However, these stayed only a week and were replaced with B-17s until they departed in December 1945 when the base closed. Between December 1943 and May 1944, the airfield was used as a RLG by Lancasters from Feltwell. It is now a motor racing circuit.

Snipe House (Alnwick/Rennington), Northumberland
This RFC second-class night LG was used for home defence from October 1916 to March 1917.

Snitterfield, Warks

This RAF station opened in May 1943 as a satellite for Church Lawford and was originally intended as a bomber base but was used instead for training. Oxfords, Ansons, and Harvards were operated here until flying ceased in September 1946. Part of the wartime airfield reopened for gliding around 1987, and today, some twenty sailplanes are resident here, mostly operated by the Stratford-upon-Avon GC.

Soberton, Hants

This opened as a dispersal site for Gosport in July 1940 and was also used as an ELG during the Second World War. Air Service Training based at Hamble used it for forced landing practice in the 1950s.

Sole Street (Wye/Crundale), Kent

This RFC third-class night LG was in use from February 1917 to June 1919. Wye LG was about 3 miles to the south-west.

Somersham, Cambs

This decoy site for Wyton was in operation during 1941. It was then used by Lysanders and Hudsons from Tempsford for night training for clandestine operations until 1944.

South Ash (Wrotham), Kent

This RFC second-class night LG was used for home defence from December 1916 to March 1919.

South Belton (Dunbar), Lothian

This RFC second-class day/third-class night LG was used for home defence from late 1916 to November 1918.

South Carlton, Lincs

This RFC training station opened in November 1916, becoming a TDS in July 1918. Types operated included FB5s, FK8s, DH4s, DH6s, DH9s, Camels, Dolphins, and Avro 504s. Flying ceased in April 1920.

South Cave, Humberside

This RFC second-class LG was used for home defence between April 1916 and June 1919. Be2s and Avro 504s were some of the types operated.

An unlicensed airfield at Mount Airy Farm 3 miles south-east of the First World War aerodrome opened in around 1993 and has a single grass runway with over a dozen resident aircraft.

South Cerney, Glos

This RAF station opened in August 1937 and was used mainly for training by various units for most of its life. Types operated included Audaxes, Magisters, Oxfords, Ansons, Harvards, Prentices, Provosts, S51s, S55s, and Chipmunks. Flying ceased in January 1968, but a VGS continued flying until June 1993. Some private flying still takes place from part of the wartime airfield.

South Elham (St Nicholas), Suffolk

This private grass airfield was in use in the 1980s and 1990s.

South Kilduff (Kinross), Central Region

This RFC third-class night LG was used for home defence from October 1916 to February 1918.

South Marston, Wilts

This aerodrome and shadow factory opened in 1939, producing Stirlings and Masters during the Second World War. After the war, Vickers Supermarine took over the facility and built Spitfires, Seafires, Attackers, Swifts, and Scimitars until 1961. These were test-flown from the adjacent airfield, which remained in use for civil flying until 1985 when it closed to make way for a Honda car factory.

South Otterington, Yorks

This RFC second-class day/night LG was used for home defence from late 1916 to late 1918 by Be2s and Avro 504s.

South Ronaldsay (Berriedale) Orkney

This civil aerodrome, also known as St Margarets Hope, was used for limited scheduled services between 1933 and 1939.

South Uist (Askernish), Hebrides

This civil aerodrome opened in late 1935 and was visited by scheduled services until closure in 1939. It was used as an ELG by the RAF from 1939 to 1945.

Southam, Warks

This RLG was used by Tiger Moths from RAF Ansty from 1940 until March 1944.

Southampton (Eastleigh), Hants

An AAP opened here in July 1918 but was used instead by the US Navy to assemble and test-fly DH9s until April 1920. Civil flying on a small scale then commenced and it became Southampton Airport in November 1932, also known as Atlantic Park aerodrome. It soon attracted scheduled services by several carriers that continued until the outbreak of the Second World War. In the mid-1930s, Vickers Supermarine set up a test-flying facility, primarily for the Spitfire but also the Walrus; the company was to stay on the airfield until 1957. The FAA took up residence on part of the airfield in November 1935; this became HMS *Raven*. They operated Swordfish, Ospreys, Sharks, Rocs, Skuas, Sea Gladiators, and Wellingtons until departing in February 1947.

The Cunliffe-Owen Aircraft Company set up a maintenance facility in 1938 and modified or repaired Hudsons, Halifaxes, Lancasters, Typhoons, Spitfires, and Seafires, as well as building their own Concordia airliner. They moved out in 1948. Civil flying resumed in September 1945 with scheduled services commencing the following year. Another manufacturer, Saunders-Roe, arrived in January 1951 and built Skeeter, Scout, and Wasp helicopters until 1961. A hard runway was eventually laid down in 1966, and today, Eastleigh is a busy airport with numerous scheduled services and some charter flights.

Southend (Rochford/Eastwood), Essex

This RNAS aerodrome opened in May 1915 and was used for home defence, mostly with Bleriots until April 1916. In the following September, these duties passed to the RFC, and it became a major flight station until June 1919. Types operated included Be2s, Be12s, SE5s, Avro 504s, Pups, Camels, and DH6s. Some gliding took place during 1930, and just to the north of the First World War site was an aerodrome known as Holt Farm, which was in use from about 1931 to 1935. It closed when Rochford came into full operation. Civil flying commenced around 1932, but Southend Airport was not opened officially until 18 September 1935. Some scheduled services were then operated here, but all civil flying ceased on the outbreak of the Second World War. An elementary flying school was set up in January 1939, which operated Audaxes, Tiger Moths, Hinds, and Ansons until September 1939. Fighters then arrived, mostly Spitfires but also some Hurricanes and Defiants, which stayed until August 1944.

An ACGS was based here from November 1943 to June 1949. It was reopened as a civil airport in January 1947 and charter flights, joy-riding, and training took place here, with car ferries arriving in 1954. Aviation Traders arrived in 1948 and overhauled Haltons and built components for Bristol Freighters. They also produced the one and only Accountant and then concentrated on converting DC4s to Carvairs. Two hard runways were laid in 1955 and 1956, and the Historic Aircraft Museum was based here from 1972 to1983. Today, London Southend Airport supports a variety of scheduled services and is also a thriving GA airfield.

Southend-on-Sea (Rochford) Airport on 9 August 1947 on the occasion of the first International Rally and Race during which heats for the Southend Cup were flown. Later in the afternoon, the official opening of the airport took place. (*Eddie Riding*)

Southfields

See Acklington.

Southport (Birkdale Sands) Merseyside

This LG situated on the beach was opened in around 1920. It was used mainly for pleasure flights by Giro Aviation; these continued until 2001 when flying ceased.

Southport (Hesketh Park), Merseyside

This was another beach aerodrome that was first used in August 1910. An AAP arrived in September 1917, which handled DH4s, DH9s, and Be2s until it closed in January 1919. It reopened for civil use in 1921 and was used mainly for pleasure flying until 1965. A hangar on land nearby was used by a CRO for the maintenance of Ansons, Mosquitoes, and Spitfires during the Second World War.

Southrop, Glos

This RAF station opened in August 1940 as a satellite for South Cerney and was used mainly as a RLG by Oxfords, Harvards, Tiger Moths, Ansons, and Magisters until April 1946. A communications flight continued to operate until the following October when flying ceased.

Southwater, Sussex

This unlicensed airfield at Jackrells Farm opened in 1987 with a single grass runway; it is home to around six aircraft, mostly microlights.

Southwold (Easton Bavents), Suffolk

This AALG was in use from 1933 to about 1939, including a couple of appearances by flying circuses. A Dart Kitten visited in 1950, and the last landing was by a glider in the late 1960s.

Spalding (Weston Marsh), Lincs

This civil airfield was used by Spalding Airways for charter flying from 1947 to 1954.

Spanhoe (Harringworth), Northants

This USAAF transport station opened in February 1944 and was home to C-47s, C-53s, C-109s, CG-4s, and Horsas. It was handed back to the RAF in April 1945 and used by a MU until closure in 1947. The Perkins Engines GC was based here from 1964 to 1967. Part of the southern area of the wartime airfield is now used by light aircraft, and around sixty are based here, operating from one hard and one grass runway, both unlicensed.

Speke

See Liverpool.

Spennymoor, Co. Durham

This RFC day LG was used for home defence from April 1916 to June 1919.

Spilsby, Lincs

This RAF bomber station opened in September 1943 as a satellite for East Kirkby and was home to Lancasters until October 1945. A detachment of Mosquitoes and Sea Mosquitoes were based here from April to June 1946 for *Highball* trials and flying then ceased. A couple of light aircraft operate from part of the old airfield.

Spitalgate, Lincs

This RFC training station, known as Spittlegate, opened in November 1916; it became a TDS in August 1918. Various types were operated here, including Be2s, FK3s, RE8s, Avro 504s, DH4s, DH6s, F2bs, and Snipes. Training continued after the First World War until February 1922 when it became a RAF bomber station equipped with DH9s, Vimys, Fawns, and Horseleys. Its role returned to training in April 1928 when it was renamed Grantham; this was to continue for the next twenty years. Types operated here included Avro 504s, Siskins, Tutors, Harvards, Oxfords, Dominies, Blenheims, Magisters, and Proctors until February 1948. Flying then ceased, but it was used as a RLG for Cranwell and Cottesmore from January 1951 to March 1961. An ACGS continued flying until January 1975 when the airfield finally closed.

Splott

See Cardiff.

Sporle, Norfolk

This RFC third-class night LG was used for home defence from the spring of 1918 to June 1919.

Sproatley (New Field), Yorks

This private grass airfield was in use from the 1970s to the early 2000s.

Squires Gate

See Blackpool.

A selection of interesting types in front of the hangars at the former USAAF transport base of Spanhoe (Harringworth). They include Auster D6 G-ARCS, Beagle Airedale G-ARNP, Taylorcraft BC12 G-BOLB, and DHC Chipmunk WD347. The photo was taken on 26 February 2009. (*Grant Peerless*)

St Albans (St Julians), Herts

This short-lived civil aerodrome opened in January 1933 for the Hertfordshire Flying Club but closed in July 1934, probably due to the proximity of Radlett aerodrome. It did, however, manage to host an appearance of Cobham's Flying Circus in May 1933.

St Andrews Sands, Central Region

This LG on the beach was used by the RFC for training during 1913 and 1914.

St Angelo

See Enniskillen.

St Athan, Glamorgan

This RAF station opened in February 1939 and was home to a variety of units, the main one being a MU. This handled Battles, Hurricanes, Blenheims, Lysanders, Defiants, Beaufighters, Mustangs, and Mosquitoes. Aircraft operated by other based units included Ansons, Oxfords, Queen Bees, Proctors, Chipmunks, and latterly Bulldogs. The main RAF units departed in March 1946 but gliding continued and a VGS was based here until 2016. Maintenance continued after the war, and most RAF types received attention, predominantly Meteors and Canberras but also 'V' bombers, Hawks, Harriers, Jaguars, and Tornadoes. The largest type dealt with was the VC10 as well as airliners for British Airways. At one time, St Athan was linked by a taxi track to nearby Llandow, which was a major storage facility. A UAS/AEF is currently based here, operating Tutors. A flight of S92s and AW189s is also based here, providing SAR duties for the MCA.

St Austell, Cornwall

Rocky Parc aerodrome opened in 1924 and was used in the 1930s for pleasure flying by the Cornwall Aviation Company. Sticker was another aerodrome used by this company during the 1930s.

St Brides, Glamorgan

This SLG was used between April 1941 and July 1945 to store Bothas, Hurricanes, Beaufighters, Defiants, Henleys, and Mustangs.

St Davids, Pembrokeshire

This RAF station opened in September 1943 and was home to mostly Coastal Command units operating Halifaxes and Liberators until placed on C&M in November 1945. The FAA took over in January 1946 and used the airfield as a RLG for Brawdy. Vampires and Attackers were based here for a few months in 1952, and a FRU operated Sea Hornets and Mosquitoes during 1955. It closed in 1958 but was again used as a RLG for Brawdy from 1974 to 1992 by the Hunters, Jet Provosts, and Hawks of a TWU.

St Eval, Cornwall

This RAF station opened in October 1939 and was used predominantly by Coastal Command units for the next twenty years. Ansons were operated initially followed by Beauforts, Hudsons, Whitleys, Halifaxes, Warwicks, Liberators, and Lancasters; they were joined, from November 1951, by Shackletons. The USAAF based B-24s here from October 1942 to January 1943 and again between July and November 1943. Fighters—in the shape of Spitfires, Blenheims, and Mosquitoes—were also based here during the war. Flying ceased in January 1959 when the last Shackleton departed although an ACGS continued flying until March 1963.

St Ives, Cornwall

This private grass airfield was in use from the 1970s to 1990s.

St Just

See Land's End.

St Marys, Scilly Isles

An aerodrome opened on a golf course in September 1937, when scheduled services commenced. These transferred to a new airport at High Cross in July 1939 and continued, to Land's End only, until November 1941. Hurricanes arrived in October 1942 and stayed until September 1944 when flying ceased. Scheduled services resumed in June 1945 and continue to this day. Two licensed hard runways are in use.

St Mawgan (Newquay), Cornwall

An AALG, known as Trebelzue, opened here in 1933, supporting a few scheduled services until the outbreak of the Second World War. It was absorbed into a RAF station in September 1941 initially with AACUs equipped with Henleys and Queen Bees. It was renamed St Mawgan in February 1943. From June 1942, it was used mainly for military and civil transport operations, some by the USAAF until November 1946 when flying ceased. Some civil flying took place in 1949 and 1950, but in January 1951, Lancasters of a maritime reconnaissance school arrived and stayed until September 1956. Coastal Command Shackletons were then based here; they were replaced by Nimrods that departed in October 1992. An SAR flight equipped with Whirlwinds, Wessexes, and later Sea Kings operated from June 1956 until 2008. Canberras were resident from May 1970 to January 1982. Civil flying returned in 1947 when limited scheduled services were operated until 1951. They resumed in 1959 and continue to this day from what is now Cornwall Airport Newquay. A flight of S92s and AW189s is based here, providing SAR duties for the MCA.

St Merryn, Cornwall

This civil aerodrome opened in 1937 but was little used until it was acquired by the FAA in 1939. It reopened as HMS *Vulture* in August 1940 and was home to Rocs, Skuas, Swordfish, Fulmars, Sea Hurricanes, Seafires, Fireflies, Corsairs, Avengers, and Sea Princes. Flying all but ceased in November 1953 when it passed to a MU as HMS *Curlew*, but an ACGS operated here until September 1955. It closed as a naval base in January 1956. In 1979, a few autogyros started flying from the site and then a parachute club arrived. Today, around a dozen microlights are based at Tregolds Farm on the eastern side of the wartime airfield.

Stag Lane, Gt. London

This RFC second-class night LG, also known as Edgware, was used for home defence and training from December 1915 to December 1918. It was also used as a RLG for Hendon. In September 1920, it became home to the de Havilland Aircraft Company, who built a factory on the site to produce their products, mostly the various Moth types. It was also used by the London Aeroplane Club and the DH School of Flying. The aerodrome closed in 1934 when de Havilland's moved to a new site at Hatfield, the last flight out being in July of that year by Geoffrey de Havilland.

Stalham (Brunstead Grange), Norfolk

This private grass airfield was in operation during the 1960s and 1970s. It was used as a sub base for Peters Aviation from 1968.

Stamford

See Wittering.

Stanley Park

See Blackpool.

Stannington, Northumberland

This RAF LG was used mainly for training from July 1918 to October 1919. The RAF airfield at Morpeth was 2 miles to the west.

Stanstead Abbots (Stanstead St Margarets), Herts

This RFC second-class night LG was used for home defence from May 1918 to May 1919. F2bs were among the types operated here.

Modern control tower and terminal building at St Mary's Airport in the Scilly Isles in May 1997. (*Grant Peerless*)

de Havilland aircraft company factory and aerodrome at Stag Lane in the early 1930s before the company moved to Hatfield in 1934 and the aerodrome closed. (*Aerofilms*)

Stansted, Essex

This USAAF bomber station opened in February 1944 and was home to B-26s until they departed in the following September. The RAF resumed control in August 1945, and the airfield reopened for civil flying in December 1946. It was officially opened as a civil airport in June 1947. Maintenance and charter flying were the mainstay for a number of years, and trooping flights were a regular feature. Scheduled flights commenced in around 1965, and today, London Stansted is a major international airport.

Stanton-by-Dale, Derbys

This RFC third-class night LG, later a day LG, was used for home defence from October 1916 to August 1918.

Stanton Harcourt, Oxon

This RAF station opened in September 1940 as a satellite for Abingdon and was used mainly as a RLG by an OTU operating Whitleys, Wellingtons, and Hurricanes until November 1945 when flying ceased.

Stapleford Tawney, Essex

This civil aerodrome opened officially on 23 June 1934 to replace Maylands. Scheduled services commenced straight away but only lasted for a year or so while private flying continued on a limited basis until the outbreak of the Second World War. An elementary flying school was formed in January 1938 with Tiger Moths, Harts, Hinds, and Audaxes; it stayed until September 1939. Hurricanes arrived in August 1940 but only stayed for a year when they were replaced with an ASR unit equipped with Lysanders, Walruses, and Defiants until December 1942. A camouflage unit was based from June 1942 to October 1944 with various types; an AOP flight with Austers and Tiger Moths was resident here between March and August 1943. It was placed on C&M in May 1945, but an ACGS continued flying here until August 1946. It reopened for civil use in 1953 by the Herts and Essex Aero Club, who relocated from Broxbourne. Edgar Percival set up a factory in 1955, which produced forty EP9s before moving out in 1958. Today, Stapleford (it has dropped the 'Tawney') is a busy GA airfield with over eighty residents operating from one hard and two grass runways, all licensed.

Staplehurst, Kent

This ALG was used by RAF Spitfires from August to October 1943 and USAAF P51s from April to July 1944.

Starveall Farm, Oxon

This SLG opened in June 1941 and was used to store Spitfires, Whirlwinds, Blenheims, Manchesters, Lysanders, Hurricanes, Bothas, Monospars, Tomahawks, Mohawks, and Kittyhawks until closure in September 1945.

Staverton (Gloucester/Cheltenham), Glos

This municipal airport opened on 16 July 1936 to replace an earlier aerodrome at Hatherley on the opposite side of the road. Scheduled services commenced soon after opening and continued up to the outbreak of the Second World War. An elementary flying school was formed in September 1938 with Harts, Hinds, and Tiger Moths; training was to be its main role for the rest of the war. Types operated included Ansons, Oxfords, Dominies, and Magisters until the RAF departed in August 1946. Several private companies were based during and after the war, including Follands, Glosters, Flight Refuelling, Rotol, and Smiths Instruments, all of which used the airfield for flight-testing various aircraft. Civil flying returned in 1950, and scheduled services recommenced in 1953. The Skyfame Aircraft Museum was based here from 1963 to 1978. Today, Staverton is Gloucestershire Airport with a thriving GA operation and over 200 resident aircraft that operate from three licensed hard runways.

Steep Down (Lancing), Sussex

This gliding site was operated by the Southdown GC from March 1933 to 1935.

Steeple Morden, Cambs

This RAF station opened in December 1940 as a satellite for Bassingbourn and was home to an OTU equipped with Wellingtons, Ansons, and Blenheims until February 1943. The USAAF then arrived with P-47s and P-51s, staying until November 1945 when flying ceased.

Stirling (Raploch), Central Region

This RFC aerodrome opened in April 1916 and was used for training and home defence until flying ceased in September 1917. Types operated included FK3s, Be2s, Avro 504s, and Martynsides. Nearby, an AALG known as Falleninch was in use between 1933 and 1939, which may have been used occasionally by scheduled services. Kincairn First World War aerodrome was 5 miles to the west.

View of the hangars and other buildings at Stapleford (known as Stapleford Tawney in its days as a RAF airfield) on 22 August 2019. (*Grant Peerless*)

Stoke (Middle Stoke), Kent

This unlicensed microlight site opened in 1975 with one grass strip and has over twenty residents. It is also open to light aircraft.

Stoke Golding, Leics

This unlicensed airfield opened in the early 1960s with a single grass runway and is home to over a dozen light aircraft.

Stoke Orchard, Glos

This RAF station opened in September 1941 and was home initially to a FTS equipped with Tiger Moths. These departed in July 1942 and were replaced by a GTS operating Hotspurs, Horsas, Masters, and Oxfords until flying ceased in July 1945. Glosters had a dispersed factory on the site during the Second World War. Some civil flying took place from the 1970s to 1990s.

Stoke-on-Trent (Meir), Staffs

This municipal airport opened officially in May 1934, but flying had commenced in July 1931. Scheduled services started in August 1934 and continued until May 1939. An elementary flying school was formed in August 1938, which operated Harts and Hinds until September 1939. Training continued after the outbreak of the Second World War with Magisters and Tiger Moths but only lasted until December 1941. An ACGS then arrived and was replaced by a VGS in September 1955. During the war, a factory near the site produced hundreds of Blenheims and Beaufighters; these were test-flown from the airfield. It later assembled and modified Harvards, Mustangs, and Liberators. Civil flying resumed after war with limited scheduled services. The VGS departed in 1963 and the Staffordshire GC, which was formed in 1962 left in 1972. The airfield closed in 1973.

Stonegate (Ticehurst), Sussex

This RFC third-class night LG was used for home defence from November 1916 to March 1917.

Stonehenge, Wilts

This RFC aerodrome opened in October 1917 and was home to various units, some American, operating Be2s, Fe2s, RE8s, FK8s, Avro 504s, DH4s, DH9s, 0/400s, and F2bs until flying ceased in January 1921. It was used by US Army liaison aircraft during the Second World War.

Stonesfield (Oaklands), Oxon

This unlicensed airfield with a single grass runway opened in the 1980s and is home to around six light aircraft.

Stoney Cross, Hants

This RAF station opened in November 1942 and was home to Mustangs, Hurricanes, Albermarles, Whitleys, Venturas, and Whitleys until March 1944. The USAAF then arrived for a short stay with P-38s and B-26s and departed the following September. The RAF returned with a transport unit operating Wellingtons, Stirlings, Dakotas, Oxfords, and Yorks and stayed until April 1946 when flying ceased.

Stormy Down, Glamorgan

This RAF station opened in June 1939 and was used mainly for training until September 1944. Types operated included Wallaces, Henleys, Battles, Whitleys, Martinets, Ansons, Defiants, and Lysanders. The airfield closed in the summer of 1945, but an ACGS continued flying here until March 1947.

Stornoway, Hebrides

This RAF station opened in November 1940, although a proposal for an aerodrome here was made in 1937. It was home initially to Walruses, which stayed until May 1941; they were followed by Coastal Command Hudsons and Whitleys. A ferry training unit was set up in December 1942, which operated Wellingtons, Ansons, Venturas, and Oxfords until March 1944; two squadrons of Halifaxes were then based until May 1945.

During the war, it was used extensively as a transit base for USAAF aircraft and also saw regular use by the FAA. Flying ceased in October 1945, but it was reopened as a civil airport in 1946. It was designated as a strike command forward base in 1973 and was used by NATO maritime patrol aircraft. Between July 1973 and July 1985, FAA Sea Kings were regularly based here. Two licensed hard runways are in use and it is served by regular scheduled services. A flight of S92s and AW189s is also based here, providing SAR duties for the MCA.

Stow Maries, Essex

This RFC home defence station opened in September 1916 and was home to Be2s, Be12s, Pups, Camels, SE5s, 1½ Strutters, and Snipes until March 1919. It has been partly restored to its First World War glory and opened to private flying in 2008. Two unlicensed grass strips are available and around a dozen aircraft are based here, including First World War replicas.

Stracathro, Tayside

This RAF station opened in June 1940 and was used mainly as a RLG for Montrose by Oxfords, Masters, Harvards, and Ansons until June 1944. A BAT flight of Oxfords was based here from April 1943 to July 1945 when flying ceased. A MU then arrived and departed in July 1948.

Stradishall, Suffolk

This RAF station opened in March 1938, remaining active for over thirty years. During this time, a wide variety of units were based here operating Heyfords, Wellingtons, Blenheims, Lysanders, Oxfords, Stirlings, Whitleys, Halifaxes, Lancasters, and Yorks. Jet equipment arrived in July 1949 in the shape of Meteors, followed by Vampires, Venoms, Hunters, and Javelins. They had departed by June 1960 and were replaced in December 1961 by an ANS operating Varsities, Vampires, and Dominies. They stayed until August 1970 when the station closed.

Memorial to pilots who lost their life flying from RFC Stow Maries between 1916 and 1919. The aerodrome, now known as Stow Maries Great War Aerodrome is being restored to its First World War condition and is home to several replica types of the period as well as being open to visiting light aircraft. The photo was taken on 4 October 2012. (*Grant Peerless*)

Stranraer (Lochans), Dumfries and Galloway

This AALG was in use in the 1930s but may have been used as early as 1925. An airfield nearby at West Galdenoch was closed in 1989.

Stratford-upon-Avon (Atherstone), Warks

This civil aerodrome was in use between 1919 and 1939 and became an AALG in 1933. Some 2 miles to the east, a RAF station known as Atherstone opened in July 1941, which was used as a RLG for Wellesbourne Mountford by Wellingtons and Ansons of an OTU. They departed in December 1944 and were replaced by a signals unit operating various types until flying ceased in January 1946. A few light aircraft are based on part of the old airfield at a site known as Alscot Park, which has been in use since before 2005.

Strathallan (Auchterarder), Tayside

This unlicensed airfield opened in around 1962 and was home from 1971 to a wartime aircraft collection. This was closed in 1980, and the site is now used mainly for parachuting. A single grass runway is in use and around six aircraft are based here.

Strathaven, Strathclyde

This field was used from 1942 by an ACGS. An unlicensed airfield opened in 1963 with three grass runways; it is home to over thirty aircraft.

Stravithie, Fife

This SLG opened in May 1941 and was used to store mostly Hurricanes and Wellingtons until May 1945. It was also used by Lysanders during the war.

Stretton, Cheshire

This FAA station HMS *Blackcap* opened in June 1942 and was home to a variety of units operating Seafires, Albacores, Barracudas, Swordfish, Wildcats, Corsairs, Sea Furies, Sea Vampires, Sea Hawks, Attackers, Fireflies, and Avengers until February 1958. It also acted as an air yard during and after the war, and hundreds of aircraft were handled here, many by scrapping. The last aircraft were flown out in August 1958, but the airfield was used occasionally by private aircraft in the 1960s; part of the wartime airfield is still used by a few resident light aircraft that operate from one hard and one grass runway.

Stretton-under-Fosse (Rugby), Warks

This RFC night LG was used for home defence from October 1916 to June 1917.

Stroma, Highland

This short-lived civil aerodrome was used as a request stop on scheduled services from June 1938 to the outbreak of the Second World War.

Stromness (Howe), Orkney

This civil aerodrome opened in May 1935 and was used by scheduled services until the outbreak of the Second World War. A nearby aerodrome at Cumminess was used for diversions in inclement weather conditions.

Stronsay, Orkney

A field at Lower Whitehall was used for scheduled services from August 1934 and closed in 1946. An airfield opened nearby in 1967 and is used for scheduled services and by visiting aircraft. One hard and one grass runway are available, both licensed.

Strubby, Lincs

This RAF station opened in April 1944 and was used initially as a RLG for Manby. It was then home to Coastal Command Warwicks for a short while until Beaufighters arrived in July 1944. Their stay was also short-lived, and they were replaced by Lancasters in the following September. They stayed until June 1945, and the base closed in September 1945. It reopened as a satellite for Manby in June 1949 and saw use by Meteors, Canberras, Vampires, Varsities, and Athenas until flying ceased in August 1972. Part of the wartime airfield is now used by gliders of the Lincolnshire GC, which operate around six sailplanes from one unlicensed hard runway. Another two unlicensed runways, one hard and one grass, are situated to the north of the wartime airfield on an old 1980s heliport site now known as Strubby North, on which around twenty light aircraft are based.

Sturgate, Lincs

This RAF station opened in April 1944 as a RLG for Hemswell and was also home to Lancasters until December 1944. Oxfords of a BAT flight arrived in September 1944 and stayed until May 1945. Lancasters then returned but only for a short while, departing in January 1946. Flying then ceased, but the airfield was reactivated in June 1953 for the USAF as a reserve base; F-84s were resident for part of this time. It closed when the Americans departed in 1964 but reopened for civil flying around 1969. Today, some thirty aircraft are based here, operating from one of the wartime runways, which is unlicensed. The Lincoln Aero Club has been resident here since 1975.

Stutton, Suffolk
This RFC second-class night LG was used for home defence from March 1917 to November 1918.

Sudbury, Suffolk
This USAAF bomber station was used between April 1944 and August 1945 by B-24s and B-17s.

Sumburgh (Lerwick), Shetland
This civil aerodrome opened in April 1933 with scheduled services commencing in June 1936, but they terminated on the outbreak of the Second World War. It opened as a RAF station in December 1939, Gladiators being the first residents, followed by Blenheims, Hurricanes, and Spitfires. Various units were based here during the war with an assortment of types, some naval, including Coastal Command squadrons operating Beauforts, Beaufighters, Hudsons, and Ansons. It was also an important diversion airfield and refuelling point. Flying ceased in June 1945, and it was placed on C&M the following August. It reopened for civil use in 1947 with scheduled services that continue today. Three hard licensed runways are available. A flight of S92s and AW189s is based here, providing SAR duties for the MCA.

Sundridge (Sevenoaks), Kent
This civil aerodrome opened in around 1910 and was home to the de Bolotoff Aeroplane Works, which built and test-flew one aircraft in 1919. It closed in 1927. It was used by the RAF for storage and salvage during the Second World War and closed finally in 1945.

Sutton Bank (Thirsk), Yorks
This gliding site was opened in 1931 by the Yorkshire GC and is home to over fifty gliders. Powered aircraft are also accepted.

Sutton Bridge, Lincs
This site was first used in 1926 for bombing and gunnery training by the RAF and FAA, which continued for the next ten years. Types operated included Bulldogs, Siskins, Harts, and Gauntlets. It became a permanent RAF station in 1936, a satellite for Westwood, and home to an armament training squadron employing Gordons, Wallaces, and Magisters. Fighters in the shape of Blenheims arrived in August 1939, followed by Battles and Spitfires, but their stay was short-lived, departing in March 1940. They were replaced by an OTU operating Hurricanes, Harvards, and Gladiators; they, in turn, were replaced in April 1942 by a gunnery school that flew Wellingtons, Hampdens, Spitfires, and Henleys. This use lasted until February 1944 when it became a RLG used mainly by Oxfords, Magisters, Harvards, and Tiger Moths. Flying ceased in April 1946, but the RAF remained until 1958. Some civil flying took place from the 1970s to 1990s.

Sutton Meadows, Cambs
This microlight site opened in around 1992, which is also open to light aircraft. It is home to over thirty aircraft, operating from three unlicensed grass strips.

Suttons Farm
See Hornchurch.

Swalecliffe (Warboys), Kent
This civil aerodrome was in operation between 1929 and 1938 and was used regularly by Cobham's Flying Circus. It reopened in August 1946 and closed finally around 1950. During this time, East Anglian Flying Services made use of the airfield.

Swannington, Norfolk
This RAF station opened in May 1944 and was home to mostly Mosquitoes; they departed in August 1945. Flying ceased in June 1947.

Swansea (Fairwood Common), Glamorgan
This RAF fighter station opened in January 1941 and was home to numerous units operating Hurricanes, Spitfires, Lysanders, Whirlwinds, Beaufighters, Mosquitoes, and Mustangs. This use continued until October 1946, and an ACGS operated for a further year when flying ceased. Private flying returned in July 1949; it became Swansea Airport in June 1956. Scheduled services then commenced, which continued until 1969, although charter flights carried on operating. A VGS arrived in May 1964 and departed in 2016. The airport is still a busy GA site with two licensed hard runways, but no scheduled services are currently operated from here. Over forty aircraft are based here; gliding also takes place.

Swanton Morley, Norfolk
This RAF station opened in October 1940 and was home to numerous units operating Blenheims, Spitfires,

Oxfords, Bostons, Mitchells, Typhoons, Mosquitoes, Ansons, Chipmunks, and Bulldogs. Norfolk Airways used the airfield for charter and pleasure flying from 1951 to the late 1960s, and the Norfolk and Norwich Aero Club was resident here from 1959 to 1995. An ACGS arrived in 1953 and gliding continued, latterly by a VGS until June 1995. The RAF departed in September 1995 and the airfield then closed. It remained grass-surfaced for the whole of its fifty-five-year life.

Swaton (Cardyke House), Lincs
This private grass airfield was in use in the 1980s.

Swinderby, Lincs
This RAF bomber station opened in August 1940 and was home to Battles, Wellingtons, Hampdens, Manchesters, Lancasters, Halifaxes, and Stirlings until November 1946. Training then took over, initially with Wellingtons and later Mosquitoes, Varsities, Provosts, and Marathons. Jets, in the shape of Vampires and Meteors, arrived in August 1955 and stayed until March 1964. Flying then all but ceased, but the airfield continued to be used occasionally until July 1979, when Chipmunks were based here for elementary training. They were resident here until April 1993 when the airfield closed.

Swingfield, Kent
This RFC second-class night LG was used as an ELG for home defence units from 1916 to 1918. From August to October 1944, it served as an ALG and was used by FAA Albacores and Swordfish.

Swinstead (Grimsthorpe), Lincs
This RFC second-class night LG was used for home defence from October 1916 to July 1919. Types based here included Be2s and Fe2s.

Sydenham
See Belfast.

Syerston, Notts
This RAF bomber station opened in December 1940 and was home to Wellingtons, Hampdens, Lancasters, and Halifaxes until October 1945. Transport Command then took over with Dakotas, Halifaxes, and Horsas until January 1948. Training then became its role and Harvards, Tiger Moths, Prentices, Provosts, Vampires, and Jet Provosts were operated until 1971 when the station was placed on C&M. It reopened in January 1975 as the RAF's central gliding school; this continues to this day. A VGS is also based here with Vikings. The airfield is open to visiting private pilots who have the choice of three hard licensed runways and eight unlicensed grass strips.

Sywell (Northampton), Northants
This civil aerodrome opened officially in September 1928, although the first landing took place in June 1927. Limited scheduled services commenced in July 1935. Elementary flying training started in June 1935 with Moths, Tiger Moths, and Harts; they were followed by Ansons, Oxfords, Prentices, and Chipmunks until June 1953. During the Second World War, a CRO (Brooklands Aviation) dealt mainly with Wellingtons, and Armstrong Whitworth opened a factory nearby that assembled Lancasters and test-flew them from the airfield. After the war, Brooklands Aviation concentrated on overhauling Valettas, Varsities, Mosquitoes, Dakotas, Vampires, and Chipmunks. It reopened for civil flying in 1947 and scheduled services operated here from 1959 to 1965. Today, Sywell is a busy GA airfield with over 150 residents operating from a hard runway laid in 2008–2009 and three grass strips, all licensed.

Tadcaster (Bramham Moor), Yorks
This RFC first-class night LG opened in March 1916 and was home to Be2s, Scouts, and Be12s on home defence duties. It later became a TDS equipped with SE5s, Avro 504s, Camels, and F2bs. Flying ceased in December 1919.

Tain, Highland
This pre-Second World War LG served nearby firing ranges. It opened as a RAF station in September 1941 and was home to various units but used mostly for Coastal Command operations with Beauforts, Hampdens, Beaufighters, Liberators, Wellingtons, and Halifaxes. Spitfires and Hurricanes were based here briefly from September 1941 to May 1942, and the FAA was frequent visitors. Flying ceased in December 1946, but a few microlights fly from part of the old airfield.

Talbenny, Pembrokeshire
This RAF station opened in May 1942 and was home initially to Coastal Command Wellingtons. It went on to host other units operating Warwicks, Venturas, and Hudsons. An armament practice camp was based here from April 1943 to September 1945 equipped with

Above: Cessna 172 G-BJVM and other types were parked in front of a T2 hangar at the RAF airfield at Swanton Morley on 5 August 1993. The notice on the hangar shows use by the Norfolk and Norwich Aero Club, which was resident from 1959 until the airfield closed in 1995. (*Grant Peerless*)

Right: A good selection of mainly DH Moth types lined up on the grass in front of the hangars at the reasonably new aerodrome at Sywell in the 1930s. (*Flight*)

Below: Aero AT3 G-SWLL and two others of the resident flying school parked in front of the control tower at Sywell at the time of a LAA rally on 2 September 2011. (*Grant Peerless*)

Martinets. In July 1944, a ferry training unit and overseas aircraft dispatch unit arrived, which collected replacement aircraft and sent them overseas. The airfield was placed on C&M in August 1945 and closed in December 1946.

Talgarth, Powys
This gliding site opened in 1980 and is home to the Black Mountains GC with about twenty-five gliders.

Tandragee (Kernan Valley), NI
This unlicensed airfield with a single hard runway opened before 2011, at which a dozen or so aircraft are based, mainly microlights.

Tangmere, Sussex
This RFC first-class LG opened in March 1918 and was used for home defence with SE5s, F2bs, and Avro 504s. A TDS was set up for the USAAS in December 1918 and operated Avro 504s, Camels, and F2bs until flying ceased in December 1919. Following expansion, it reopened as a Fighter Command station in December 1926 and was to retain this role until March 1958. A wide variety of types were operated here, including Gamecocks, Siskins, Furies, Gladiators, Hurricanes, Blenheims, Spitfires, Havocs, and Typhoons.

After the war, Mosquitoes, Meteors, Vampires, and Hunters were employed here. From October 1940, Lysanders employed on SOE operations were regular visitors. The CFE was based from January to October 1945 with various types. A signals unit arrived in August 1958 equipped with Canberras and Varsities, staying until October 1963. A flight of ASR Whirlwinds was based here from 1961 to 1964, and flying ceased in October 1970, although a VGS continued operating here until 2016. The Tangmere Aviation Museum opened on part of the wartime airfield in June 1982.

Tarrant Rushton, Dorset
This RAF station opened in May 1943 and was home to mainly gliding and transport units operating Halifaxes, Stirlings, Hamilcars, and Horsas. They departed in September 1946, but the RAF returned in August 1952 with an AFS operating Meteors and Vampires until April 1954. Flight Refuelling Ltd arrived in June 1948 and stayed until the airfield closed in January 1981. The Dorset GC was based here during the 1970s.

Tatenhill (Burton-on-Trent), Staffs
This RAF station opened in 1940 as a satellite for Wheaton Aston and was used as a RLG for various training units. Types operated included Magisters, Tiger Moths, Wellingtons, Ansons, Oxfords, and Masters. Flying ceased in January 1945, but it reopened in the 1950s for civil use. Today, it is home to over sixty aircraft that operate from a single licensed hard runway.

Tatton Park, Cheshire
This area was first used in September 1940 as a parachute landing site. The aircraft involved operated from nearby Ringway but occasionally landed in the park. This use continued until March 1946. In August 1941, an SLG was set up that stored Lysanders, Bothas, Halifaxes, and Wellingtons until April 1943.

Taunton (Haydon), Somerset
Two AALGs on adjoining sites were in use here between 1933 and 1939.

Taverham, Norfolk
This RFC second-class night LG was used for home defence from 1916 to 1918.

Tealing, Tayside
This RAF station opened in March 1942 as a satellite for Errol and was home to an OTU operating Hurricanes, Masters, Lysanders, Harvards, Spitfires, and Typhoons until July 1944. It was then used by an AFU equipped with Masters, Harvards, and Hurricanes until flying ceased in June 1945.

Tebay Fell, Cumbria
This gliding site was used by the Furness GC (Lakes GC from 1957) between 1956 and 1964.

Teddesley Park, Staffs
This SLG was used to store Venturas, Hudsons, Hotspurs, Typhoons, Avengers, Proctors, and Seamews from June 1941 until February 1946.

Teignmouth
See Haldon.

Telscombe Cliffs (Newhaven), Sussex
This RFC first-class day LG opened in October 1916 and was used for home defence by Be2s and Be12s. An AAP was resident from August 1917 to March 1918. A coastal patrol flight arrived in June 1918 and operated DH6s until flying ceased in January 1919.

Temple Bruer, Lincs
This field was used as a RLG for RAF Avro 504s during 1929. An unlicensed airfield at Griffins Farm opened

before 1989 and is home to over fifteen light aircraft that operate from a single grass runway.

Temple Guiting, Glos
This civil aerodrome was in operation in the 1930s and was later used as an ELG by the RAF from December 1944 to September 1945.

Templeton, Pembrokeshire
This RAF station opened in November 1942 as a satellite for Withybush and was home to mostly training units operating Beauforts, Ansons, Mosquitoes, Martinets, and Spitfires. The latter two were used for target-towing. It closed in June 1945, but an ACGS continued flying here until June 1946. The West Wales GC was based here from 1985 to 1993.

Tempsford, Beds
This RAF station opened in December 1941 and was home to Wellingtons that stayed until April 1942. The next unit that arrived made Tempsford famous as it was the squadron that delivered SOE agents to occupied Europe. It operated Lysanders, Halifaxes, Whitleys, Hudsons, and Stirlings until June 1945. A flight of Liberators was then based here until April 1946 when flying ceased. A MU then took over, handing mostly Harvards and Mosquitoes until September 1947.

Tern Hill (Stoke Heath), Salop
This RFC aerodrome opened in November 1916 and was used mainly for training with Camels, Avro 504s, Be12s, Fe2s, 0/400s, and DH6s until flying ceased in March 1920. Following expansion, it reopened for the RAF in January 1936, again mainly in the training role. Numerous units operated Harts, Audaxes, Tutors, Oxfords, Harvards, Masters, Hurricanes, Spitfires, Tiger Moths, Provosts, and Prentices until July 1961. The CFS helicopter wing then arrived with Sycamores, Whirlwinds, and Sioux until they transferred to Shawbury in September 1976. A MU was set up during the war, which continued until February 1959. It handled many types including Lysanders, Wellingtons, Swordfish, Lancasters, and Spitfires. The airfield is still open to helicopters, mostly from RAF Shawbury that use it as a RLG but fixed-wing aircraft are not allowed here, apart from gliders. A VGS is currently based here with Vikings.

Thakeham (Billingshurst), Sussex
This RFC first-class night/day LG was used for home defence from March 1917 to February 1918.

Thame
See Aylesbury.

Thaxted, Essex
This RFC second-class night LG was used for home defence from January 1917 to June 1918.

Theale (Sheffield Farm), Berks
This RLG for Woodley opened in September 1939 and was used mainly by Magisters and Tiger Moths until July 1941. A FTS equipped with Tiger Moths was then based until July 1945. A communications flight arrived in 1942 and operated Mentors, Dominies, and Puss Moths until May 1944. An ACGS was based here from July 1944 to July 1948 when flying ceased.

The Hyde, Gt. London
This LG was used by Airco for test-flying aircraft during the First World War.

Therfield Heath (Baldock), Herts
This RFC LG was used for home defence from 1917 to late 1918, mainly with Be2s and Be12s.

Thetford (Lodge Farm), Norfolk
This civil aerodrome was first used in July 1932 by Cobham's Flying Circus, but its subsequent use is unknown.

Thetford (Snarehill), Norfolk
This LG was used in 1911 and 1912 for army manoeuvres. It opened as a RFC second-class LG in November 1915 and was used mainly for training but with a home defence presence as well. A wide variety of types were operated here, including Bleriots, Shorthorns, Longhorns, Be2s, Fe2s, RE8s, FK8s, Avro 504s, DH4s, DH6s, DH9s, and Camels until flying ceased in April 1919. It was considered as a civil airport for Thetford in 1927–1928 and may have been used in the 1930s by Suffolk and Eastern Counties Aero Club based at Hadleigh.

Thirsk, Yorks
This LG on the racecourse was used by the RFC for home defence with Avro 504s and Be2s during 1916 and 1917. On a nearby site, an AALG was in use in the 1930s.

Tholthorpe, Yorks
This RAF bomber station opened in August 1940 as a satellite for Linton-on-Ouse, but it did not host any

resident units until June 1943 when Halifaxes arrived. These were followed by Lancasters that stayed until June 1945 when the station closed.

Thornaby (Yarm), Cleveland
This RFC ELG opened in August 1914 and later became a second-class night LG that was used for home defence from 1916. Following expansion, it reopened as a RAF station in March 1930 and was home to a wide variety of units operating Wapitis, Demons, Audaxes, Hinds, Ansons, Bothas, Blenheims, Battles, Spitfires, Hudsons, Fortresses, Halifaxes, Liberators, Warwicks, Oxfords, and Sea Otters. Flying ceased in June 1946 but resumed in September 1950 when Meteors from Middleton St George used it as a RLG. Vampires arrived in July 1951, which were followed by Hunters; a flight of ASR Sycamores was resident here from November 1954 to October 1957. It closed in October 1958.

Thorne, Yorks
This RFC first-class night LG was used for home defence from October 1916 to November 1918

Thorney Island, Hants
This RAF station opened for Coastal Command in March 1938 with a brief stay by Vildebeests. A reconnaissance school was formed here a month later and operated Sharks, Nimrods, Ospreys, Ansons, Beauforts, Hampdens, Liberators, Wellingtons, and Hudsons. It became a fighter station during the Second World War with Spitfires, Blenheims, and Typhoons. A naval detachment was also based with Swordfish, Avengers, Barracudas, Fireflies, and Sea Mosquitoes, which stayed until May 1948.

After the war, RAF Beaufighters, Mosquitoes, and Meteors were resident. An ANS arrived in May 1950 and operated Wellingtons, Marathons, Ansons, Vampires, Meteors, and Varsities until January 1962. This was followed by an OCU equipped with Valettas, Hastings, Argosies, Beverleys, Andovers, and Hercules, which stayed until October 1975. A flight of SAR Whirlwinds was based here from February 1955 to June 1969. The airfield closed in March 1976, but Britten-Norman used a hangar for Islander and Trislander production from mid-1977. A few microlights fly from part of the old airfield.

Thornhill, Central Region
This private grass airfield at Easter Poldar Farm opened in around 1989, which is home to a dozen aircraft, mostly microlights.

Thorpe Abbotts, Suffolk
Originally intended as a satellite for Horham, it opened instead for the USAAF as a bomber station in June 1943. It was home to B-17s until December 1945 when flying ceased. A lone PA28 flies from part of the old airfield.

Thrapston, Northants
This RFC third-class LG was in use for a short period from October 1916 to March 1917.

Throwley (Faversham), Kent
This RFC night LG was used for home defence from October 1915, becoming a flight station in February 1917. Types operated included Be2s, Be12s, Pups, Camels, Snipes, and Avro 504s until flying ceased in May 1919. It may have been used as an ELG for RAF Detling during the Second World War.

Thruxton, Hants
This RAF station opened in July 1941 and was home to a variety of units, mostly training and transport ones that operated Lysanders, Oxfords, Whitleys, Albermarles, Blenheims, and Ansons until 1946. The USAAF put in a brief appearance with P-47s between March and June 1944. Civil flying commenced in 1947 and continues to this day with around seventy aircraft being based here. Thruxton motor racing circuit, which opened in 1967, occupies most of the wartime airfield, and the runways—one hard and one grass—are inside the circuit, both being licensed.

Thurgarton, Notts
This RFC/RAF second-class night LG was used for home defence during 1918.

Thurleigh (Bedford), Beds
This USAAF station opened in September 1942 and was home to B-17s until December 1945. After the war, the airfield was developed for test-flying by the RAE and opened officially in June 1957. Numerous service and experimental types used the facility until it closed in March 1994. The FAA based a flight of Wyverns here between June and October 1954. The eastern end of the east–west wartime runway was licensed in 2010 and is available to visiting aircraft.

Thurrock, Essex
This unlicensed airfield at Kings Farm opened in 1990 and is home to over twenty aircraft that have the use of one hard and one parallel grass runway.

Second World War control tower with later glass house addition at Thruxton on 21 June 1999. The airfield is situated inside the motor racing circuit. (*Grant Peerless*)

Thurso (Clardon), Highland

This civil aerodrome opened in June 1935 when it became a request stop for scheduled services, but these ceased on the outbreak of the Second World War.

Thurso (Scrabster), Highland

This civil aerodrome was first used in 1931 before coming into use as a request stop on scheduled services a couple of years later. It was also used by charter flights. It closed around 1936 when services transferred to nearby Clardon aerodrome.

Tibenham, Norfolk

This RFC second-class night LG opened in October 1916 and was used for home defence by Avro 504s, Be2s, Be12s, Pups, and F2bs until closure in late 1918. Priory Farm airfield opened on the same site in 1982 and is home to over forty light aircraft that operate from a single unlicensed grass runway. Approximately 2 miles to the east, a USAAF bomber station opened in October 1942 and was home to B-26s and B-24s, which departed in May 1945. The RAF then resumed control and extended the main runway in 1955, but little flying took place and the airfield closed in March 1959. The Norfolk GC arrived in 1960 and continues to use the site today, visiting light aircraft also being welcome. Three unlicensed hard runways are available. Over sixty aircraft are based here, including gliders.

Tilshead, Wilts

This RAF LG opened in June 1918 and was used mainly for artillery co-operation until the following November. Types operated included Pups, RE8s, and Avro 504s. It was again used by army co-operation units in 1925 with F2bs, Atlases, Hectors, and Lysanders. The latter type departed in September 1941 and little use was made of the airfield until Proctors from Yatesbury used it as a RLG from June 1944 to July 1945. Flying then ceased.

Tilstock (Whitchurch), Salop

This RAF station opened in August 1942 and was home to several training units operating Wellingtons, Ansons, Whitleys, Stirlings, Halifaxes, Spitfires, and Hurricanes. It was placed on C&M in March 1946 and was used periodically during the 1950s for training exercises. Part of the wartime airfield reopened for private flying in 1964, mostly parachuting; a few aircraft are based here. One unlicensed hard runway is available.

Tiree (Reef), Hebrides

This civil aerodrome was first used in July 1936 for scheduled services that continued on a limited basis during the Second World War. It opened as a RAF station in April 1942 and was home initially to Coastal Command Hudsons, Wellingtons, Liberators, and Halifaxes. A meteorological reconnaissance unit operated Halifaxes here from September 1943 to

Sign welcoming visitors to Priory Farm, Tibenham on 24 July 2008. An RFC aerodrome occupied this site during the First World War. (*Grant Peerless*)

September 1945, and ASR Warwicks were based here from February 1944 to September 1945. Flying then ceased but the airfield reopened as a civil airport in July 1946 and scheduled services are still operated. Parts of three of the hard wartime runways are in use and are all licensed.

Tisbury, Wilts

This civil aerodrome was in use during the 1930s.

Tollerton (Nottingham), Notts

Possibly a RFC home defence LG during the First World War, it was officially opened on 19 June 1930 as Nottingham Airport. Scheduled services commenced in May 1932 and continued until 1936 when the aerodrome became too small for larger aircraft. An elementary flying school arrived in June 1938 with Hinds, Ansons, Magisters, and Harts but was disbanded on the outbreak of the Second World War. Field Aircraft Services set up a repair facility in 1938 and went on to overhaul hundreds of aircraft, including Dakotas, Hampdens, Halifaxes, Manchesters, Liberators, Bostons, and Lancasters.

During the war, it was a dispersal site for Hampdens from RAF Waddington. Between July 1941 and December 1946, it was a RLG for Hucknall and used by Harvards, Oxfords, and Ansons. After the war, Field Aircraft Services broke up large numbers of redundant Lancasters and finally left the airfield in 1957. It became a RLG again in November 1951, this time for Syerston and was used by Harvards, Prentices, and Provosts until January 1958. It reopened for civil flying after the war, and some scheduled services were operated from here. Today, it is a busy GA airfield with over fifty resident aircraft that operate from two licensed hard runways.

Toome, NI

This RAF station opened in July 1943 and was home to an OTU operating Wellingtons, but their stay was short-lived and they departed two months later. The USAAF then arrived and operated A-20s and A-26s in the training role until November 1944 when flying ceased. It was reactivated in September 1953 as a RLG for Cluntoe and used by Harvards and Prentices until June 1954.

Topcliffe, Yorks

This RAF bomber station opened in September 1940 and was home initially to Whitleys, which were followed by Halifaxes, Wellingtons, and Lancasters until October 1945. An ANS arrived in September 1946 equipped with Ansons, Wellingtons, and Oxfords and stayed until July 1949. Transport Command then took over with Hastings until May 1953. In August 1952,

Grumman American AA-5 G-PURR on the apron in front of the control tower at Tollerton (Nottingham) on 27 October 2005. This author is sitting on the wing. (*Grant Peerless*)

Coastal Command came on the scene with Lancasters and Neptunes, which were resident until February 1957. An ANS then returned, this time with Marathons and Varsities and soldiered on until October 1973. A communications flight was based from October 1964 to January 1969, which operated Devons, Pembrokes, Ansons, and Bassetts. The army took over the base in April 1969 with helicopters, but the RAF returned in April 1993 and used the airfield as a RLG for Linton-on-Ouse with Fireflies followed by Tucanos. This use continues today, and a VGS with Vigilants is also based here, together with a few private light aircraft.

Tottenhill, Norfolk
This RFC third-class night LG was used for home defence from late 1916 to November 1918.

Townsend, Wilts
This FLG was first used in 1940 by Tiger Moths from RAF Yatesbury. In August 1941, it became an SLG and stored various types of aircraft until November 1944. It was used again as a RLG for Yatesbury, this time by Proctors from 1943 until July 1945, when flying ceased.

Towyn, Gwynedd
This RAF station opened in September 1940 and was used mainly for AACU duties. Queen Bees, Henleys, Martinets, Tiger Moths, Lysanders, and Hurricanes were operated from here until closure in July 1945.

Tranent
See Macmerry.

Tregantle, Cornwall
This was a RNAS storage depot at Tregantle Fort, but it is believed that some aircraft, possibly DH6s, were flown from an adjacent field during 1918.

Treligga, Cornwall
First used as a gliding site before the Second World War, it was selected by the FAA as a firing range in late 1939, known as HMS *Vulture* 2. It became a RLG for St Merryn and closed at the end of 1955.

Treswell, Notts
This unlicensed airfield at Forwood Farm opened before 2011 with a single grass runway; it is home to around six light aircraft.

Trimley, Suffolk
This RLG for Martlesham Heath was used for test-flying from December 1916 to May 1918. Types operated included Pups and DH4s.

Trowbridge, Wilts
This small AALG was in use in the 1930s.

Truro, Cornwall
This unlicensed airfield opened before 1982 with a single grass runway and has a few resident aircraft.

Tuddenham, Suffolk

This RAF bomber station opened in October 1943 and was initially home to Stirlings, which were followed by Lancasters that stayed until November 1946 when flying ceased. Thor missiles were deployed on the site between July 1959 and July 1963.

Turnberry (Girvan), Strathclyde

This RFC aerodrome opened on the golf course in January 1917 and was home to a gunnery school equipped with Avro 504s, Camels, Dolphins, FB9s, DH2s, FK3s, Be2s, Fe2s, DH4s, DH9s, SE5s, and F2bs until April 1919. It was an AALG during the 1930s and opened as a RAF station in May 1942. Its first resident was an OTU equipped with Beauforts, Hampdens, Ansons, and Oxfords, which stayed until December 1942. It returned in February 1944 with some of the foregoing types but also Venturas and Warwicks until August 1945.

A target-towing unit arrived in November 1942 and operated Beaufighters, Wellingtons, Bothas, Lysanders, and Hampdens until May 1944. A Coastal Command flying instructors school was formed in June 1945, equipped with Beaufighters, Wellingtons, Mosquitoes, Liberators, and Warwicks that stayed until April 1946. Flying then ceased, although an ACGS continued flying until 1948. It reopened for civil use in the 1960s and was popular during matches at the adjacent golf course. It closed around 2002.

Turnhouse

See Edinburgh.

Turweston, Bucks

This RAF station was first used by Blenheims for a short period just before the Second World War. From October 1942, it became a RLG for Silverstone and was used by an OTU operating Blenheims, Wellingtons, Ansons, and Mitchells until December 1945. A ferry training unit was based here briefly between May and October 1943, which operated Blenheims, Bostons, Havocs, Wellingtons, and Beaufighters. Flying ceased in November 1945. Limited private flying took place after the war until it opened as an unlicensed airfield in 1989. Part of one of the wartime runways was refurbished in 1994; it is now unlicensed, and today, the airfield is a busy GA facility with over eighty resident aircraft.

Twatt, Orkney

This FAA station HMS *Tern* opened in April 1941 and was used mainly by units on 'shore leave' from aircraft carriers. Types based here included Swordfish, Fulmars, Walruses, Albacores, Sea Hurricanes, and Seafires. Flying ceased in August 1945, but it was retained as a reserve station until January 1949, finally closing in 1957.

Twinwood Farm, Beds

This LG was in use during the 1930s and at one time considered as a municipal airport for Bedford. It opened as a RAF station in June 1941 as a satellite for Cranfield and was used mainly by an OTU operating Blenheims, Beaufighters, Mosquitoes, Oxfords, Ansons, and Harvards until closure in June 1945. Tomahawks, Mustangs, and Typhoons of various units were also based here during the war. It was used by communication flights until 1955 and then by a civil flying and gliding club until 1984, possibly later. During the 1960s, some test-flying by Kestrels and Harriers took place.

Tydd St Mary (Wisbech), Lincs

This RFC home defence flight station opened in the summer of 1916 and was used by Fe2s and Avro 504s. The USAAS arrived in July 1918 and operated DH6s, Avro 504s, and Be2s until they departed in the following September. The LG closed in June 1919.

Tynehead, Lothian

This RFC first-class LG was used for home defence from February 1917 to November 1918.

Tynemouth (Cullercoats), Tyne and Wear

This RFC second-class night LG opened in December 1916 and was used for home defence until May 1918. A coastal patrol flight was then based here, operating DH6s until flying ceased in June 1919.

Udny (Pitmedden), Grampian

This unlicensed grass airfield, operated by Udny and Dudwick Estates, opened before 1974 and closed in around 1984.

Unst (Baltasound), Shetland

This unlicensed airfield opened in 1968 with a single hard runway. Scheduled services were operated from the 1970s to 1996, but only limited flying now takes place. It is the most northerly airfield in the British Isles.

Upavon, Wilts

This RFC training station opened in May 1912, which was home to Camels, SE5As, DH4s, FK8s, Avro 504s, and F2bs. Training continued after the First World

The futuristic control tower at Turweston on 1 August 2018. It was brought into use in December 2016 and houses the Flight Deck Café and Turweston Flight Centre. The Light Aircraft Association's head office is on the left. (*Tony Yarnold*)

War and into the Second World War, finally ceasing in May 1946. A wide assortment of aircraft was operated here, including Avro 504s, Snipes, Woodcocks, Tutors, Harts, Bulldogs, Siskins, Masters, Magisters, and Oxfords. Flying then became sporadic, mostly by a communications flight until April 1964. From May 1959 to May 1960, some Pioneers and Twin Pioneers were based here. A VGS commenced operations in November 1978 and is still operating, currently with Vikings. The base was transferred to the army in August 1993, but two licensed grass strips are still available to visiting aircraft. A dozen or so gliders belonging to the Wyvern GC and Army GC are also based here.

Upottery, Devon

This RAF station opened in February 1944 but was used by the Americans for most of its life. The USAAF operated C-47s, C-53s, Horsas, and Hadrians until September 1944. It then transferred to the RAF as a satellite for Westonzoyland, but the following January, it was back in American hands, this time the US Navy with PB4Ys. They stayed until June 1945 when flying ceased. The base then passed to a MU but closed in November 1948.

Upper Dysart (Montrose), Tayside

This LG was in use by the RFC from February to December 1913 when operations moved to Broomfield. Be2s were among the types based here.

Upper Heyford, Oxon

This RFC LG was opened in 1916, but no units were based here until July 1918 when a TDS was formed. This saw little action and flying ceased in February 1920. Types operated included Dolphins, Salamanders, and DH9s. Following expansion, it reopened as a RAF station in November 1927, its first resident being a station flight with Avro 504s. Various units then operated Hyderabads, Hinaidis, Heyfords, Virginias, Audaxes, Blenheims, and Wellesleys up to the outbreak of the Second World War. It became a bomber base during the war, supporting operations by Hampdens, Ansons, Wellingtons, and Mosquitoes. From March 1946, parachute and gliding training took place with Dakotas, Halifaxes, Wellingtons, and Horsas, continuing until June 1950. The base passed to the USAF in May 1951; they went on to operate B-29s, C-47s, B-50s, B-47s, B-36s, C-97s, B-66s, F-4Cs, HH-34s, HH-43s, and F-101s. F-111s were the last aircraft to be based here, and they departed in December 1993 when flying ceased.

Upton (Poole), Dorset

This LG was in use by the RFC and RAF during 1918.

Upwood, Cambs

A RFC night LG, known as Bury or Ramsey, opened for home defence and later training in January 1917. Types operated from here included Be2s, DH6s,

Fe2s, and Avro 504s until closure in May 1919. Following expansion, it reopened as a RAF station in February 1937 and was home to numerous units operating Hinds, Battles, Audaxes, Blenheims, Oxfords, Mosquitoes, Liberators, Lancasters, and Lincolns. Canberras arrived in December 1952 and stayed until January 1959. Operational flying ceased in September 1961, but some private aircraft are still based on the airfield as well as gliders of the Nene Valley GC—around twenty in all.

Usk (Gwernesney), Gwent

This gliding site opened in 1970, operated by the South Wales GC; it is home to over forty gliders.

Usworth, Tyne and Wear

This RFC home defence aerodrome, known as Hylton, opened in October 1916 and was home to Fe2s and Scouts until June 1919. It was reactivated for the RAF in March 1930, and many different units were based here for the next thirty years. The first residents were Wapitis followed by Demons, Gladiators, Hinds, and Battles. Hurricanes were based here briefly between September 1940 and January 1941, and an OTU then arrived with Hurricanes, Masters, Defiants, Blenheims, Ansons, and Wellingtons. This stayed until July 1943 when operational flying virtually ceased apart from a UAS formed in March 1944, which used Tiger Moths and Harvards followed by Chipmunks, Ansons, Prentices, and Balliols until October 1957. An RFS operated similar types between February 1949 and July 1953. An AOP flight of Austers was based here from February 1954 to March 1957, and Ansons belonging to training flights were resident between April 1951 and October 1957. Flying then ceased, but an ACGS continued operating until September 1962. It reopened for civil use in July 1962 as Sunderland Airport and closed in May 1984 when it was developed into the Nissan car factory.

Valley, Gwynedd

This RAF station opened in February 1941, initially as a fighter base, and was home to Hurricanes, Beaufighters, and Defiants. In October 1941, its role changed to ASR when Lysanders, Walruses, and Ansons were operated. This continued until 2015 when Sea King helicopters were withdrawn. Between June 1943 and September 1945, it was used as a USAAF ferry terminal and numerous types were handled here, including B-24s, B-17s, B-25s, and C-47s. Flying ceased in June 1947 and it was placed on C&M until March 1951 when training returned with Vampires, Meteors, Swifts, Javelins, Gnats, Chipmunks, and Bulldogs. Hawks and Texans are currently used and today, Valley remains a busy RAF training airfield. Scheduled services to Cardiff began in 2007 and are still operating today by Flybe.

Waddington, Lincs

This RFC first-class LG opened in November 1916 and was used as a training station, which later became a TDS. Types operated here included Shorthorns, DH4s, DH6s, DH9s, RE8s, FK8s, Dolphins, and Avro 504s until closure in December 1919. Following expansion, it reopened as a RAF bomber station in October 1926 and was to continue in this role for the next fifty-eight years. The first residents were Fawns, Hyderabads, and Wallaces, then later, there were Hinds and Blenheims, which were followed during the Second World War by Hampdens, Battles, Manchesters, and Lancasters. After the war, Lincolns and Washingtons were based here, followed in May 1955 by Canberras and then later, by Vulcans; the former only stayed a couple of years but the latter were retired in March 1984. The USAAF put in various appearances between July 1948 and May 1955 with B-29s, B-50s, and C-47s. Nimrods arrived in December 1984 and departed in 2011. Sentries appeared in June 1990, and these are still based here today, together with Shadows, Sentinels, and RC-135 Rivet Joints.

Wakefield, Grampian

This field was used as a FLG for RAF Montrose between 1942 and 1945.

Waldershare Park (Dover), Kent

This gliding site opened in 1985 and is operated by the Channel GC at which around six gliders are based.

Wallasey, Merseyside

This LG on the beach was used by Northwest Air Services for pleasure flights in the early 1960s.

Wallingford, Oxon

This AALG was in use in the 1930s.

Walmer (Hawksdown), Kent

This RNAS aerodrome opened in May 1917 and was used by a home defence flight operating Be2s, Scouts, and Pups. A coastal patrol flight arrived in June 1918 equipped with Camels, DH4s, and DH9s; they stayed until flying ceased in September 1919.

Walney Island
See Barrow-in-Furness.

Walsall (Aldridge), W. Midlands
This RFC second-class night LG, known as Great Barr, was used for home defence for only a short time from April to December 1916. About 3 miles to the north, a site came into use in May 1934 and was opened officially as Walsall Airport in July 1935. Helliwells set up a facility in 1938 to manufacture aircraft components and later went on to service and repair RAF aircraft as a CRO. Types handled included Harvards, Spitfires, Hurricanes, and Bostons. A branch of the CAG was set up in July 1938, and an ACGS operated here from October 1943 to December 1946. Helliwells assembled several Globe Swifts imported from the USA in the early 1950s, but this enterprise was not a success. The airfield closed in 1956.

Waltham (Cheapside/Grimsby), Humberside
This civil aerodrome was opened in June 1933 by the Lincolnshire Aero Club with scheduled services commencing soon afterwards. An elementary flying school was formed in June 1938 with Tiger Moths, Magisters, and Hinds but departed on the outbreak of the Second World War when the airfield closed. It was then developed into a RAF bomber station that opened in November 1941, initially equipped with Wellingtons, which were followed by Lancasters. A detachment of Sea Hurricanes was based from January 1943 to December 1944. The Lancasters departed in April 1945, and flying then ceased, although an ACGS continued flying until August 1950.

Waltham St Lawrence, Berks
This RLG for White Waltham, Fairoaks, and Woodley was in use from August 1940 to July 1947, mostly by Tiger Moths and Magisters.

Walton, Cambs
This airstrip was used by Frederick Sage and Co. to test-fly aircraft built by them at an adjacent factory during the First World War. Types produced included Be2s and Avro 504s.

Walton Wood (Thorpe Audlin/ Pontefract), Yorks
This unlicensed airfield opened in the 1980s with a single grass runway and is home to around six or so aircraft.

Wanborough, Wilts
This RAF training station opened in August 1941 and was used mainly as a RLG for Watchfield until May 1945. Types used included Tiger Moths, Harvards, Oxfords, and Ansons. Glider training took place from December 1943 to May 1944 with Masters and Hotspurs. The school of flying control was based here briefly from June to December 1943 and operated Ansons, Dominies, and Oxfords. Flying ceased in May 1945.

A nearby microlight site at Redlands opened in 1991 and is home to over forty aircraft as well as being used for parachuting. Three unlicensed grass strips are in use. Another private grass strip in the vicinity at Lotmead Farm, in use since before 2001, has around six residents.

Warboys, Cambs
This RAF bomber station opened as a satellite for Upwood in October 1941 and closed in January 1946. Types operated included Stirlings, Blenheims, Wellingtons, Lancasters, Halifaxes, and Mosquitoes. Bloodhound missiles were deployed here between 1960 and 1963.

Warmwell (Woodsford), Dorset
This RAF station opened in May 1937 and was home initially to training units operating Tutors, Hinds, Seals, Wallaces, Battles, and Ansons. Fighter Command took over in July 1940 and employed Spitfires, Hurricanes, Whirlwinds, and Typhoons until September 1945. The USAAF put in a brief appearance between March and August 1944 with P-38s, and the airfield was placed on C&M in October 1945, closing down soon afterwards.

Warton, Lancs
This RAF station opened in 1941 as a satellite for Squires Gate, but no flying took place until August 1942 when it became a USAAF base air depot. Nearly 10,000 aircraft were handled during its two years of operation, mostly P-51s and B-24s but also A-26s, P-47s, B-17s, and C-47s. It returned to the RAF in November 1945 and was used by a MU until February 1951 and an ACGS from November 1951 to September 1955. English Electric acquired the site in 1949 for building and test-flying Canberras, which were followed by Lightnings, Jaguars, Tornadoes, and Typhoons, latterly as BAE Systems. A single licensed hard runway is in use but it is only available to aircraft on BAE business.

Warwick, Warks
This RLG for RAF Church Lawford was used by Oxfords, Tutors, and Ansons from July 1941 to May 1945.

Watchet (Doniford), Somerset
This LG was opened in 1928 to accept communication flights for a nearby gunnery range. It was used by AACUs from July 1937, which operated Queen Bees, Magisters, and Tutors until October 1940. It was then used mainly for communications and training by Lysanders, Austers, and L-4s. It also saw use as an ELG. It may have been in use until 1956, still in support of gunnery ranges.

Watchfield, Berks
This civil aerodrome was licensed in July 1939 but was little used until it closed on the outbreak of the Second World War. It reopened as a RAF station in July 1940 and was used initially for training with Tiger Moths, Ansons, and Magisters until December 1941. From September 1940, it became the home of blind landing development and the school of air traffic control until February 1950 when the RAF departed. These units employed Ansons, Oxfords, Dominies, Masters, and Harvards. During the 1950s, it was used for parachute training and by gliders in the 1970s.

Waterbeach, Cambs
This RAF bomber station opened in March 1941 and was home to Wellingtons, Stirlings, and Lancasters. It transferred to Transport Command in September 1945, who operated Liberators, Yorks, and Dakotas. Another change took place in May 1950 when Fighter Command took over, initially with Meteors, which were followed by Swifts, Hunters, Venoms, Vampires, and Javelins. The last aircraft, a Hunter, departed in August 1963, but it was used as a RLG for Oakington until 1974.

Watergate Wath, Yorks
This gliding site was operated by the Watergate Wath GC in the late 1970s and early 1980s.

Waterloo Sands (Blundellsands/ Bootle), Merseyside
This civil aerodrome was opened in 1911 by the Liverpool Aviation School, which operated a few Bleriots, along with the Avro Transport Company with 504s. It was used by the RFC and RAF as a day LG during the First World War and closed in around 1920.

Wath Head, Cumbria
This SLG was used for storing Hampdens, Wellingtons, Halifaxes, Oxfords, and Bostons from April 1941 to December 1945.

Watnall, Notts
This microlight site at Brooksbreasting Farm opened in the 2000s and has around a dozen residents.

Wattisham, Suffolk
This RAF station opened in May 1939 and was home initially to Blenheims and Beaufighters. In October 1942, the USAAF arrived with P-38s, P-39s, and P-51s; they stayed until November 1945. The RAF then returned, and a year later, jet fighters came on the scene in the shape of Meteors, followed by Hunters, Javelins, Lightnings, and Phantoms. The latter were withdrawn in October 1992 and the RAF then departed. Suckling Airways operated briefly from here during 1988 because of soft grass runways at Ipswich Airport. Bloodhound missiles were deployed here between 1983 and July 1991. The army took over in March 1993 with Lynxes, Gazelles, and Apaches; the latter are still operated today. The Anglia GC and Army GC are also based here, and visiting private aircraft are accepted with prior permission.

Watton, Norfolk
This RAF station opened in March 1939 and was home to mostly Blenheims until December 1941. Masters of an AFU then arrived and stayed until May 1943 when the USAAF came on the scene. They operated B-17s, B-24s, and Mosquitoes in the reconnaissance role until they departed in July 1945. Various RAF units then took over and operated Canberras, Washingtons, Varsities, Lincolns, and Argosies until June 1976 when flying ceased. Bloodhound missiles were deployed here between June 1959 and June 1963. A VGS was based here until April 2012, but some gliding still takes place.

Welford, Berks
Originally proposed as a RAF bomber OTU, it was instead taken over by the USAAF in November 1943. They operated C-47s, C-53s, and CG-4s until February 1945. RAF Transport Command then took over with Dakotas, Oxfords, Horsas, and Proctors, staying until March 1946. Elliots of Newbury used the airfield for flight-testing their gliders from August 1947; it closed in August 1952.

Welham, Leics
This small RFC LG was used for home defence for a few months in 1916.

Wellesbourne Mountford, Warks
This RAF station opened in April 1941 and was home to an OTU operating Wellingtons and Ansons until July

1945. A ferry training unit employed Wellingtons from April to December 1943, and a photographic school used Ansons from January 1948 to August 1963. The CFS made use of the airfield as a RLG between January and December 1951; an FTS then flew Oxfords until May 1954. Part of the wartime airfield reopened for civil flying in 1964, and around eighty aircraft are currently based here. It has now dropped 'Mountford' as is just known as Wellesbourne. Two licensed hard runways and an unlicensed grass strip are in use.

Wellingore (Welbourn), Lincs

This RNAS LG was used as a RLG for Cranwell from mid-1917 by Be2s, Camels, and Avro 504s. It was again used as a RLG for Cranwell by the RAF from 1937 until September 1940. It then became a fighter station, which operated Hurricanes, Blenheims, Beaufighters, and Spitfires until March 1944. It then reverted to its former role as RLG for Cranwell and was used by Harvards, Ansons, and Oxfords until closure in June 1946.

Welshpool, Powys

Initially a grass airfield at Trehilig Farm which opened in 1987, it was later developed into what is now—Mid Wales Airport. A hard runway was laid in the early 1990s, which is now licensed, and about forty aircraft are based here.

Wembley (North Wembley) Gt. London

This field was used from 1917 to June 1919 by Hoopers, car motor bodybuilders to test-fly aircraft built by them. Types included 1½ Strutters, Camels, Dolphins, and Buzzards.

Wendling, Norfolk

This USAAF bomber station opened in July 1943 and was home to B-24s until June 1945.

West Fenton

See Drem.

West Freugh, Dumfries and Galloway

This RNAS station, known as Luce Bay, was predominantly an airship base but was also home to a RAF coastal patrol flight that operated DH6s and Fairey 3s from June 1918 to June 1919. It was redeveloped and reopened as a RAF station in October 1937 and went on to host various units, mostly training ones operating Wallaces, Seals, Henleys, Battles, Bothas, and Ansons. A bomber training unit arrived in August 1942 and operated Hampdens, Halifaxes, and Mitchells, followed by Lancasters, Mosquitoes, and Lincolns until disbanding in January 1957. A sub storage unit stored Mosquitoes from July 1945 to October 1946. It was transferred to the RAE in May

Grumman American AA-5 G-PURR in front of the control tower and hangars at the former RAF station at Wellesbourne Mountford on 3 December 2014. (*Grant Peerless*)

Hangar with control tower on top at Welshpool on 9 September 2000. General Avia F22 G-FZZA and a Piper Tomahawk are parked on the apron. It is now known as Mid Wales Airport. (*Grant Peerless*)

1956, who operated various military types until April 1995, using Devons and Jetstreams for communication purposes. The RAE departed in 2001, but it was then taken over by QinetiQ, who keep the runways open for emergency use.

West Hartlepool (Greatham), Cleveland

Construction of a municipal airport at Greatham commenced in December 1935, but it was not opened officially until 15 April 1938. An elementary flying school was formed in April 1939 with Audaxes, Tiger Moths, Ansons, and Hinds, but it moved out on the outbreak of the Second World War. In September 1941, it became a satellite for RAF Thornaby, and Spitfires from various squadrons were detached here from March 1942 to June 1943. An AACU arrived in April 1942 with Henleys and Tiger Moths but only stayed until February 1943. The RAF departed in June 1943 but an ACGS continued to operate here until November 1944. The airfield returned to civil use after the war, and Northern Air Charter arrived in May 1946, staying until 1948. BKS commenced scheduled services in May 1953; these continued until 1956 when the airfield closed.

West Malling, Kent

This RFC second-class night LG, known as Kings Hill, was used for home defence from March 1917 to August 1919. It was opened for civil use in 1930 by the Maidstone School of Flying and became Maidstone Airport on 22 July 1933. Civil flying ceased on the outbreak of the Second World War when it was taken over by the RAF as West Malling. Its first residents, in June 1940, were a flight of AACU Lysanders, but these only stayed for a couple of months. They were replaced by Defiants, Spitfires, Beaufighters, Hurricanes, Havocs, Mosquitoes, and Mustangs until August 1944. Fighters returned in October 1945 when Spitfires, Mosquitoes, Meteors, and Javelins were based here until September 1960. The US Navy then arrived with R4Ds, R4Ys, SNB-5s, and C-131s, which was resident until June 1964. It was then returned to the RAF, but they had no further use for the airfield. Shorts set up a maintenance facility in 1967 that dealt with Varsities and Chipmunks until the early 1970s; it was used by Metair for painting Saab 340s during 1990. The airfield closed in 1992 but a VGS continued flying until March 1995.

West Raynham, Norfolk

This RAF station opened in May 1939 and was home to a variety of units using Blenheims, Wellingtons, Lysanders, Defiants, Mitchells, Bostons, Beaufighters, and Mosquitoes until January 1946. The CFE then took over and operated Meteors, Vampires, Hunters, and Javelins. This unit stayed until October 1962, but before this, in September 1960, the airfield became operational again with Javelins, Hunters, Meteors, and Canberras until flying ceased in December 1975. Between 1945 and 1956, it was home to a FAA squadron, which operated Fireflies, Hellcats, Seafires,

DH60G Moth G-AACZ belonging to Malling Aviation in front of the company's hangar at West Malling on 1 April 1936. Following use by the RAF and civil operators, it closed around 1992. (*Eddie Riding*)

Attackers, Seahawks, and Wyverns. Bloodhound missiles were deployed here from 1964 to July 1991.

West Rudham, Norfolk
This RFC second-class night LG was used for home defence from December 1916 to November 1918

Westcott, Bucks
This RAF station opened in September 1942 and was home to an OTU operating Wellingtons, Hurricanes, and Masters until September 1945. Between October 1942 and February 1945, an engine control development unit was based here with Wellingtons, Beaufighters, and Lancasters. In April 1946, Westcott became involved in rocket propulsion; this continued in various forms until 1994.

Westenhangar, Kent
Folkestone Racecourse was used for a flying meeting in September 1910, but it was not used again until 1940–1941 when it became a decoy for Lympne. Austers were based here from April to July 1944 but flying then appears to have ceased.

Westgate (Mutrix Farm/St Mildreds Bay), Kent
This RNAS and RAF aerodrome was in use from 1915 to 1920 by JN3s, Be2s, Avro 504s, and Fairey 3Bs.

Westhampnett
See Goodwood.

Weston-on-the-Green, Oxon
This TDS opened in July 1918 and was used by Camels, Avro 504s, Salamanders, and DH9s until December 1919. Following expansion, it reopened for the RAF in September 1939 and was used briefly by Blenheims and Ansons. It became a RLG for an OTU operating various types in April 1940; this continued until the following November. A FTS then flew Harvards and Oxfords until December 1941 when a GTS took over. This operated Hectors, Hotspurs, Audaxes, and Masters until departing in April 1943. It was next used as a RLG by Oxfords, Ansons, and Masters of an AFU until June 1945. Dakotas used the airfield for parachute drops from March 1946 to August 1950; it is still used for this purpose today. An ACGS was based here until September 1955, and gliding is still an important activity by civilian clubs including the Oxford GC. Around twenty gliders are based here, operating from three unlicensed grass runways.

Weston Park, Staffs
This SLG was used to store mainly Spitfires, Swordfish, and gliders from June 1941 to June 1945. In early 1944, it also became a satellite for Hinstock, known as HMS *Godwit* 2. Oxfords were based here until the summer of 1945.

Weston-super-Mare, Avon

Weston Airport opened on 25 June 1936 and soon attracted scheduled services that operated until the outbreak of the Second World War. Just before this, in July 1939, an elementary flying school was formed with Magisters and Harts; this was followed by a variety of RAF units operating an assortment of types mainly in the training role. These included Ansons, Tiger Moths, Harvards, and Oxfords, which stayed until July 1945. In 1940, a shadow factory was built just outside the airfield boundary at Old Mixon, which produced over 3,000 Beaufighters until September 1945. It went on to build Bristol helicopters from 1955, particularly the Sycamore and Belvedere, as well as over thirty Bristol Freighters; it was taken over by Westland in 1960. Components for helicopters were manufactured until 2002. Civil flying resumed in March 1946, including scheduled services; this continued until the operating license was relinquished at the end of 1978. A VGS went on to operate here until June 1993, and part of the site is now occupied by the British Rotorcraft Museum, established in 1978.

Westonzoyland, Somerset

This LG was used in association with a RAF summer camp for nearby gunnery ranges from 1926 to 1936. Types used included Fawns and Horsleys. It became home to a number of AACU and training units from May 1936, operating Wallaces, Lysanders, Masters, Martinets, Tiger Moths, Mustangs, Tomahawks, Henleys, Defiants, Oxfords, Vengeances, and Mosquitoes until August 1946. Warwicks were based here for a few months from September 1943 to February 1944, and the USAAF appeared briefly between June and October 1944 with C-47s, C-53s, and CG-4s. The airfield was placed on C&M in August 1946 but reopened in June 1952 for use by Vampires, Meteors, and Canberras. Flying ceased in March 1957, and it closed in January 1958. Part of one of the wartime runways and a couple of unlicensed grass strips have been used by mostly microlights since before 1982, some fifty being based here.

Westpole Farm, Gt. London

This RFC third-class night LG near East Barnet was used for home defence from 1916 to June 1919.

West Town Moor, Tyne and Wear

This RFC LG was in use for only a short time from May to October 1916. It was closed in favour of Hylton just to the west.

Westray, Orkney

This aerodrome at West Gretna opened in August 1934 and was used by scheduled services until the outbreak of the Second World War. It reopened in 1967 and has one hard and two grass runways, all licensed. It is served by scheduled services, including the world's shortest sector to Papa Westray, which takes approximately two minutes.

Westwood Ho!, Devon

This LG was used by a RAF coastal patrol flight equipped with DH6s and DH9s from June 1918 to March 1919.

Wethersfield, Essex

This USAAF station opened in February 1944 as a satellite for Ridgewell and was home to A-20s until the following September. The RAF operated various types from March 1944 to January 1946, including Stirlings, Dakotas, Halifaxes, and Oxfords. The station was then placed on C&M until June 1952, when the USAF returned with F-84s followed by F-100s and H-21s. These stayed until April 1970 when the base was reduced to standby status and only occasional flying then took place. A VGS operating Vikings is currently based on the airfield, but it is due to close by 2024.

Weybourne, Norfolk

This LG was used for launching Queen Bee radio-controlled target aircraft between May 1939 and April 1942. Private flying has taken place since before 1998 from two unlicensed grass strips on the site, which also houses the Muckleburgh Military Collection of wartime vehicles.

Weymouth (Chickerell), Dorset

This aerodrome was used from June 1918 to January 1919 by a coastal patrol flight operating DH6s and later that year, briefly, by HP 0/400s on a service from Cricklewood. Between 1923 and 1929, FAA units were resident here with Fairey 3Fs and Walruses. It saw use in the 1930s by the Dorset GC and various flying circuses. It was used during 1937 as a forward base for nearby bombing ranges and again by the FAA during the Second World War, this time with Rocs, Masters, and Defiants. The navy returned for a short time in 1953 with Dragonfly helicopters, and the airfield closed in 1959.

Derelict Second World War control tower at Westonzoyland on 19 September 2009. Parts of the wartime airfield are still used by light aircraft, mostly microlights. (*Grant Peerless*)

Terminal building at the small grass airfield at Weybourne in Norfolk, on the site of the Muckleburgh collection of military vehicles. The photo was taken on 10 September 2009. (*Tony Yarnold*)

Weymouth (Lodmoor), Dorset

A LG on Weymouth Cricket Club's ground was used by the RFC and RAF for training from 1912. An aerodrome at Lodmoor was used by a scheduled service from Ensbury Park (Bournemouth) in 1919–20 and by Cobham's Flying Circus in 1932, but it closed in 1933.

Whalsay, Shetland

This unlicensed airfield opened in 1972 with a single hard runway. Scheduled services were operated in the 1970s, but today, it is mainly used for air ambulance operations; it is also open to visiting aircraft.

Wheatley Hill, Co. Durham

This unlicensed micolight site at Greenhills Farm is operated by East Durham Microlights and is home to nearly twenty aircraft.

Wheaton Aston, Staffs

This RAF station opened in December 1941 as a RLG for Shawbury. It was home to several training units until flying ceased in December 1946. Types operated included Oxfords, Harvards, Battles, Magisters, Spitfires, Ansons, and Tiger Moths.

Whitchurch

See Bristol.

Whiteacre Hall, Warks

This RLG for Castle Bromwich and Elmdon was used from September 1939 to February 1946. Types operated here included Tiger Moths, Magisters, Ansons, and Oxfords.

Whiteburn (Grantshouse), Northumberland

This RFC/RAF LG was used for home defence from November 1916 to December 1918.

Whitefield, Tayside

This RAF station opened in December 1939 as a RLG for Perth and was used by Tiger Moths, Magisters, and Masters until closure in July 1945.

Whiterashes (Leslie), Grampian

This unlicensed airfield at Pittrichie Farm opened around 1999 with two grass runways and is home to eight or so aircraft, mostly microlights.

White Waltham, Berks

This civil aerodrome opened in November 1935 for an elementary flying school operated by de Havillands, equipped with Harts, Audaxes, Tiger Moths, Hinds, and Ansons until December 1940. It became the headquarters of the ATA in February 1940, and its ferry pool operated Arguses and Ansons until departing in March 1946. An assortment of communication flights then operated a wide variety of types until April 1964, and an AEF and UAS was based here with Chipmunks from July 1958 to August 1973. Fairey Aviation set up a facility in 1947 to test-fly Fireflies and Gannets as well as the Rotodyne. A VGS was resident here until May 1963, and the RAF finally departed in August 1973. It then reverted to civil use, and today, over 150 residents operate from three licensed grass runways.

Whitley Bay, Tyne and Wear

This RNAS LG was used for home defence from late 1914 to May 1916. Types operated included TB8s, Be2s, and G3s.

Wick, Highland

A civil aerodrome at Hillhead opened in May 1933, which was used by scheduled services until the outbreak of the Second World War. A RAF airfield just to the north opened in October 1939 and was home to various units, mostly Coastal Command ones until the end of the War. Ansons, Hudsons, Wellingtons, Hampdens, Beauforts, Whitleys, and Beaufighters were the main types operated. Hurricanes were based here briefly between February and October 1940, and Spitfires and Mosquitoes of a PRU were resident here from April to October 1941. A meteorological flight arrived in May 1941 equipped with Hampdens, Spitfires, Hudsons, Venturas, Fortresses, and Halifaxes and stayed until August 1945. Mustangs were based briefly from January to March 1946 and it then reverted to civil use. Scheduled services are operated and a few aircraft are based here. A single licensed hard runway is in use. It is now known as Wick John O'Groats Airport.

Wickenby, Lincs

This RAF bomber station opened in September 1942 and was home to Wellingtons and Lancasters until closure in October 1945. Part of the Second World War airfield reopened for civil use in 1963, and today, it is a thriving GA airfield with around sixty residents. Two licensed hard runways are in use.

Widford, Essex

This RNAS night ELG was in use from January to September 1915, mainly by Gunbuses and G3s.

White Waltham in January 1936 with mainly DH Moth types lined up on the grass in front of the hangar. It is still grass-surfaced today and a popular GA airfield. (*Flight*)

Luscombe Silvaire G-BTCH and a Piper PA28 parked on the grass in front of hangars and control tower at White Waltham on 21 June 1991. (*Grant Peerless*)

Wight
See Cowes.

Wigsley, Notts
This RFC second-class night LG was used for home defence from October 1916 to November 1918. Following expansion, it reopened as a RAF bomber station in September 1942 and was home to Hampdens, Manchesters, Lancasters, and Stirlings until September 1945. It remained open after the war as a satellite for Swinderby and closed in July 1958.

Wigtown (Baldoon), Dumfries and Galloway
This RAF station opened in September 1941 and was home to an observers school equipped with Bothas, Ansons, Blenheims and Lysanders until November 1945. A bomber training unit was based here from June 1947 to May 1948, operating Lancasters, Lincolns, Mosquitoes, and Ansons until May 1948. It closed in July 1948; part of the airfield was reopened for civil use before 1974, but the runway surface is now virtually unusable.

Willian (Hitchin), Herts
This RFC second-class day LG was in use from 1916 to early 1919.

Willingale
See Chipping Ongar.

Willingham, Cambs
This private grass airfield at Cold Harbour Farm opened before 1985; it is home to about fifteen aircraft, mostly microlights.

Willoughby Hills (Halltoft), Lincs
This RFC second-class day/night LG was used for home defence from September 1916 to June 1918.

Wilmington (Milton Gate), Sussex
This civil aerodrome was opened in early 1933 by the Sussex Aero Club and Eastbourne Flying Club, which remained active until the outbreak of the Second World War. It was used by the RAF as a RLG in the 1930s, by a RAF communications flight in February and March 1940, and by USAAF liaison aircraft later in the war.

Wilmslow, Cheshire
This civil aerodrome was in use in the 1920s and was home to an ACGS from March 1944 to January 1946.

Wimbledon Common, Gt. London
This RFC LG opened in 1914, which later became a third-class night LG that was used for home defence until March 1919. It continued to be used by the RAF into the 1930s.

Wincanton, Somerset
This private grass airfield at Westleaze Farm was in use from the 1970s to the 1990s.

Windrush, Glos
This RLG for RAF Little Rissington was used mainly by Oxfords and Ansons from January 1940 to July 1945. Civil flying took place sporadically after the war, including use by an Islander for parachute dropping in the 1990s. The private grass airfield was still open in 2016 and is believed to be in use today.

Winfield, Borders
This RFC second-class night LG, known as Horndean, was used for home defence from December 1916 to December 1917. It was developed into a RAF station and opened in May 1942 as a satellite for Charterhall. Its main resident was an OTU that operated Blenheims, Hurricanes, Beaufighters, Wellingtons, and Mosquitoes until May 1945 when flying ceased. Part of the airfield reopened for civil flying in 1963 but closed in the 1990s.

Wing, Bucks
This RAF station opened in January 1942 and was home to an OTU that operated Ansons and Wellingtons until March 1946. A communications flight equipped with Wellingtons, Tiger Moths, and Moth Minors was based here from January 1945 until April 1946 when flying ceased.

Winkfield, Berks
This RLG for Fairoaks opened in May 1941 and was used mainly by Tiger Moths and Ansons until closure in July 1945.

Winkleigh, Devon
This RAF station opened in January 1943, but it saw little use until the following October, when the USAAF arrived for a brief stay of two months with Spitfires, B-25s, B-26s, P-61s, and C-47s. Lysanders of the SOE used the airfield for fifteen months during 1943 and 1944. The RAF came on the scene in April 1944 when several units operated Beaufighters, Mosquitoes, Defiants, Hurricanes, Martinets, Oxfords, Swordfish,

and Albacores, some with Canadian crews, until November 1944. It was then used for nearly a year by a Royal Norwegian Air Force training flight equipped with Harvards, Cornells, and Oxfords. Flying ceased in November 1945, but the AAC carried out exercises on the old airfield in 1975 and 1978 with Lynxes and Gazelles.

Winkton, Hants

This ALG was used by USAAF P-47s from April to July 1944.

Winterseugh, Dumfries and Galloway

This SLG opened in May 1941 and was used to store mostly Battles until April 1944. It was used briefly from July 1940 as a RLG by Bothas and Battles from RAF Dumfries.

Winterton (Roxby), Humberside

This RFC second-class night LG was used for home defence from December 1916 to June 1919 by Be2s and Fe2s.

Winthorpe, Notts

This RAF station opened in September 1940 as a satellite for Swinderby and was used mainly by Bomber Command until September 1945. Types operated included Battles, Wellingtons, Hampdens, Manchesters, Lancasters, Halifaxes, and Stirlings. Transport Command then took over and used the airfield for training. In February 1953, the central servicing development unit was formed with Ansons, Meteors, Varsities, and Valettas and stayed until January 1958 when flying ceased. It finally closed in June 1959 but was used for gliding until June 2006. The Newark Air Museum was opened on the site in April 1973, and today, it is a popular attraction.

Wisborough Green, Sussex

This civil aerodrome was in use before the Second World War.

Wisley, Surrey

This relief airfield was opened in 1943 by Vickers Armstrongs in connection with their factory at nearby Brooklands. It became their main flight-test centre after the war, and many types made their first flights from here, including Viscounts, Vanguards, Valiants, and VC10s. A hard runway was laid in 1952 and the airfield closed in 1973 mainly due to the proximity of Heathrow and Gatwick airports.

Witchford, Cambs

This RAF bomber station opened in July 1943 and was home to Stirlings and Lancasters until closure in September 1945.

Witham-on-the-Hill (Careby), Lincs

This gliding site was operated by the Welland Soaring Group (formerly Perkins Engines GC) from 1977 to 1980.

Withnoe, Cornwall

This was a RNAS storage depot, but it is believed that some aircraft operated from an adjacent field during the First World War.

Derelict control tower at the former RAF station at Winkleigh in August 2016. (*Grant Peerless*)

Withybush

See Haverfordwest.

Witley, Surrey

This AALG in Witley Park was in use in the 1930s.

Witney, Oxon

This RFC training station opened in March 1918, equipped with Avro 504s, F2bs, DH6s, FK8s, Camels, and RE8s until flying ceased in October 1919. Civil use returned in November 1925 with Berkshire Aviation Tours and their Avro 504s, which stayed until December 1927. Universal Aircraft Services arrived in 1933, and Chilton Aircraft used the aerodrome from 1937 for test-flying their products. In September 1939, it became a RLG for Brize Norton and was used mainly by Oxfords. de Havilland's set up a civilian repair unit in 1940, which dealt not only with DH products, mostly Dominies and Moths but also Hurricanes and Spitfires. Flying ceased in 1946. A private grass airfield in the vicinity known as Black Bourton was in use from the 1970s to the 1990s.

Wittering, Cambs

This RFC night LG, known as Stamford, opened in October 1916 and was used initially for home defence with Be2s and Fe2s. A TDS was formed in July 1917 and was in use until March 1919. It operated Avro 504s, DH4s, DH6s, DH9s, RE8s, F2bs, and Camels. Some USAAS units were also based from January to August 1918. Flying resumed by the RAF in October 1926 when the CFS arrived with F2bs, DH9s, Snipes, Grebes, Gamecocks, Siskins, Bulldogs, Tomtits, Harts, and Atlases, which stayed until September 1935. A FTS was then based here, operating Furies, Audaxes, Harts, Ansons, and Oxfords until May 1938. It then became a fighter station for the next ten years, and numerous types were employed here, including Demons, Gauntlets, Hurricanes, Spitfires, Blenheims, Defiants, Beaufighters, and Mosquitoes.

'Turbinlite' Havocs, Bostons and Hurricanes were based here between July 1941 and January 1943. The USAAF put in a brief appearance from January to April 1943 with P-47s and again between August 1943 and April 1944 with P-38s and P-51s. An air fighting development squadron was formed in October 1944 and operated Tempests, Meteors, Vampires, Javelins, Sabres, and Hunters here until September 1959. Bomber Command took over in August 1953, initially with Lincolns, which were followed by Canberras, Valiants, and Victors until February 1970. The Harrier, the type for which Wittering is most famous, arrived in January 1969 and stayed until they were withdrawn from use in January 2011. It was then placed on C&M until it was reactivated in April 2014 for flying training, including by two AEF and UASs. Tutors are the main type flown but King Airs are also used. A few gliders are also based on the airfield.

Woburn Park, Beds

An airstrip on the Woburn estate was used by the Duchess of Bedford during the early 1930s. In July 1941, the site became an SLG and was used to store Spitfires, Hurricanes, Battles, Masters, Tiger Moths, Magisters, Swordfish, Albacores, Stirlings, and approximately 200 Lancasters until closure around May 1947. Some of these aircraft were broken up here. A grass strip on the estate has been used in the past for DH Moth rallies, the last one taking place in 2015.

Wold Newton (Willy Howe), Yorks

This private grass airfield was in use from around 1992 to 2000.

Wolverhampton (Dunstall Park), W. Midlands

Flying first took place on the racecourse here by the Midland Aero Club in June 1910 and continued until March 1912 when flying ceased.

Wolverhampton (Pendeford), W. Midlands

This municipal aerodrome opened officially on 24 June 1938, but flying had started before this when Boulton Paul established a factory on the site in 1936. They built over 1,000 Defiants, 100 Rocs, and nearly 700 Barracudas. After the war, they produced Balliols until manufacturing ceased in 1956. A FTS was set up in September 1941 which operated Tiger Moths and Hinds. This became an RFS after the war equipped with Ansons, Prentices, and Chipmunks and was disbanded in March 1953. An AOP flight operated Austers and Chipmunks between July 1949 and March 1957. Civil flying resumed in January 1946, and a few scheduled services were operated here between 1953 and 1956. The airfield closed in 1971.

Wolvey, Warks

This RLG for OTUs based at RAF Bramcote was used during the Second World War.

Wombleton, Yorks

This RAF bomber station opened in October 1943 and was home to a HCU operating Halifaxes, Lancasters, Spitfires, Hurricanes, and Oxfords until flying ceased in August 1945. Part of the wartime airfield reopened for private flying before 1982, and around six aircraft are based here, operating from parts of two of the wartime hard runways, both unlicensed. It is approximately 1.5 miles south-west of the now-closed Kirkbymoorside airfield.

Woodbridge (Northumberland)

See Milfield.

Woodbridge, Suffolk

Construction of this RAF station commenced in July 1942, but the first units did not arrive until May 1944. These operated Mosquitoes, Lancasters, Lincolns, and Halifaxes until April 1946, with the RAF departing in March 1948. During the latter part of the Second World War, it served as an emergency diversion airfield as it had an extra-long runway; over 4,000 aircraft in difficulties made successful landings. This was one of three airfields designated for this purpose, the others being Carnaby and Manston. In June 1952, the USAF arrived with F-84s; these were followed by F-100s, F-101s, F-4s, A-10s, HC-130s, and HH-3s. The Americans stayed until August 1992, when flying ceased. However, occasional use of the long runway is still made, and it is to remain open indefinitely. A Pilatus PC24 spent two weeks test-flying here in 2018.

Woodchurch, Kent

This ALG was used by RAF Mustangs from July to October 1943 and USAAF P-47s from April to July 1944. A few light aircraft are based on an unlicensed grass strip just to the north of the old LG at Little Engeham Farm. Just to the south-west is another private grass strip at Little Robhurst Farm, at which a few aircraft are based.

Woodford, Gt. Manchester

This civil aerodrome opened in February 1925 to replace Alexandra Park and was used initially by the Lancashire Aero Club. Avro set up a factory on the site and started by producing Avro 504s followed by Avians, Audaxes, Ansons, Blenheims, and Lancasters. After the war, they went on to build Tudors, Shackletons, Vulcans, 748s, ATPs, 146s and modified Nimrods until the factory closed in 2010. It was not used operationally during the Second World War but received many interesting visitors, particularly American aircraft. An ACGS was based here from May 1945 to September 1955, and the airfield closed in August 2011.

Woodford Green, Gt. London

This RFC LG was used for home defence from June 1916 to December 1917. Types operated included Be2s and Be12s.

The Avro Aircraft Company's aerodrome at Woodford, *c.* 1936, featuring some of their products. Anson K6177 and a Tutor are parked outside the hangar while another Anson lurks inside. Hawker Audax K5175 is also present. Flying ceased at Woodford in 2011. (*Eddie Riding*)

Woodhall Spa, Lincs

This RAF bomber station opened in February 1942 as a satellite for Coningsby and was home to Lancasters and Mosquitoes until flying ceased in October 1945. It was reactivated in 1964 for Bloodhound missiles, which stayed until 1965.

Woodham Mortimer, Essex

This RFC LG was used for home defence from September 1916 to June 1918. Types operated included Be2s, Be12s, Pups, RE7s, and SE5s.

Woodley (Reading), Berks

This civil aerodrome opened at Easter 1929 and was used for training, sales, and maintenance. F. G. Miles opened a factory in 1932 and built Hawks, Falcons, Magisters, Masters, Martinets, and Monitors. They also overhauled Spitfires during the Second World War. An elementary flying school was set up in November 1935, equipped with Tiger Moths, Harts, Magisters, Battles, and Ansons; training continued until March 1953, latterly by a RFS that operated Tiger Moths, Ansons, and Chipmunks. A few communication flights were based during and after the war until flying ceased in March 1953. Marathons and Heralds were built here by Handley Page in the former F. G. Miles factory until it closed in 1963.

Woodvale, Merseyside

This RAF station opened in December 1941 and was home to a wide variety of units operating Spitfires, Hurricanes, Defiants, Typhoons, Beaufighters, Oxfords, Martinets, Rocs, Skuas, Vengeances, Blenheims, Meteors, Chipmunks, and Bulldogs. It became a satellite for RNAS Burscough (as HMS *Ringtail 2*) in April 1945 and operated various types until October 1945. A RAuxAF squadron arrived in July 1946 and flew Spitfires and Meteors until July 1951. This was followed by a meteorological flight that used Spitfires, Mosquitoes, and Meteors until May 1959. Training carried on after the war and continues to this day by a VGS operating Vigilants and a couple of UAS/AEFs with Tutors. Between 1955 and 1957, Silver City Airways operated a car ferry service to Belfast with Bristol Freighters. A CAACU operated Mosquitoes, Meteors, and Vampires from January 1958 to June 1971. Private flying takes place from two licensed hard runways, and around fifteen private aircraft are based here.

Wooler

See Milfield.

Woolfox Lodge, Leics

This RAF station opened in December 1940 and was used initially as a RLG for Cottesmore until August 1941 by Hampdens, Herefords, and Ansons. It then became a bomber base that operated Hampdens, Manchesters, Lancasters, Wellingtons, and Stirlings until flying ceased in July 1945. It reopened as a RLG for Wittering in May 1951 and was used by Harvards, Balliols, and Prentices until April 1954. It then closed to

FG Miles' factory and grass airfield at Woodley (Reading) in July 1947. It was taken over by Handley Page who eventually departed in 1963 although flying ceased in 1953. (*The Aeroplane*)

flying but was reactivated in 1960 for the deployment of Bloodhound missiles, which remained until 1964.

Woolsington
See Newcastle.

Worcester (Perdiswell), Worcs
This civil aerodrome opened in 1935. Battles built at nearby Longbridge were flight-tested between 1938 and 1942. It was used by the RAF for training from April 1942 with Tiger Moths and Magisters until flying ceased in July 1945.

Workington (Distington), Cumbria
This civil airfield was operated by the British Steel Corporation from the 1950s to about 1975.

Worksop (Scofton), Notts
This RAF station opened as a satellite for Finningley in September 1943 and was used mainly for training until January 1946. Various types were operated, including Wellingtons, Martinets, Oxfords, Tomahawks, and Lysanders. Several minor units were then based here until it was placed on C&M in June 1948. It reopened in August 1952 for an AFS equipped with Meteors, Provosts, and Vampires until flying ceased in June 1958.

Wormingford, Essex
This RFC first-class night LG, known as Bures, was used for home defence from December 1916 to June 1919. Following expansion, it reopened as a USAAF station in November 1943 and was home to P-47s, which were followed by P-38s and P-51s. These departed in July 1945, and the station passed to the RAF, who stayed until January 1947. Some civil flying then took place and continues to this day in the form of gliding by the Essex and Suffolk GC. Over fifty sailplanes are based here.

Worth Matravers (Swanage), Dorset
This civil aerodrome opened in August 1928 for the Isle of Purbeck Light Aeroplane Club but closed in 1939. It was used for a short while from June 1940 for glider towing trials with Avro 504s. Communications aircraft visited occasionally, but the airstrip closed in 1941.

Worthy Down, Hants
This LG opened on the old Winchester racecourse in January 1918 and was home to AACUs equipped with FK8s, Be2s, RE8s, F2bs, Avro 504s, DH4s, DH9s, and Camels until flying ceased in March 1920. It reopened as a RAF bomber station in April 1924 with Vimys, Virginias, Heyfords, Hinds, Gordons, and Wellesleys; this use continued until April 1938. It was then taken over by the FAA and became HMS *Kestrel* in May 1939. They operated Nimrods, Gladiators, Skuas, Sharks, Swordfish, Fulmars, Rocs, Avengers, Barracudas, Firebrands, Seafires, Proctors, Hellcats, and Wildcats until departing in November 1945. The airfield was used by Vickers Supermarine for Spitfire development flying from December 1940 to March 1944. An UAS flew Tiger Moths and Oxfords from November 1942 to June 1946 when flying ceased. It passed to the navy again in 1952 as HMS *Ariel 2* and was home to an air electrical school until 1960, but no aircraft were operated by them.

Wratting Common, Cambs
This RAF bomber station opened in May 1943 and was home to Stirlings and Lancasters. Flying ceased in July 1946, and it then became a storage sub unit until September 1947 when the airfield closed.

Wrexham (Borras), Clwyd
This RAF station opened in June 1941 as a satellite for Calveley and was home to mostly training units that operated Blenheims, Lysanders, Defiants, Hurricanes, Beaufighters, Masters, Oxfords, and Harvards. Flying ceased in June 1945. It reopened for civil flying after the war but closed in the late 1990s.

Wrexham (Rhos Uchaf), Clwyd
This AALG was in use in the 1930s.

Writtle (Chelmsford), Essex
This RFC LG was used for home defence by several units for short periods from October 1914 to September 1915. Types operated included Longhorns and Be2s.

Wroughton, Wilts
This RAF station opened in April 1940 and was used mainly for maintenance, storage, and packing until March 1972. Types handled included Blenheims, Hurricanes, Masters, Albacores, Defiants, Spitfires, Swordfish, Mosquitoes, Meteors, and Canberras. In April 1972, it became a Royal Navy air yard that maintained Scout, Gazelle, Lynx, and Sea King helicopters until September 1992. A communications flight was based here from April 1940 to March 1972, and glider training took place between March 1943 and August 1945 with Whitleys, Albermarles, Hudsons, and Ansons. The Science Museum began to use some

of the wartime hangars for storing their larger exhibits in 1978. Since 2016, it has been home to the test track for the TV series *The Grand Tour*.

Wycombe Air Park

See Booker.

Wye, Kent

This RFC third-class LG opened in May 1916 and was used for home defence and training with Be2s, RE8s, FK8s, Pups, Camels, DH4s, DH6s, and Avro 504s until May 1919. The USAAS operated DH4s from January to December 1918 and it closed in June 1919.

Wymeswold, Leics

This RAF station opened in May 1942 for bomber training with Wellingtons, Lancasters, Halifaxes, Stirlings, and Oxfords. Transport Command took over in October 1944 and flew Dakotas until December 1947 when flying ceased. It resumed in April 1949 when Fighter Command arrived with Meteors and Hunters that remained until January 1957, albeit for short periods only. A detachment of AOP Austers was based here between July 1954 and March 1957. Field Aircraft Services set up a maintenance organisation in 1957, which handled F-86s, T-33s, DC4s, and Viscounts before moving out in 1968. Part of Field's hangar was occupied from December 1964 by the Beagle Aircraft Company, who flight-tested Bassets for the RAF. From January 1958, the airfield was used as a RLG by Provosts from Syerston and Fulbeck until January 1970. It then closed, but some flying continued for a few years, possibly as late as 1978.

Wyton, Cambs

This RFC aerodrome opened in April 1916 and was used mostly for training with Be2s, DH2s, DH9s, and Camels until closure in June 1919. Following expansion, it reopened as a RAF station in September 1936 and a wide variety of units were based here during its long life operating Hinds, Blenheims, Wellingtons, Stirlings, Mosquitoes, Lancasters, Lincolns, Canberras, Valiants, Victors, Comets, Devons, Bassets, Varsities, and Nimrods. The USAF put in a brief appearance between July 1950 and August 1951 with B-50s and B-29s. Bloodhound missiles were deployed between 1983 and July 1991. The last Canberra departed in October 1994 and the airfield closed in March 1995, but an UAS and AEF continued flying their Tutors until 2014. Some private flying also takes place from an unlicensed grass strip, and around thirty light aircraft are currently based here. The airfield is due to close by 2024.

Yapton

See Ford.

Yarcombe, Devon

This private grass airfield at Watchford Farm opened in around 1992; it is home to over twenty light aircraft.

Yate (Chipping Sodbury), Avon

This RFC aerodrome opened in October 1917 and was home to an ARD. This handled Camels, Snipes, and F2bs, until closure in April 1920. It was reopened by Parnall Aircraft in 1925, who built experimental aeroplanes, followed by Gulls for Percivals. The company merged with Hendy and Frazer Nash in 1935 and went on to build Hecks, gun turrets, and components for Spitfires. The airfield closed at the end of the war but continued to be used by an ACGS until February 1948.

Yatesbury (Calne/Cherhill/Compton Bassett), Wilts

This RFC training station opened on two adjacent sites in November 1916, operating Avro 504s, DH5s, RE8s, Be12s, Pups, SE5s, and Camels. Flying ceased in October 1919 but recommenced from a combined site in January 1936 when an elementary flying school arrived with Tiger Moths and Harts. Training for the RAF then continued until October 1965, most importantly for radio operators. Types employed included Ansons, Magisters, Bothas, Dominies, and Proctors. Communications aircraft then made use of the airfield until it closed in April 1969. Part of the wartime airfield has been used by microlights since 1995 and over twenty are based here. One unlicensed grass runway is in use.

Yeadon (Leeds Bradford Airport), Yorks

The municipal airport for Leeds and Bradford opened on 17 October 1931. Scheduled services commenced in August 1934 until terminated at the outbreak of the Second World War. The RAF arrived in February 1936 with Harts and later Spitfires and the CAG trained pilots from 1938. It was used as a dispersal site for Whitleys at the start of the War and a communications flight was resident from December 1940 to July 1945 operating a variety of aircraft. An FTS operated Tiger Moths from March 1941; this use continued with a UAS until December 1945. In 1940, Avro built a shadow factory on the airfield to produce and test-fly Ansons, Lancasters, Lincolns, and Yorks. In September 1946, the RAux AF arrived with Mosquitoes and Spitfires; these stayed until October 1950. Civil flying resumed in January 1947 and scheduled services recommenced in 1955. An AOP flight of Austers was based here from September 1949 to March 1957 and Chipmunks of a UAS/AEF were resident here from March 1954 to November 1959. Today, Yeadon is the busy Leeds Bradford Airport, which supports scheduled and charter flights as well as GA operations.

Yearby, Cleveland

This unlicensed airfield at Turners Arms Farm opened in 1972 with a single grass runway and is home to around ten aircraft.

Yelling (St Neots), Cambs

This RFC LG was used for home defence from October 1916 to October 1917, mainly by Be2s.

Yeovil (Judwin), Somerset

Petters Ltd (which became the Westland Aircraft Company in 1934) opened a factory here in April 1915 and an associated aerodrome two years later. Types built by the company over the years included DH4s, DH9s, Vimys, Wapitis, Hectors, Lysanders, Whirlwinds, Spitfires, Seafires, Welkins, and Wyverns. Modifications were also carried out to Mohawks, Tomahawks, and Kittyhawks. In the early 1950s, the company decided to concentrate on helicopters and is still building them today, albeit under the Leonardo banner. Significant types built include Dragonflies, Whirlwinds, Wessexes, Sea Kings, Lynxes, and Merlins. AW159 Wildcats are currently being produced here. The airfield saw little military use during the Second World War, although an ACGS was based between October 1943 and November 1947. It is open to visiting aircraft, for which one licensed grass runway is available.

Yeovilton, Somerset

This FAA station HMS *Heron* opened in May 1940 and has been home since then to virtually every type of naval aircraft, many on shore leave from aircraft carriers. Significant types operated included Swordfish, Albacores, Fulmars, Masters, Martlets, Sea Hurricanes, Corsairs, Seafires, Fireflies, Sea Furies, Sea Venoms, Sea Vixens, Gannets, Phantoms, Hunters, Canberras, Jetstreams, and Sea Harriers. During the Second World War, Westland had a facility on the site to repair, assemble, and test-fly Spitfires and Seafires. Today, Yeovilton is an important naval base and Merlins, Wildcats, and Hawks are currently based here, together with Tutors of the naval air squadron and gliders of the Heron GC. It is also home to the Fleet Air Arm Museum, which opened in 1964.

York (Clifton/Rawcliffe), Yorks

York Airport was opened on 4 July 1936 and used for club and charter flying until the outbreak of the Second World War when it requisitioned by the Air Ministry. It was used initially as a RLG for RAF Linton-on-Ouse, and various units were based here, some for only short periods, operating Lysanders, Blenheims, Dominies, Tomahawks, Mustangs, Fulmars, Oxfords, and Austers. The RAF departed in June 1945. Over 2,000 Halifaxes were repaired or overhauled by a CRO during the war, and many were scrapped on site afterwards. Civil flying resumed after the war until the airfield closed in 1955.

York (Knavesmire), Yorks

York racecourse was first used for flying in 1912 and was occupied by the RFC as a night LG for home defence with Be2s from April 1916. It was soon reclassified as a day LG and flying continued until 1919.

Yoxford, Suffolk

This private aerodrome on Sir Guy Hambling's Rookery Estate was in use from 1934 until the outbreak of the Second World War. About 1 mile to the north-west is a private strip at Hill Farm, which is home to a lone Cessna.

Zeals, Wilts

This RAF fighter station opened in May 1942 and was home to various units operating Defiants, Hurricanes, Spitfires, and Mosquitoes. Glider training commenced in October 1944, when Masters, Hotspurs, Dakotas, and Hadrians were operated until March 1945. The airfield was then taken over by the FAA as HMS *Humming Bird*, who used it for training with Corsairs, Hellcats, Wildcats, Mosquitoes, Seafires, and Oxfords. Flying ceased in January 1946 and the airfield closed soon after.

Above: Control tower and office buildings at Westland Helicopters's (now Leonardo) factory and airfield at Yeovil on 7 May 2014. (*Grant Peerless*)

Left: Temporary air traffic control trailer at Yeovil airfield in use while the control tower was being renovated in 2014. (*Grant Peerless*)

Below: Fairy Swordfish LS326 of the Royal Navy Historic Flight in front of the standard navy pattern control tower at RNAS Yeovilton during an air day in July 1982. North American P-51 G-BTCD can be seen in the background. (*Grant Peerless*)

Bibliography

A great number of books, magazines, and websites were consulted during the preparation of this book but the main ones were as follows:

Books

Ashworth, C., *Action Stations Vol, 5: Military Airfields of the South West* (Patrick Stephens, 1982)

Ashworth, C., *Action Stations Vol. 9: Military Airfields of the Central South & South East* (Patrick Stephens, 1982)

Automobile Association Register of Aircraft Landing Grounds (The Automobile Association, first published 1932)

Barrymore, B., *Action Stations Vol. 2: Military Airfields of Lincolnshire & East Midlands* (Patrick Stephens, 1981)

Bowyer, M. J. F., *Action Stations Vol. 1: Wartime Military Airfields of East Anglia* (Patrick Stephens, 1979)

Bowyer, M. J. F., *Action Stations Vol. 6: Military Airfields of the Cotswolds & Central Midlands* (Patrick Stephens, 1983)

Butler, P. H., *British Isles Airfield Guide* (Merseyside Aviation Society, 1985)

Chorlton, M., *Forgotten Aerodromes of World War 1* (Crecy Publishing, 2014)

Curtis, H. J., *Military Aircraft Markings* (Crecy Publishing)

Halpenny, B. B., *Action Stations Vol. 4: Military Airfields of Yorkshire* (Patrick Stephens, 1982)

Halpenny, B. B., *Action Stations Vol. 8: Military Airfields of Greater London* (Patrick Stephens, 1984)

Hamlin, J. F., *Peaceful Fields: A Directory of Civil Airfields and Landing Grounds in the United Kingdom 1919–1939* (GMS Enterprises, 2007)

Hoddinott, D., Hoddinott, R., Cross, K., and Vasek, J., *British Isles Civil Aircraft Register 2019* (LAASdata)

Merton-Jones, A. C., *British Independent Airlines 1946 to 1976* (The Aviation Hobby Shop, 2000)

Smith, D. J., *Action Stations Vol. 3: Military Airfields of Wales & the North West* (Patrick Stephens, 1981)

Smith, D. J., *Action Stations Vol. 7: Military Airfields of Scotland, the North East & Northern Ireland* (Patrick Stephens, 1983)

The LAAS British Isles Airfield Guide (LAASdata)

VFR Flight Guide UK 2019 (Aviation Flight Equipment Ltd)

Willis, S. and Holliss, B., *Military Airfields in the British Isles 1939–1945* (Enthusiast Publications, 1987)

Magazines

Air Pictorial

Airfield Review (journal of the Airfield Research Group)

Flight International

Flyer

Pilot

Popular Flying

The Aeroplane/Aeroplane Monthly

CDs

Bases—database of military airfields published by *Air Britain* (2012)

Websites

Numerous websites were consulted but the main ones were as follows:

abct.org.uk—database of airfields compiled by the Airfields of Britain Conservation Trust.
streetmap.co.uk—Ordnance Survey maps.
ukairfieldguide.net—UK Airfields and Airports: A guide to the history of British flying sites within the United Kingdom by Dick Flute and Lee Merritt.

Index